AF412050

THE ACTIVATION OF CITIZENSHIP IN EUROPE

Manchester University Press

SERIES EDITORS THOMAS CHRISTIANSEN AND EMIL KIRCHNER

The formation of Croatian national identity ALEX J. BELLAMY

The European Union and the accommodation of Basque difference in Spain ANGELA K. BOURNE

Theory and reform in the European Union, 2nd edition DIMITRIS N. CHRYSSOCHOOU, MICHAEL J. TSINISIZELIS, STELIOS STAVRIDIS AND KOSTAS IFANTIS

From integration to integrity: administrative ethics and reform in the European Commission MICHELLE CINI

The transatlantic divide OSVALDO CROCI AND AMY VERDUN

Germany, pacifism and peace enforcement ANJA DALGAARD-NIELSEN

The changing European Commission DIONYSSIS DIMITRAKOPOULOS (ED.)

Supranational citizenship LYNN DOBSON

Reshaping Economic and Monetary Union SHAWN DONNELLY

The time of European governance MAGNUS EKENGREN

Adapting to European integration? Kaliningrad, Russia and the European Union STEFAN GÄNZLE, GUIDO MÜNTEL, EVGENY VINOKUROV (EDS)

An introduction to post-Communist Bulgaria EMIL GIATZIDIS

Mothering the Union ROBERTA GUERRINA

Non-state actors in international relations: the case of Germany ANNE-MARIE LE GLOANNEC

Globalisation, integration and the future of European welfare states THEODORA ISMENE-GIZELIS

European internal security : towards supranational governance in the area of freedom, security and justice CHRISTIAN KAUNERT

Turkey: facing a new millennium AMIKAM NACHMANI

Europolis: constitutional patriotism beyond the nation state PATRIZIA NANZ

The changing faces of federalism SERGIO ORTINO, MITJA ŽAGAR AND VOJTECH MASTNY (EDS)

The road to the European Union
Volume 1 The Czech and Slovak Republics JACQUES RUPNIK AND JAN ZIELONKA (EDS)
Volume 2 Estonia, Latvia and Lithuania VELLO PETTAI AND JAN ZIELONKA (EDS)

A political sociology of the European Union: reassessing constructivism MICHEL MANGENOT AND JAY ROWELL (EDS)

Democratising capitalism? The political economy of post-Communist transformations in Romania, 1989–2001 LILIANA POP

Europe and civil society: movement coalitions and European governance CARLO RUZZA

Constructing the path to eastern enlargement ULRICH SEDELMEIER

Governing Europe's new neighbourhood: Partners or periphery? MICHAEL SMITH, KATJA WEBER , AND MICHAEL BAUN (EDS)

Two tiers or two speeds? The European security order and the enlargement of the European Union and NATO JAMES SPERLING (ED.)

Recasting the European order JAMES SPERLING AND EMIL KIRCHNER

The Europeanisation of conflicts: Integration and conflict resolution from the 1950s to the twenty-first century BOYKA STEFANOVA

Political symbolism and European integration TOBIAS THEILER

Rethinking European Union foreign policy BEN TONRA AND THOMAS CHRISTIANSEN (EDS)

The Europeanisation of the western Balkans: EU justice and home affairs in Croatia and Macedonia ... FLORIAN TRAUNER

The European Union in the wake of Eastern enlargement AMY VERDUN AND OSVALDO CROCI (EDS)

Democratic citizenship and the European Union ALBERT WEALE

Inclusion, exclusion and the governance of European security MARK WEBBER

THOMAS PFISTER

THE ACTIVATION OF CITIZENSHIP IN EUROPE

MANCHESTER UNIVERSITY PRESS
Manchester and New York

*distributed in the United States exclusively
by Palgrave Macmillan*

Published by Manchester University Press
Oxford Road, Manchester M13 9NR, UK
and Room 400, 175 Fifth Avenue, New York, NY 10010, USA
www.manchesteruniversitypress.co.uk

Distributed in the United States exclusively by
Palgrave Macmillan, 175 Fifth Avenue, New York,
NY 10010, USA

Distributed in Canada exclusively by
UBC Press, University of British Columbia, 2029 West Mall,
Vancouver, BC, Canada V6T 1Z2

British Library Cataloguing-in-Publication Data
A catalogue record for this book is available from the British Library

Library of Congress Cataloging-in-Publication Data applied for

ISBN   978 0 7190 8 3310 *hardback*

First published 2011

The publisher has no responsibility for the persistence or accuracy of URLs for any external or third-party internet websites referred to in this book, and does not guarantee that any content on such websites is, or will remain, accurate or appropriate.

Edited and typeset
by Frances Hackeson Freelance Publishing Services, Brinscall, Lancs
Printed in Great Britain
by the MPG Books Group, UK

Contents

Figures and tables   *page* vi
Abbreviations   vii
Acknowledgements   viii

1 The transnational quest for a new welfare paradigm   1

2 From citizenship to citizenship in practice   16

3 The EU debate: gender equality in the EES   27

4 Germany – reservations and reforms   41

5 The United Kingdom – teaching activation   57

6 Hungary – openness and rights without access   73

7 Conclusion: the activation of citizenship – transnationally negotiated   91

   Appendix: author interviews   113
   References   114
   Index   137

Figures

2.1	Dimensions and analytical elements of citizenship	*page* 22
7.1	Activation as reorganisation of policy spheres	93
7.2	Overlapping activation debates	96

Tables

3.1	Key events in the EES and the Lisbon Strategy	34

BA	Bundesagentur für Arbeit; before 01.01.2004 Bundesanstalt für Arbeit (German Federal Employment Service)
BEPG	Broad Economic Policy Guidelines
BMFSFJ	Bundesministerium für Familie, Senioren, Frauen und Jugend (Federal Ministry for Family, Senior Citizens, Women and Youth)
CDU	Christlich Demokratische Union Deutschlands (Christian Democratic Union of Germany)
CEDAW	Convention/Committee on the Elimination of Discrimination against Women
CSU	Christlich Soziale Union (Christian Social Union)
DfEE	Department for Employment and Education
DGB	Deutscher Gewerkschaftsbund (German Trade Union Federation)
DJB	Deutscher Juristinnenbund (German Women Lawyers Association)
DSS	Department for Social Security
DTI	Department for Trade and Industry
DWP	Department for Work and Pensions
ECJ	European Court of Justice
EES	European Employment Strategy
EHRC	Equality and Human Rights Commission
EMCO	Employment Committee
EOC	Equal Opportunities Commission
ESF	European Social Fund
EU	European Union
FCO	Foreign and Commonwealth Office
FDP	Freie Demokratische Partei (Free Democratic Party)
FIDESZ	Fiatal Demokraták Szövetsége (Alliance of Young Democrats)
IHF	International Helsinki Federation for Human Rights
IMF	International Monetary Fund
JSA	Jobseeker's Allowance
MSZP	Magyar Szocialista Párt (Hungarian Socialist Party)
NAP	National Action Plan
NRP	National Reform Programme
OECD	Organisation for Economic Co-operation and Development
OMC	Open Method of Coordination
SPD	Sozialdemokratische Partei Deutschlands (Social Democratic Party of Germany)
TUC	Trade Union Council
UK	United Kingdom
UN	United Nations

*A*CKNOWLEDGEMENTS

Prior to taking up the academic considerations of this book, I want to mention the many people who helped me with it at various times and in various ways and express my gratitude to them. To begin with, this book would not exist without those people in Berlin, Bonn, Brussels, Budapest, and London who devoted their precious time to answering my questions and to sharing their priceless insights with me. The project took off while I was a Ph.D. student at the School of Politics, International Studies and Philosophy at Queen's University Belfast. During that time, Antje Wiener and Andrew Baker offered multifaceted support and valuable feedback as my supervisors. Moreover, by employing me as a research assistant between April 2004 and March 2007 Antje Wiener contributed to my survival in a more substantive sense. In this context, the financial support of the British Academy is also gratefully acknowledged. I completed the manuscript when I was a post-doc fellow at the Centre of Excellence 'Cultural Foundations of Integration' at the University of Konstanz (Germany), which provided exactly the right context and adequate support to bring such a project to a close. The finishing touches were applied during my time in the Program on Science, Technology, and Society at the Kennedy School of Government, Harvard University, benefiting from this immensely inspiring intellectual environment.

The Center for Policy Studies (CPS) and particularly its Director Viola Zentai at the Central European University in Budapest (Hungary) provided generous hospitality between April and August 2006. Without their institutional and intellectual support I would not have been able to include a full case study on Hungary.

Furthermore, I gratefully acknowledge financial support from the University Association for Contemporary European Studies (UACES), the Queen's University Alumni Fund and the Department for Education and Learning (Northern Ireland). Margaret Hagan, Anna Horvath, Sandra Kröger, Joanne McEvoy, Aidan McGarry, Erhan Içener, Mairead Ni Choileain, Richard Traill, and Edvin Vink read parts at different stages of the project and I profited from many discussions and exchanges with them. David Brenner has seen through the whole manuscript and offered invaluable help with language and presentation. I am also grateful to the series editors, the anonymous referee and everyone at Manchester University Press for their help in realising this book. Diana Schmidt-Pfister always was the most patient and accurate reader during the whole process of writing the book. Her critical as well as encouraging comments were immensely important at all times. So much more important, however, is her companionship, her support and the time we share beyond academic discussions. Johannes and Eva are to be thanked for simply being there and constantly reminding us of all the other things which make our lives worth living.

1

The transnational quest for a new welfare paradigm

The activation agenda and citizenship: problem, approach, and argument

Both the practices and concepts of citizenship are transforming in a variety of ways across Europe. This book contributes to the deeper understanding of such developments by investigating how a transnational conceptual debate around the key concepts of 'activation' and the 'activating welfare state' interacts with those transformations. It demonstrates that the implications of the former reach far beyond the boundaries of social and employment policy, critically affect the exclusionary element of citizenship, and therefore raise fundamental questions about the constitution of our societies and their democratic governance. In general, the transnational activation agenda poses a risk to the delicate balance of citizenship. As a consequence, this requires a strengthened element of political citizenship. The present study is based on the following main research questions:

1   How does the increasing dominance of a Europe-wide activation discourse affect the concepts and practices of citizenship?
2   What are the implications of this transformation in terms of exclusion and inequality?
3   What exactly is the role of the European Union in this process?

Throughout Europe, we are witnessing a large-scale reshuffling of welfare economies. While the causes for this development might be multiple and complex, it is possible to identify one dominant discourse that vitally informs and shapes the way the reforms are undertaken: a new welfare paradigm which promotes activation and an activating welfare state as guiding principles for social and economic modernisation (see the two sections that follow below). In fact, countries with very different institutions and histories regarding welfare and employment – such as the old and new EU member states examined in the present study – have been receptive to that discourse, actively engaged in it and putting it into practice.

Moreover, because the activation discourse is a fundamentally transnational phenomenon, the examination of these questions has to go beyond analysing national welfare systems. The European Union (EU) especially has become a major driving force as well as the key locus of this conceptual debate. In particular, based on its European Employment Strategy (EES), the Union has managed to crucially expand its activities into the realm of employment and social policy (in the broadest sense). The Strategy is of key importance as an arena where the activation discourse is promoted, shaped, and endowed with meanings. Furthermore, in the context of this conceptual debate, the Union has won the ability to actively get involved in national renegotiations of welfare and citizenship.

In general, the move towards such an activating welfare state implies shifts of the central problems for social policy, the basic objectives of the welfare state and of the practices with which those goals should be realised. In the process, this trend also intervenes in the institutionalised social relationships that constitute citizenship. This development is of particular importance since citizenship can be seen as a main source of social integration and political legitimacy of the European post-war welfare state – now it is even being renegotiated at the level of the EU.

Citizenship constitutes the main interest and the central theoretical category of the study and will be discussed in detail in Chapter 2. All phenomena are interpreted from a comprehensive citizenship perspective, understood in this book as not only the object of empirical research but also an analytical lens to assess social and political relationships. At the same time, the book also demonstrates that citizenship studies are able to generate theoretical conclusions which are of high normative relevance but equally based on empirical evidence.

However, any study in transformations of citizenship has to acknowledge its ambivalent nature. Citizenship does not only mean integration and legitimacy but it also (and always) generates distinct patterns of exclusion and inequality – even among citizens who are formally equal (for example, women, gays and lesbians, people with disability, children, and linguistic, national, ethnic, or cultural minorities). Therefore, it is necessary to pay special attention to already existing areas of exclusion from full citizenship in order to fully evaluate such a transformation. Since the consequences of the activation agenda for those exclusionary aspects will become particularly visible in the dimension of gender, the book chooses the gender equality dimension of the activation discourse – and in particular within the EES – as a main empirical focus. On the one hand, gender inequalities in the labour market and the social security system, which originate in specific gender relations and the related division between public and private spheres underlying each European society, constitute a key element of inequality in contemporary European democracies. On the other hand, based on its core norm of universal labour market participation, the activation paradigm implies shifting gender contracts – from a male breadwinner/female caregiver model towards an adult worker model.[1] In addition, such a transnational perspective is especially relevant with regard to gender, because the EU has a strong track record of promoting gender equality among its member states and because related provisions have always been part of the EES (though they have lost much of their initial force). However, under which conditions this transformation might be achieved is less clear and has to be established in each particular case.

Following this brief outline of the main questions and problems examined in this book, the remainder of this section will introduce the approach for examining them and the conclusions that follow. The present study is committed to a reflective approach to social research, thus locating itself towards the interpretive end of the methodological spectrum. Consequently, the main emphasis of the comparisons is not on the careful manipulation of variables, in order to isolate causal effects and more on deeper understanding of the particular cases by contrasting them with each other. Above all, the interest in the linkages between activation discourses and citizenship requires an approach which is capable of engaging in what Anthony Giddens has coined 'double hermeneutics' (Giddens 1976) or the challenge of interpreting the meanings that actors ascribe to the language and practices within a particular socio-historical context. In addition, the study looks at the overall picture of how discourses on welfare reform in different political contexts overlap and interact with each other and how they inform shifts in citizenship. It therefore follows a vision of social science that emphasises contextual and historical knowledge (rather than parsimony or causal explanation) and which is open to a wide repertoire of qualitative inquiry.

Citizenship can be seen as a historical process, driven by its essential contestedness. The EES can be understood as pushing the EU member states to modernise their labour market institutions and social security systems as well as developing specific discourse on the direction and necessity of such reforms. Ultimately, this will also have consequences for citizenship although it is not yet evident what those consequences are. In this respect, this study concentrates mostly on reconstructing the different debates about welfare modernisation at the EU level as well as in three EU member states: Germany, the UK, and Hungary. It traces how different actors from these countries engage in the activation discourse mainly developed in the context of the EES. In particular, the focus is on the role of that debate with regard to contestations of existing and newly emerging citizenship practices from the transnational and the national level. Since the EES is understood here as a specifically structured space for discursive interaction, the empirical part of this book asks only to a lesser extent about the Strategy's effectiveness in terms of effects and causes (contrary to most other studies). Instead, it enquires how the dynamic system of meanings that evolves within it interacts with the meanings, concepts, and practices of citizenship in different contexts.

Two of the selected EU member states, Germany and the United Kingdom (UK), have been described as strong male breadwinner models (Lewis & Ostner 1995) which is also illustrated by the indicators of the EES. For both display high overall gender gaps: that is an unequal ratio of women and men with regard to employment and unemployment and the problem of unequal pay. At the same time, both countries belong to different welfare regimes (Esping-Andersen 1990) and have experienced very different economic and labour market performances in the last decade or so. Germany encountered manifest problems with slow growth, high unemployment rates, and widespread perceptions of crisis from the

1990s onwards. In contrast, the economy of the UK largely prospered with high growth and employment rates (at least until the massive economic crisis in 2008). Moreover, given their specific gender contracts, the implications of the activation paradigm should become particularly visible. The inclusion of Hungary reflects a new aspect of diversity within the EU. Since the spreading activation discourse and the EES are so closely (though not causally) connected, it would generally be inappropriate to study them without considering the 2004 enlargement. For example, some see a fundamental tension between the EU's programme of social and economic modernisation and its Eastern enlargement (Ingham & Ingham 2003; Ingham *et al.* 2005). Hungary's post-communist legacy certainly adds a very specific context that cannot be found in any of the old member states. Citizenship, labour markets, social security systems, and the state as such have been undergoing massive transformations since the end of communism. Against this background, it is extremely interesting to see how such changes affect the reception of the activation paradigm, the engagement in the communicative processes within the EES and citizenship.

The study covers the activation debate in the EU from the beginning of the EES (1997) until around 2009. Yet acknowledging the specific temporality and contextual characteristics of each case, the case studies might also look further back in time or beyond the limits of employment policy to do justice to the specific circumstances of each case. In this respect, the tension between a common focus and the need for integrating such particularities in the narrative has been most significant in the chapter on Hungary.

The empirical research proceeded in three main steps. First, starting with the documents exchanged within the EES, it was possible to reconstruct the national debates on labour market and welfare reforms for each case. As mentioned, the Strategy produces unique material since the member states are nowhere else requested to comprehensively report and reflect on the state of their employment and social policy as well as on ongoing and future welfare reforms. Of course, especially the national reports submitted to the EU have to be read with some care and should be seen as material for further analysis of a political process rather than collections of facts. After that, the reconstruction of these national reform projects was extended to national sources in order to provide more detail and clarification. In the second step, these transformations were examined from a citizenship perspective and translated in terms of shifting citizens' rights and duties, participation, and access to societal resources. The final step involved tracing the various contestations which became visible during the political debates about welfare reform. On the one hand, focusing on contestations makes visible the politics, particularly struggles about diverging goals and strategies, behind such transformations. On the other hand, tracing contestations is essential to uncover issues of inequality and exclusion – as result of governance as well as from the process itself – and to relate them back to the activation agenda. These three steps of the research process are also reflected in the structure of the empirical chapters.

Regarding the empirical material, the investigation draws on an extensive qualitative data set which comprises all relevant documents and reports generated within the framework of the EES, further EU documents, which are relevant for better understanding the conceptual debate about social and political modernisation at the supranational level, and national documents necessary for tracing the emergence of national welfare reforms. Furthermore, the data set contains different sources reflecting those critical voices that contest how social policy reforms in general and activation in particular are debated and put into practice. Finally, the analysis is based upon thirty-eight interviews not only with EU and national officials but also with trade unionists, activists, and academics from all four contexts. The collection and interpretation of the data have been guided by a constructivist grounded theory methodology (Charmaz 2000, 2005; Mills, Bonner, & Francis 2006; Strauss & Corbin 1998; Titscher, *et al.* 2000) and critical discourse analysis (Fairclough & Wodak 1997; van Dijk 1993); van Dijk 2001; Wodak 2003).

On the whole, I argue that the European Employment Strategy is a key site where the conceptual debate about activation is taking place and where the conceptual foundations of citizenship are re-negotiated on a transnational scale. Importantly, since this process mainly affects knowledge construction, underlying concepts, and world views, it is not a purely supranational influence but national and supranational elements are being blurred.

Furthermore, focusing on the gender equality dimension within the EU level conceptual debate allows for particularly significant insights. Here, the ambivalences of the activation agenda with regard to shifting patterns of inclusion/exclusion and equality/inequality become clearly visible. Most importantly, gender equality is less and less associated with women's human rights to personal autonomy but rather seen as a functional requirement for female employment. Moreover, concentrating on this dimension from a citizenship perspective also demonstrates the significance of this change of underlying concepts. Finally, the significance of transnational conceptual debates and their affect on social citizenship raises a number of much more fundamental questions about political citizenship and democracy. If key parameters of citizenship are redefined in a transnational conceptual debate, such a debate should be opened up to the views and potential contestations of those affected by its outcomes: the citizens. Therefore, that debate strongly requires a new element of European political citizenship based on a right to participate.

Most studies of activation, social policy and comparative welfare state research merely focus on social citizenship (as a constellation of rights and duties) which they see as an element of welfare. This study, however, suggests we investigate the link between these entities from a perspective including all dimensions of political membership and grounded more deeply in citizenship theory. At the same time, it will become plain that discourses about welfare state reform are deeply political and affect citizenship in a way that cannot be adequately expressed in terms of social rights alone. As a consequence, this book contributes to the better understanding of European transformations of citizenship. In particular, it complements comparative or global perspectives on transformations of national citizenship and citizenship of the EU with a specific perspective on European renegotiations of national citizenship (see Chapter 2 for a detailed discussion).

The activation discourse is the fairly recent dominant response to a widely perceived need to modernise social and employment policy. The next sections of this chapter examine this trend by looking at some of its most important characteristics: its epistemic substance (i.e. its underlying knowledge), related practices, and its transnational character. The discussion leads to the assumption that this new paradigm transforms the basic terms and conditions of social and political membership. It is therefore suggested we study these changes from a comprehensive citizenship perspective rather than from a narrower institutional one.

New goals: welfare in a globalised world

To begin with, the activation agenda becomes manifest in a reorientation of social and employment policy towards new goals deriving mainly from academic and political discourses of the mid-1990s. Van Berkel and Møller make clear that this new emphasis on active policies has to be attributed to the emergence of a new underlying welfare paradigm (van Berkel & Møller 2002b). As a consequence, it is necessary to go beyond mere typologies of activating policies and to consider the broader discursive context including perceptions of key problems, preferred solutions, and underlying norms in order to understand the full implications of activation for citizenship. At the core of this agenda, the authors identify the objective of universal participation in the labour market. Beyond that central norm, however, there are various active social policies and many nuances why and how this goal should be achieved.

Looking for a more detailed account of the normative framework, Jane Jenson and Denis Saint-Martin – using the ironic label 'LEGO™ paradigm' (Jenson & Saint-Martin 2006) – provide a concise overview of the main themes of activation. Moreover, they also demonstrate quite clearly that this process does not stop at the boundaries of the labour market but that it constitutes a massive transformation of the fundamental building blocks of a society. Their paradigm is characterised by international convergence around a set of new ideas, while remaining differences between national policies would result from different implementations.[2] It consists of three key features: first, notions of human capital and learning over the life-course (Jenson & Saint-Martin 2006) reflect the widely perceived need to enable citizens to individually confront and adapt to the challenges of a constantly changing globalised world. This emphasis implies the necessity to activate men and women equally since otherwise the human capital, especially of women, would be wasted. More generally, the orientation towards lifelong learning and investment in social capital also mirrors a pure supply-side approach to employment. State responsibility is increasingly limited to guaranteeing and managing a skilled and flexible labour force. The second element consists in an essential orientation towards the future (Jenson & Saint-Martin 2006) which generally motivates active measures (as active investment in contrast to passive expenditures) and turns the attention from workers to children – especially to education as key requirement and to child poverty as main hurdle to becoming self-responsible, independent and economically active citizens (see also Lister 2006). The third element 'asserts that activity and investments enrich the collective good' (Jenson & Saint-Martin 2006: 445). In other words, the new paradigm involves a general appraisal of economic activity as being morally most valuable and the assumption that there is no trade-off between system needs and individual needs. The idea of a forward-looking welfare state which invests in the social capital of its citizens rather than compensating them for any hardships is crucial for understanding the widespread depiction of activation/LEGO™ as reconciling a maximum of flexibility with social security in a win-win situation. In contrast, Jenson is sceptical towards such a scenario according to which both individuals' and systemic needs could be brought together so smoothly. Viewing the developments in a citizenship context, she sees a particularly high risk for the objective of gender equality to be sidelined, especially, because the supply-side and future orientation of the new paradigm would systematically obscure present structural inequalities (Jenson 2008).

The relational implications of activation – i.e. its influence on the relationships between state and citizens, their rights, duties and access to resources – is made even more explicit by Amparo Serrano Pascual who rather emphasises its negative potential (Serrano Pascual 2007; see also Crespo & Serrano Pascual 2004; Serrano Pascual & Crespo Suarez 2007a). In addition to the core norm of universal labour market participation as a sole path to social inclusion, the new 'activation paradigm' (Serrano Pascual 2007) is said to consist of an individualised approach which would redistribute risk and responsibility from the society to the individual. Accordingly, policies under the paradigm are said to draw on atomistic notions of a rational individual and to tackle individual behaviour rather than structural problems. As a further characteristic, the metaphor of the contract had become a central metaphor which guides the different active policies targeting individuals and which would also be used with reference to a new social contract underlying the active welfare state. Stressing the disciplinary aspects of activation, Serrano Pascual observes a general weakening (if not replacement) of social citizenship (see also Handler 2004).

What all these approaches have in common is a view of the activation agenda as not only a shift in policies but also a fundamental transformation of idioms and underlying worldviews. Importantly, this transformation goes beyond political norms in the narrow sense but includes a much broader range of normative, phenomenological, and analytical issues – in short, of knowledge. Moreover, there is consensus among all authors that those new objectives are crucially developed and promoted by the EU and especially within the context of the EES. Concerning their specific contents, all the accounts mentioned agree on the core objective of universal labour market participation as the perceived sole way to social inclusion, growth, and competitiveness. In addition, they all see an individualised and/or supply-side approach towards the activation of 'inactive' citizens as further key element. However, why and how those primary goals should be achieved remains vague.

At this point, it is important to highlight a fundamental tension inherent in the activation agenda. Its origins are twofold in the emphasis on economic activity combined with the individual approach, and in the vagueness concerning the reasons behind those objectives or the appropriate instruments for achieving them. On the one hand, according to optimistic assessments, an activating welfare state should seek the substantive empowerment of the targeted citizens according to their needs. On the other hand, activating policies can simply function as instruments to control and discipline individual behaviour in order to increase employment rates. While van Berkel and Møller (2002a) see some potential for empowerment, Serrano Pascual (2007) tends to emphasise the disciplinary elements while Jenson in turn stresses the particular risks for women and the cause of gender equality (Jenson 2007; 2008). To complicate things further, even measures targeted at empowerment can show ambivalent characteristics (Marinetto 2003; Newman 2005b).

This study contributes to the understanding of the relationship between the activation agenda's normative framework and citizenship in two ways. First, the book's comprehensive citizenship perspective lets us understand how the objectives of the activation discourse affect the institutionalised relationships between polity and citizens and among the citizens themselves. Moreover, it lets us place the normative framework of activation in the context of other norms, which are fundamental for the constitution of our societies, such as justice or democracy. Secondly, the citizenship perspective also offers ways to engage in critical and normative reflection about the implications of the activation agenda which point beyond narrow analytical accounts and provide a broader picture. As Dora Kostakopoulou has pointed out, citizenship studies is not only about analysing political realities but also about reflecting on what could and indeed should be (Kostakopoulou 2008).

However, any attempt to understand activation as a mere set of objectives for social policy would be incomplete. In contrast, in order to fully grasp its key characteristics we have to expand our research and to consider two further crucial aspects: first, a parallel trend towards new means and instruments; second, the essentially transnational character of the activation paradigm.

New means: governance

The reorientation of social policy towards new objectives is embedded in another, much broader transformation which affects the practices of how benefits and services are provided as well as the constellation of actors involved in these operations – governance being the keyword here. As will be demonstrated below, this process also made it possible for key tasks of sovereign nation states to now be subject to contestations and redefinitions in a transnational conceptual debate. Taking into account these shifts in the organisational settlement as well as the shifting objectives is a key requirement for understanding the activation agenda and its consequences for citizenship (Clarke & Newman 1997). As Lascoume and Le Galès point out (2007), it is necessary to analyse policy instruments and the process of policy instrumentation separately from political objectives. On the one hand, instruments always have effects which are independent from their initial aims. On the other hand, analysing instruments reveals underlying theorisations of the specific problems targeted or insights about the relationship between those who govern and those who are governed.

Characterising these transformations in the field of social policy, John Clarke identifies a process of 'dispersal of the state' which implies a reorganisation of the 'vertical and horizontal relationships within which public services are framed' (Clarke 2004: 118). With regard to the horizontal dimension, systems of service provision have become increasingly disintegrated through the externalisation of services, increased competition or new forms of collaboration and co-production. The state has retreated in many cases from the direct provision of services, instead steering and setting the general policy objectives and frameworks (van Berkel & Valkenburg 2007). Importantly, this does not imply the hollowing-out or withering away of the state. For the state remains a vital site for meta-governance and the most important legitimating agency through which most processes of governance have to pass (Clarke 2004). Especially in the course of the individualisation of public services, even individual public agents have gained completely new competences and discretion (van Berkel & Valkenburg 2007). On the one hand, power and competences are moved downwards to decentralised organisations, local tiers of government, or individual agents and clients/consumers. On the other hand, the practices of governing social policy are moved upwards to supranational institutions, most importantly the EU. At the same time, each trend itself involves a wide range of diverse meanings and practices. Overall, these dynamics massively increase the complexity of the institutionalised social relationships within a state. Eventually, it will be shown how such developments can pose a challenge to a society's capacity for democratic self-governance.

Before taking a closer look at the activation paradigm as a transnational phenomenon in the next subsection, at least two critical points should be made about the dominant governance narrative in political science, sociology, public administration, and EU studies. First, this narrative is often not linked with the basic concepts of social and political theory necessary for understanding modern democratic societies (Clarke 2004). Debates address the changing actors, capacities, and institutions involved in the regulation of public affairs. However, the consequences of these processes in constituting specific norms, subjects, identities, or spaces have largely been neglected. Second and closely connected with this weak social theoretical foundation, the shift towards governance often entails a shift towards a new post-ideological image of politics (Newman 2005a; Offe 2008; Walters 2004). Instead of assuming that politics is characterised by antagonistic interests and identities, many governance arrangements and theories seem to be based on ideas of pragmatic, technical problem-solving and the possibility of reconciling conflicting political standpoints in win-win situations. The transnational activation debate in the EES is a very good example of this trend. As will be shown in Chapter 3 in particular, the Strategy constantly promotes a rebalancing of flexibility and security in a free-market framework which nevertheless benefits everyone – the state, the economy, and the socially excluded.

In contrast, this book embeds its investigation in a rich account of human interaction and aims to specifically examine the political and contested nature of that interaction. This is mainly accomplished through its citizenship perspective, which is discussed in detail in the next chapter. This approach offers valuable insights on the situation of individual citizens or groups of citizens. Moreover, it is capable of uncovering various alternative demands, which might run counter to current social policies. And finally, it is capable of identifying shifting patterns of inclusion and exclusion resulting from the dominant discourse. At the same time, it can be shown how specific governance practices (in this case the EES) develop a dynamic independent of their explicit objectives, for such practices intervene in the constitution of politics in general and citizenship in particular.

The transnational character of the activation agenda

With regard to the governance of social policy beyond the state, the activation paradigm is a brilliant example of the increasingly transnational interconnectedness of discourses surrounding state reform and the modernisation of welfare. In addition, these discourses are increasingly embedded in and structured by transnational modes of governance which interact with reorganisations of national welfare states. The most important instance in this respect is the EU's EES which also constitutes the procedural blueprint and a vital element in the Union's broader Lisbon Strategy. The latter strategy was launched by the Lisbon European Council in 2000 as a massive political programme in order to 'become the most competitive and dynamic knowledge-based economy in the world, capable of sustainable economic growth with more and better jobs and greater social cohesion' (European Council 2000, No. 5). Most governance processes under this umbrella were based on the open method of coordination (OMC), based on the procedures of the EES.

Social policy and the welfare state were long seen as determined chiefly by national legacies, shielded by national sovereignty and, therefore, largely unaffected by external influences. The same was deemed true for citizenship. Furthermore, the EU had tried to expand its activities into the realm of employment and social policy for quite some time but with very little success. If nothing else, developments were restricted or enacted piecemeal because the Union lacks a clear legal competence in this regard. In relation to the different historical, institutional, and cultural contexts of national social policies, European regulation is generally controversial although some argue that globalisation poses similar challenges to all welfare regimes and that the best response might lie beyond the state (see Esping-Andersen 2002; Zeitlin 2003). However, although the Amsterdam Treaty could not solve this 'regulatory conundrum' (Rhodes 1995), it nevertheless changed its composition since the Union managed to extend its competences and activities into this domain by inventing the EES.

Launched in 1997, the Strategy was modelled after the coordination process of EU economic policies based on the Broad Economic Policy Guidelines

(BEPG) and has its legal foundation in Chapter VIII of the Amsterdam Treaty. In particular, the Strategy does not introduce supranational regulation. Instead, the member states commit themselves to common objectives and targets, which are formulated in the European Employment Guidelines (approved by the Council of the EU). They also produce National Action Plans (NAPs), respectively National Reform Programmes (NRPs since 2005) to report on their efforts to implement these guidelines, which are then synthesised and monitored by the Commission. On that basis, the Council can also issue country-specific employment recommendations (proposed by the Commission). However, it does not have the power to issue tougher sanctions.

Regarding its substance, activation constitutes the core theme of the EES and is portrayed as the best way to combine a strong focus on flexibility, growth, and competitiveness with social security and high job quality. Moreover, even though the OECD has been depicted as the 'principal ideational artist' setting the agenda and generating new ideas (cited in Noaksson & Jacobsson 2003), the EES is now perceived as the most important supranational influence on national welfare reforms as well as the strongest supranational driver of the activation agenda in Europe (Jenson 2007; Serrano Pascual 2007; Serrano Pascual & Crespo Suarez 2007b; van Berkel & Roche 2002). Therefore, the empirical focus of the present study of the impact of activation on citizenship is particularly on the EES. Thanks to the invention of the EES, the EU has become able to contest national policies and consequently elements of national citizenship in a comprehensive European conceptual debate – in a field where this was impossible before. At the same time, such a framework could also provide new opportunities and resources for other actors to contest national policies. Moreover, from a practical standpoint, the data and material provided within the Strategy offer valuable access to national reform debates and their transnational links and interdependencies.

Because the EES does not involve sanctions, it depends on the success of a continuous communicative process rather than compliance with legal norms. Drawing on approaches that emphasise the Strategy's discursive nature (Carmel 2005; Pfister 2008; Serrano Pascual & Crespo Suarez 2007b), this study understands the EES as a vital site for conceptual debate. This idea highlights that the EES is constituted by discursive interaction and therefore the social construction of knowledge. While constantly negotiating definitions of problems, possible solutions, and strategies, the member states and the Commission create a specific conceptual language where technical terms link certain problems with solutions. Beyond naming and selecting particular concepts, the EES is about their interplay and relative weight. Finally, the configuration of concepts has semantic implications because the context in which a term is used delineates the scope of its potential meanings. The different terms thus support, explain, and sometimes contradict each other. Of all the exchanges within the EES, the employment guidelines and the employment recommendations are most vital because they fix the Strategy's contents at a certain point of time. In general, in its essence as a conceptual debate, the EES makes specific practices 'of European governing thinkable and practicable, and … excludes other objects and forms from the remit of public or political action' (Carmel 2005: 42). It is a central argument of this book that this conceptual debate is not only about the parameters of social policy but also the concepts, meanings, and practices of citizenship.

It ought to be noted that the relationship between discourse and action or even political change is always complex and mediated (Fairclough & Wodak 1997; Titscher *et al.* 2000; van Dijk 1997; Wodak & Meyer 2001). If we understand the EES as discursive interaction, any investigation of it cannot be limited to the EU level but has to focus on the member states – yet without attributing every national development to the Strategy. Moreover, it would be mistaken to search for direct causal links in accordance with the positivist research tradition. Rather, our enterprise is an interpretive one, surveying the discourses and meanings within the Strategy.

On this basis, it is possible to outline a refined account of activation as a major trend which intervenes in historical developments of citizenship. Hence, activation is best understood as a dynamic construction consisting of practices and discourses. Its elements acquire different meanings in different contexts and at different times. Moreover, actors' ideas (what they think) are not separable from their practices (what they say, write, and do). It is impossible to extract an original or pure idea of activation from the various activating discourses and practices that may be observed and experienced. However, it is possible to distinguish (and compare) different kinds of practices, such as formulating a strategy in a policy paper, agreeing on benchmarks, contracting out a public service, consulting stakeholders, or making social benefits conditional on cooperation with a case manager. Each practice also expresses norms, conceptual knowledge and invites new interpretations which again generate new meanings. As a result, the concepts that characterise the activation agenda are constantly being interpreted and reproduced but also contested by the various actors involved in formulating and implementing social policy. Thus far, the core norms of universal labour market participation and a supply-side orientation have remained stable. However, the instruments and the conditions under which those norms are to be realised may vary widely. Hence, the paradigm may take different shapes in different political contexts and therefore affect citizenship in different ways. In addition, the paradigm clearly involves tensions, contradictions, and contestations which always have to be interpreted and negotiated in the particular case (Valkenburg 2007). As mentioned, the tension between the promise of empowerment and the risk of mere control requires particular attention when citizenship is involved.

To summarise, this book perceives the EES as a particular conceptual debate. This supranational communicative process does not determine national policies but rather interacts with national debates about welfare reform. Generally, and most essentially, this debate is not only about policies and solving technical problems but also about a society's fundamental principles, norms, and institutionalised social relationships. Much of this can be subsumed under the concept of citizenship. The new goals, for example, imply new legitimation for redistributing responsibilities, new definitions of risk, and new images of society and the citizen. Moreover, shifting governance procedures entail that social policies have new ways of intervening in the everyday lives and biographies of citizens. Finally, the significance of the transnational activation debate relocates debates about social policy – and implicitly about citizenship – within a new framework of political actors and processes. Analysing and evaluating the relational implications of this process constitutes a key challenge for social research such as that taken up by this study. Thus, the relational dimension of the activation paradigm is understood as a fundamental shift in the parameters of social and political membership and therefore best approached from a citizenship perspective. Such an approach opens up new insights about politics and the consequences for citizens because it translates transformations of social policy into citizens' rights and duties, participation, and access to societal resources. In the process, it will also become evident how a discourse on welfare restructuring affects citizenship on a much broader scale. Furthermore, it allows us to analyse activation with a particular view to inclusion and exclusion.

Before turning our attention to citizenship as the central theoretical category of this study (in Chapter 2), the final section of this chapter outlines the structure of the book.

Outline of the book

Following these introductory thoughts, the next chapter elaborates on citizenship as the key theoretical concept and the main point of interest of the study. Besides the foregoing discussion of the general conditions and trends affecting citizenship, the theoretical discussion of the following chapter constitutes the conceptual foundation of this study.

The next part of the book contains four case studies. Chapter 3 traces the development of the debate about activation and particularly about gender equality in this context at the EU level. In particular, it demonstrates how activation is developed as a network of concepts and meanings within the structures and practices of the EES. It is followed by three chapters which reconstruct and compare the debates on activation and transformations of citizenship in Germany, the UK, and Hungary respectively. Those three chapters largely follow the same basic structure: first, they outline the most relevant welfare reforms and identify the gender dimension of those reforms. Second, each chapter interprets these changes in terms of shifting citizenship practices. And finally, each chapter gives an account of the different contestations behind these new citizenship practices. Including contestations from national actors as well as from the transnational level allows for linking national reforms with the broader activation discourse. At the same time, the book pays close attention to the specific characteristics of each national case study since a comprehensive analysis of discourses in general and conceptual debates in particular would be impossible without being embedded in rich contextual information. In this manner, the developments in Germany and the UK are rather similar as we can see the gradual – though often substantive – adjustment of existing welfare and citizenship regimes. The Hungarian case, however, displays a much more rigorous break in many dimensions reaching far beyond the welfare state – welfare institutions, citizenship practices, the country's role in the international and European realm, cultural orientations, and the economy are all in a state of essential upheaval. Therefore, the scope and the time frame of this chapter are slightly different in order to account for those specific circumstances.

The book's final chapter presents the findings of the study and discusses their implications. Regarding the empirical findings, it reaffirms the view that a transnational conceptual debate about social and economic modernisation is taking place at the level of the EU and that this debate has implications for how we understand and practice citizenship. Moreover, the activation agenda as a large-scale programme for contemporary welfare is affecting citizenship in all three countries. All these cases share a tendency towards individualised duties which are mostly based on contract-like relationships and bolstered by new disciplinary regimes. In contrast, the inherent promise of increased access to societal resources did not result in a substantial decrease of gender inequalities in any of the cases. Moreover, apart from some exceptions concerning family policies and education, each case also displays a turn away from rights and rights language, as had been first expressed in a shift towards quantitative targets. Yet the national approaches are quite diverse in kind and degree and they should not be misunderstood as merely applying European standards or complying with European norms.

Rather, at the EU level, the basic concepts of the activation discourse have been developed collectively. The EES can be understood as a process of political knowledge production, meaning that it is politically more significant in terms of meaning making than in terms of redistribution or potential influence on behaviour. Hence, within the Strategy, the European Commission and the member states negotiate the epistemic foundations (i.e. the underlying knowledge) for transformations of welfare and citizenship on a transnational scale. Among the most important effects of this debate is the fact that gender equality has ceased to be debated in a context of human rights or as an objective in its own right. Instead, it has increasingly become seen as a functional requirement for economic and demographic objectives. In general, the individualistic perspective inherent in the activation discourse, combined with a neglect of rights and rights language impedes attempts to put the gender equality agenda back on track. The activation paradigm can therefore have potentially negative impacts on citizens in terms of reproducing and newly generating specific forms of exclusion and inequality.

With respect to the political and theoretical implications of those findings, the chapter concludes that in order to guarantee an inclusive, progressive, and balanced development of citizenship in times of massive institutional and epistemic transformations, it is indispensable to open up the conceptual debates surrounding such developments to the participation of the affected citizens. In other words, since the activation of the welfare state is a deeply political process, it requires an element of political citizenship.

Notes

1 Concerning the socially constructed nature of work, see Grint (1998), for a particular gender perspective see Brush (1998). For an argument concerning the interdependence between gender and work, see Lewis (2004).
2 International in this context should not mean global but a group of actors including Canada, many Western European states, the EU, the OECD and the World Bank.

2
From citizenship to citizenship in practice

A citizenship perspective relates the EU-wide activation debate to the terms and conditions of political membership in the EU and its member states. It thus provides a very comprehensive framework in which to analyse and evaluate how the spreading activation paradigm reacts with different social and political contexts. In this context, it should be stressed that each historical citizenship formation is closely entangled with the historically dominant forms of political organisation. For example, the meanings of 'citizenship' and 'citizen' have differed notably in the Greek polis, the Roman Empire, the city republics in Renaissance Italy, and the modern nation states. Even the modern nation state is not a static phenomenon. While it did not disappear as suggested by some contributions to the early globalisation debate (for example Ohmae 1995), its character is constantly changing and citizenship constitutes the key relational feature in such a state. For example, the idea of the state as the collective expression of a homogenous nation has been successfully challenged by different social movements whose claims are mirrored in academic debates about exclusion and inequalities stemming from the wide-ranging diversity of life situations (Benhabib 1996; Phillips 1993; Tully 1995; Young 1989; 1990); the feminist movement certainly plays a major role in such developments (Turner 1994). Others have demonstrated how the boundary of national citizenship is being blurred by an emerging human rights regime (Delanty 2000; Jacobson 1996; Soysal 1994) and by a variety of (more or less formal) elements of citizenship in the European Union.

Therefore, the notion of citizenship to be developed in this chapter has to be able to identify the widest possible range of changes – in degree and in kind – and should be able to understand citizenship in its dynamic nature.

A developing institution – historical process and essential contestedness

One of the most promising starting points for a theoretical discussion of citizenship is still provided by T.H. Marshall's (1992) seminal essay first published in 1950. In his account of its historical emergence in Britain, citizenship is most generally defined as 'full membership in a community' (Marshall 1992: 18), thus implying rights and duties. Moreover, he distinguishes three dimensions of citizenship – civil, political, and social – which had developed in consecutive periods. However, Marshall's text should not be read as a general theory of citizenship that can be simply applied to the present case (see Giddens 1995; Mann 1987; Turner 1990). Rather, we can approach it as a classic text which might have outlived the circumstances of its origin but still offers illuminating insights. The most intriguing idea in this respect is its understanding of citizenship as a 'developing institution' (Marshall 1992: 18):

> There is no universal principle that determines what those rights and duties shall be, but societies in which citizenship is a developing institution create an image of an ideal citizenship against which achievement can be measured and towards which aspiration can be directed. (Marshall 1992: 18)

This idea elicits the insight that citizenship is always the result of a historical process and that change is a constitutive feature. This historically contingent notion of citizenship has also been confirmed by other studies which show how particular configurations emerged through interaction between citizens and the state or between groups of citizens in a specific context (for example Bellamy, Castiglione, & Santoro 2004; Bendix 1964; Brubaker 1992; Hanagan & Tilly 1999; Therborn 1977; Tilly 1975;). However, while Marshall's historical view on citizenship is convincing, his account of the driving forces behind this historical process is somehow unsatisfactory. Theoretically speaking, while ideal citizenship serves here as a hypothetical reference point, it is not clear where this ideal comes from. Moreover, when arguing that the opposed dynamics of citizenship and the capitalist class system were finally reconciled with the advent of social citizenship granting all citizens a 'modicum of welfare and security', he seems to suggest this historical process has an endpoint. However, against the background of older and newer structural and discursive challenges to the welfare state and its normative foundations, such historical finality is hardly convincing. The advent of the activation paradigm is an excellent example for such a large-scale challenge. Furthermore, the transformation of citizenship in the course of European integration demonstrates that the political space in which citizenship is developing is not a natural given.

An alternative and more compelling account of the driving force behind citizenship as historical process is provided by Ruth Lister who, drawing on Gallie (1956), characterises citizenship as an essentially contested concept (Lister 2003a).[1] This attribute is vital for understanding the dynamic nature of citizenship. In Marshall's case, its historical development is driven by a discrepancy between actual and ideal citizenship. However, that process seems to steer towards an endpoint while the origin of the ideal as such is unclear. Moreover, for all the differences between actual and ideal citizenship, Marshall seems to assume significant societal consensus about the ideal. This changes radically under the condition of essential contestedness, for citizenship will always be subject to disagreement and conflict. In other words, the historical process of citizenship is not only about a gap between actual achievements and ideal citizenship but also about a multiplicity of competing ideals. Chapter 1 indicated how the paradigmatic shift to activation has produced an entire body of new concepts, norms, and objectives. Moreover, given its dynamic discursive nature the various ideals are not fixed but once again contested, both from outside and within the new paradigm. Finally, in accordance with the transnational character of the activation discourse, the institutions of the EU (and the other member states) have become involved in this debate and are now contesting national social policy. Of course, the mere existence of contestation does not tell us anything about its outcome.

Disagreement, conflict, and competing ideals can be observed in academic debates as well as in political and social action. In discussing citizenship theories, Gerard Delanty identifies three main strands: liberal approaches emphasising rights and the equal status of all citizens, republican approaches stressing political participation and/or collective identities in a specific political community, and lastly a more diverse strand of radical approaches.[2] The final strand may come from quite different directions but is nevertheless said to share a threefold model of citizenship consisting of a politics of voice, difference, and justice (Delanty 2000: 46; see also Kostakopoulou 2008). Beyond academic disputes, citizenship is also contested in practice. Even though not all social struggles explicitly refer to the concept of citizenship, they are mostly targeting the terms and conditions of membership in a particular society at a specific point of time. Examples of active and practical interventions in existing citizenship regimes can be found in all periods, such as labour movements, gay and lesbian movements, struggles for recognition by migrants or ethnic minorities, the disability movement, and feminism. The degree of such dissent can vary from friendly and cooperative conversation to revolutionary opposition. Even governments themselves often alter the terms of citizenship although such interventions are more likely to be labelled as reform, modernisation, or simply objective necessity. Against this background, a wide range of actors can be expected to be involved in contesting European welfare states and their activation: national politicians, the EU and its institutions, other international organisations, courts, civil society organisations, trade unions, academics, and the media. This historical contestedness and open-endedness of citizenship has further implications which are vital for understanding it in the context of this study. On the one hand, the paradigmatic character of the aforementioned trend towards activation also affects the classical association of the welfare state with social citizenship. Marshall's trinity of civil, political, and social citizenship should not be seen as given or as independent entities. Instead, it is essential to investigate developments in citizenship with a view toward inter-relationships and interdependencies between its different dimensions. In addition, the emergence of entirely new dimensions of citizenship is possible as well (see Figure 2.1). Therefore, this research opts for a comprehensive perspective on citizenship as a whole rather than a narrower focus on social rights. On the other hand, a closer look at the demands of many radical theoretical and practical contestations reveals a further key characteristic requiring our special attention: the Janus-faced nature of citizenship.

The Janus-faced nature of citizenship

In Western European democracies, citizenship can be seen as the historical explanation as well as the institutionalised locus of social integration and political legitimacy. At the same time, however, each historical citizenship formation also establishes a certain order of inclusion and exclusion. This 'Janus-faced nature' (Lister 2003a: 4) of citizenship constitutes a key interest of this research, making it highly relevant for understanding the activation paradigm. To begin with, citizenship distinguishes citizens from non-citizens, insiders from those outsiders who are excluded from all the benefits arising from the status of citizenship. Each citizenship regime also creates specific types of partial citizens or denizens who are excluded from some aspects of citizenship while enjoying others (see Bauböck 2006; Castles & Davidson 2000; Hammar 1994; Soysal 1994). Lastly, citizenship can have quite different effects on different groups of citizens and therefore lead to considerable inequalities among citizens who are formally equal. This ambivalent characteristic of citizenship has been uncovered by a number of diverse approaches challenging the dominant liberal and republican schools. Among them, feminism is a particular strong voice criticising such exclusion from within. This aspect of exclusion is crucial to consider when studying and attempting to evaluate the activation paradigm.

Citizenship has therefore become a central theme in feminist welfare state research (Borchorst 1998). The labour market and welfare state have always been identified as key sites of women's exclusion from full citizenship. Social policy and the institutions of the welfare state play a crucial role in constituting and reproducing those inequalities. Even though female employment rates have greatly increased and even though women have the same formal rights as men in most countries, the gender contracts and institutions of most welfare states are still based on an unequal distribution of labour. On the one hand, women are still seen as the main providers of care work. On the other hand, they face substantive disadvantages in the labour market, for example, unequal pay or concentration in jobs with poorer working conditions and lower career chances. The significance of such instances of exclusion is best understood in relation to the fundamental critique of the distinction between a private and a public sphere (see Okin 1998; Pateman 1989), sometimes taken for granted in liberal as well as republican political theory. This dichotomy produces inequality for women as they are mostly associated with the 'private' (and therefore subordinated to men as the public heads of households or breadwinners). Moreover, this distinction obscures the fact that the private sphere is also highly subject to and structured by political, legal, and social institutions.

Institutions of the welfare state, the labour market, and/or the educational system play a vital role in constructing and reproducing gender relations within a society. They affect highly private issues such as pregnancy, childcare, custody, marriage, divorce, and many other aspects of personal autonomy. Furthermore, with respect to the public sphere, liberal and republican approaches might disagree about the size and extent of citizens' activity. Yet, both have been equally criticised for their blindness to the various forms of unequal access to the public sphere – as well as unequal power within it. In the process, critics have indicated that public spheres are not characterised by a homogenous citizenry but by difference and diversity (see Dietz 1992; Phillips 1993, 1991; Young 1989, 1990). In fact, despite the universalising language of citizenship, most citizenship regimes are biased towards male, heterosexual, white, working and able-bodied citizens, thereby excluding others.

In this context, I have already pointed out that the core norm of the activation agenda – universal labour market participation – covers the entire population and not just male breadwinners. Therefore, it should be expected that the arrival of the activation discourse also implies significant shifts in the gender norms and relationships underlying European welfare states. Moreover, in the same way, the shift towards activation intervenes in a crucial aspect of exclusion from equal citizenship: those gender inequalities constituted by the welfare system and the labour market. However, how this transformation should be evaluated from a perspective on gender equality cannot be established in advance since it likewise implies risks and opportunities. In contrast, it is a shift that has to be analysed empirically. If activation has the potential to trigger and shape changes in citizenship, a focus on gender can work as a litmus test for changing patterns of exclusion and inclusion, in particular when considering the shift towards an adult worker model as basic gender norm associated with the activation paradigm. In this context, it is essential to differentiate between the gender norms underlying political discourses and practices and the actual social realities within a specific society at a certain point of time. While traditional family structures corresponding to a male breadwinner/female caregiver model are actually being eroded (Crompton 1999), the gender norms of the adult worker model are not an adequate description of the emerging social realities either (Lewis 2001; Lewis & Giullari 2005). The best strategy for uncovering potential instances of exclusion from full citizenship empirically is to trace contestations of social policy reforms and developments of citizenship – especially by those who directly experience disadvantages.

To sum up, citizenship is seen in the present study as a historical process driven by its essential contestedness. Among the most crucial contestations – raised by feminists but also by multiculturalists, post-colonialists, radical democrats, and others who focus on structural inequalities potentially hidden behind the universal language of citizenship – is the insight that citizenship is not only about inclusion and rights, but also exclusion and differences in the access to its benefits. Since the turn to activation also intervenes in these exclusionary elements, an empirical focus on gender should provide key insights of broader relevance. Yet, given the internal complexity of citizenship already outlined, the next paragraphs address the question of how to understand citizenship in empirical research.

Citizenship in practice

In order to identify the widest range of possible changes and account for the dynamic character of citizenship as a historical process, it is first of all necessary to decouple the empirical concept from purely normative notions of citizenship. In contrast, it is assumed that each existing citizenship formation will display a mix of features emphasised by different normative theories. It is thus useful to investigate the characteristics and developments of this composite concept in terms of particular practices. This approach is particularly inspired by studies of an emerging EU citizenship which have uncovered the incremental development of EU citizenship (see also next section). In particular, they pointed to the significance of rights and resources which may not be explicitly designated as parts of EU citizenship but constitute citizenship in practice.[3] A very helpful account is provided by Antje Wiener (1998, see also Wiener 1997, 2005) who highlights the processes of institution-building and the contribution of citizenship to the 'stateness' of the EU. In this respect, citizenship practice is said to be that 'dynamic citizen-polity relation' (Wiener 1998: 7) consisting of:

> [t]he historical elements of rights, access and belonging which in turn specify the historical variability of the institutionalised link between the citizen and the polity/ community. The historical elements tie individuals to the state by law and identity, on the one hand, and they reflect the constraints and opportunities for access to political participation, on the other. (Wiener 1998: 31)

In contrast to normative conceptualisations, this notion of citizenship allows for a much more comprehensive picture of actual historical formations. By contextualising citizenship and treating it as an open-ended historical process, it becomes possible to translate previously static aspects of rights and status into a more dynamic framework of historically contingent institutions and practices, which can include rights just as well as participatory patterns. Moreover, by focusing more broadly on routinised relationships, we can better understand those more informal and discursive elements of citizenship which are not explicitly spelled out in legal terms. Furthermore, this broader notion allows us to include the social, cultural, and economic realities of particular citizenship configurations. What ultimately matters for the individual citizen is not only her formal status but its realisation through specific institutions and everyday practices. In other words, a broader empirically oriented focus is capable of testing formal citizenship rights against their practical and material implementation. Finally, and most important in the context of this research, this approach is most suited for identifying and assessing even subtle changes.

However, for the objectives of our project, Wiener's account has to be modified in some points. To begin with, the focus should be broadened from the immediate link between the state/polity and the citizens (i.e. the vertical dimension of citizenship) to those institutionalised relationships between citizens themselves, which are predetermined by the polity (horizontal dimension).[4] Incorporation in the economy or gender contracts are just two examples. Ignoring the horizontal dimension runs the risk of subsuming all intrasocietal relations to the private realm, thereby reproducing a strong public/private divide and overlooking important patterns of inclusion and exclusion.

Figure 2.1 Dimensions and analytical elements of citizenship

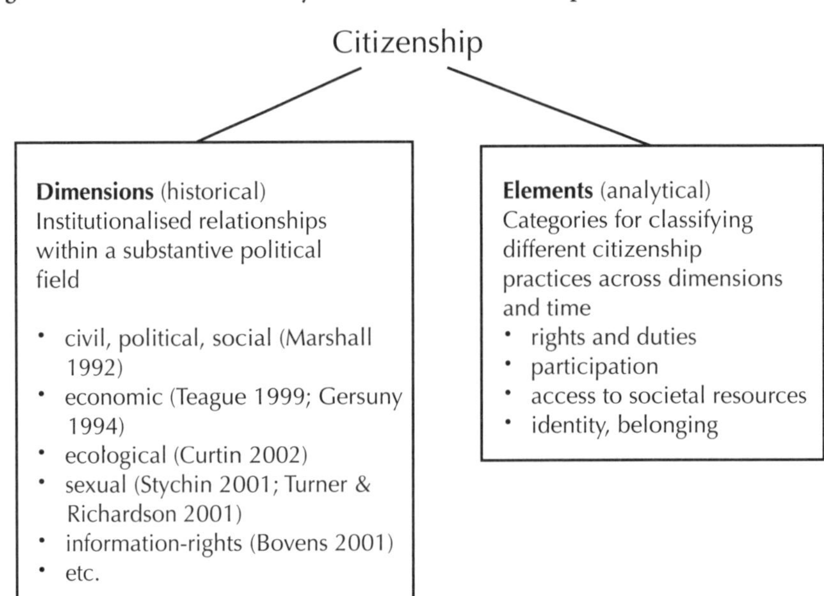

Furthermore, Wiener's basic elements of citizenship (cited above) should be reconsidered (see also Figure 2.1). With regard to the rights element it is important to complement citizenship rights with a notion of duties and responsibilities, especially when exploring the social and economic dimension.[5] Moreover, her access element contains aspects of participation (which is the main element of republican approaches) as well as the insight that there is a difference between having a right and having the real opportunity to benefit from it. In contrast to Wiener I suggest distinguishing more clearly between participatory and access elements in order to increase analytical clarity. Especially when our investigation is expanded to the horizontal dimension of citizenship, the number of different patterns of participation and access will multiply quickly. At the same time, participatory practices will always be characterised by an element of voice. One could, for instance, mention participation in the workplace, in schools, the local community or civil society. Moreover, these practices contain a constructive potential inasmuch as they can provide opportunities for citizens to shape their own environment (within the constraints of unequal power relationships). Looking at participation only with regard to access to participation might expose those barriers which exclude certain groups of citizens in practice. However, that would still disregard the diversity of participatory practices, and different distributions of power within them as well as their constructive input into society. Moreover, having taken participation out of the access element and demarcated them more clearly, I suggest interpreting access in the broadest possible sense: as access to societal resources. Again, when we consider the horizontal dimension, equal citizenship is not just a question of access to the welfare state but of a much broader range of resources. These can range from access to material benefits provided by the welfare state, all the way to education, labour market access, and access to social resources in terms of time, social networks, social roles, or personal autonomy. In more general terms, while participation involves notions of democracy and voice, access to societal resources refers to substantive notions of justice, equality, and opportunity. The element of belonging, in contrast, is seen here as a second-order attribute that follows citizenship practices rather than preceding them. Hence, the identity dimension of citizenship is acknowledged but not included in the conceptual and empirical investigation of this study.[6]

Finally, I suggest taking the notion of citizenship practice in a more literal sense. While Wiener mostly uses it in singular form as abstraction representing the total of all institutional ties between the citizenry and their polity at a certain time, this study is interested in the multiplicity of actual citizenship practices on the ground – both as citizens' activity and as the practices of political, legal, or administrative institutions. For example, the present study encountered family policies increasing entitlements to parental leave (rights), the sanctions against 'non-cooperative' unemployed benefit claimants (duties), large scale childcare programmes (access to societal resources), or public consultations about policy proposals (participation). In other words, this book is particularly interested in understanding citizenship in practice and as an aspect of the patterned everyday life of citizens and institutions. It breaks with accounts of citizenship which imagine it as a unified entity that can be demonstrated in its totality rather easily. Instead, the account of citizenship developed in this discussion stresses contextualisation over theoretical idealisation. Citizenship understood that way can be seen in analogy to other complex and composite concepts such as 'the state' or 'social order' which also elude a comprehensive vision.

It was already mentioned in Chapter 1 that the activation agenda constitutes a fundamental shift of objectives, governance practices, and scope in social policy debates. Moreover, its paradigm redefines the normative, analytical, constitutional, and even ontological key concepts underlying social policy. If citizenship is thus about rights and duties, participation, belonging, and access to resources, it is highly likely that such fundamental changes would affect citizenship in various ways. At the same time, it is of particular interest in the present study how potentially shifting citizenship practices linked with the activation paradigm also imply shifting patterns of inclusion and exclusion. The previous discussion has repeatedly noted the ambivalent character of activation and the key tension between activation policies that attempt to empower and those that merely attempt to control the behaviour of the targeted citizens. In addition, the particular relevance of gender has been highlighted as a realm in which the exclusionary implications of activation will become particularly visible. Now, this ambivalence can be approached from a citizenship perspective and translated into a language of citizenship practices. On the one hand, redefinitions of risk and demands for redistributing responsibilities between citizens and state are most likely to intervene with the rights and duties element of citizenship. Especially when such a redistribution of responsibilities is combined with the supply-side perspective, which emphasises individual resources and behaviour over structural factors, and with new notions of the citizens as self-contained and self-responsible life-course entrepreneurs, the most likely result will be limitations of rights and/or new duties. That is to say: rights might be abolished, and new duties introduced. It can be assumed that an activation regime which focuses primarily on limitations of rights or new duties is more likely to seek to control and discipline individual behaviour than to empower citizens and enhance their capabilities.

On the other hand, we can interpret claims for investment in social capital and needs-based individual empowerment from a citizenship perspective, as promises of increased access to societal resources. Similarly, claims for the inclusion of stakeholders or the participation of civil society can be read as inherent promises of increased participation. There are other promises as well. Just how they interact and whether the inherent possibilities of increased access and participation eventually materialise has to be assessed in each particular case. On the whole, given the existing gender inequalities in the labour market and the welfare state, realising the new gender contract promoted by the activation paradigm will reproduce old patterns of gendered exclusion from full citizenship and even produce new ones, unless that transformation is based on policies and substantive provisions which clearly seek to empower women (and men) and to increase their ability to equally share work and care responsibilities. Moreover, this study is mainly interested in the role of the EU within the far-reaching activation of citizenship. Therefore, the next section situates this specific development of citizenship within the context of a broader transformation of citizenship in the course of European integration.

The 'European' transformation of citizenship

The discussion has thus far addressed citizenship as the general terms and conditions of political membership. In addition, it has pointed to various characteristics of activation that call for a citizenship perspective. Moreover, Chapter 1 outlined activation as an essentially transnational phenomenon, in particular highlighting the conceptual debate within the EES. Therefore, in the following, the activation agenda and its impact on citizenship will be situated within the context of broader transformations of citizenship in Europe.

The Maastricht Treaty introduced the legal concept of Citizenship of the European Union as a status awarded to every citizen of an EU member state.[7] In addition, elements of citizenship can be identified which historically precede and substantially exceed the narrow legal meaning of citizenship in the EU (for example Maas 2007; Meehan 1993; Olsen 2008; Wiener 1998, 2003). These elements are primarily based on rights to free movement and anti-discrimination legislation (Shaw 2007) which were framed as citizenship rights and subsequently elaborated and expanded through the case law of the European Court of Justice (ECJ) (see, for example, Kostakopoulou 2005, 2007; Mather 2005). In earlier interpretations, EU citizenship has been described as a space for development or as a set of possibilities rather than a fixed and clear status (Preuss 1995b; Shaw 1998). However, Shaw has made it clear that the direction and scope of this development are strictly confined by the limited competences conferred upon the EU by the member states (Shaw 2007). These limitations include only partial competences in the realm of social and employment policy. Nevertheless, there is evidence for elements of social citizenship at the EU level (for example Castle-Kanerova & Jordan 2001; Faist 2001; Jenson 2007; Magnusson & Strath 2004).

Since the relevance of the EES for the investigation has been repeatedly emphasised, particular attention has to be paid to relate this policy process to citizenship. At least in the Strategy's beginning, its provisions on gender equality were highlighted as highly significant for the promotion of gender equality and gender mainstreaming in Europe.[8] Even although the EES has a legal base in the Treaties, it is not linked to the legal provisions concerning EU citizenship. Nor can it prescribe binding social rights to the member states. In other words, the EES does not have the capacity to generate any new formal European citizenship rights or duties. Yet its conceptual debate might be relevant with regard to substantive citizenship practices beyond explicitly formulated legal rights at the EU level. On the one hand, at the EU level such a debate could lead to the instalment of practices that may be seen as substantive elements of citizenship. On the other hand, it could intervene in developments of national citizenship. In this regard, particularly the employment recommendations can be seen as European contestations of national citizenship. Moreover, as indicated above, the conceptual debate at the EU level creates a rich body of new norms, concepts, meanings, and practices. These are in turn received, interpreted, used, and often co-produced by national actors, which could affect national debates about social policy reforms. Finally, the EES might affect the position of specific national actors and thereby lend force to contestations of citizenship. In fact, the present study finds that the European activation debate is to a lesser extent about citizenship at the EU level and more about EU level re-negotiations of national citizenship.

This specific characteristic of a legal formulation of citizenship as intentionally limited and explicitly complementary reveals the paradox character of the EU polity, which is not meant to be a nation state but nevertheless includes a 'touch of stateness' (Shaw & Wiener 1999). In this regard, it should not be forgotten that the objective of gaining legitimacy from successful problem-solving is important in spreading new modes of governance in areas where the Union did not have clear legal competences. More generally, citizenship is certainly one of the central strategies for achieving legitimacy in the history of Western democracies (see Tilly 1975; for more critical accounts Hindess 1998; Mann 1987).

To sum up, inasmuch as citizenship is viewed as an open-ended historical process driven by continuous contestation, it can be understood as a composite of different citizenship practices establishing and reproducing institutionalised relationships. More specifically, citizenship can be about rights and duties, about participation and about access to societal resources. At the moment, it is not yet clear how the conceptual debate within the EES might affect citizenship and whether this will influence national citizenship, EU citizenship, or just blur the boundary between them.

Notes

1 According to Vandenberg (2000), essentially contested concepts are, first 'ascriptive', that is normative and analytical elements are inextricably linked; second, they are 'internally complex' and open to divergent interpretations; and, third, they refer to an (historical) 'exemplar', which is also open to diverging interpretations of its exemplary meaning (pp. 4–5).

2 Although the radical school might be even more diverse, liberal and republican approaches also involve various conceptual subtypes and stretch across the entire political spectrum.

3 For studies exploring EU citizenship beyond the formal concept of a *Citizenship of the Union* (Article 17 to Article 22 EC Treaty) see, for example, Kostakopoulou (2005, 2007), Maas (2007), Meehan (1993), Shaw (1998, 2007), Bellamy and Warleigh (2001) and Wiener (1997, 1998, 2003).

4 The distinction between a vertical and a horizontal dimension is borrowed from Siim (2000; see also Voet 1998).

5 Although he is much vaguer on duties than on rights, even Marshall states that the duty to work is of 'paramount importance" (Marshall 1992: 45); on the broader political and normative debate about 'citizenship duties' see Kymlicka and Norman (1994).

6 Concerning the interplay between citizenship and identity/political community, Jo Shaw (1997) argues that when looking at historical examples both aspects seem to be related but that this relationship is theoretically under-determined. Maurizio Ferrera (2005) makes the convincing point that it was more likely the condition of being 'locked-in' the nation state that allowed extensive patterns of redistribution to emerge; some form of common identity can be assumed as a further consequence of this process. For relevant contributions discussing the role of identity in citizenship, see Bader (2002), Delanty (1995), Habermas (1992), Isin and Wood (1999), Miller (2000), Münch (2001), Pfister (2005), or Preuss (1995a).

7 The legal provisions of Citizenship of the European Union are contained in Articles 17 to 22 of the EC Treaty. They were crucially amended by the Treaty of Amsterdam in 1995.

8 In 1998 the Council of Europe defined gender mainstreaming as 'the (re)organisation, improvement, development and evaluation of policy processes, so that a gender equality perspective is incorporated in all policies at all levels and at all stages, by the actors normally involved in policy-making" (Council of Europe 1998: 15).

3

The EU debate: gender equality in the EES

Having outlined the conceptual basis and the broader context of this study, the following four chapters discuss four empirical case studies. This chapter opens up the investigation by providing an account of the debate on welfare modernisation within the EES with a particular focus on gender equality. The development of this equity has experienced a gradual loss of visibility and relative weight since 2002. However, while explicit struggles about the status of gender equality have been limited this loss of visibility has to be seen against the background of shifts in the overall context of the Strategy towards growth, competitiveness, and more efficient policy advice. As a consequence, the disappearance of the gender equality dimension of the EES drastically weakens the Strategy's capacity to analyse, to identify, and combat instances of substantive inequality.

The history of social policy at the EU level has always been fraught with difficulty. Most attempts to extend the Union's activities and competences in such fields have encountered fierce resistance from most member states. Regarding social policy in general, Leibfried and Pierson (1995) claim that activist policies by the Commission had been rather unsuccessful (until the mid-1990s) but that a process of negative market integration would nevertheless impose constraints on the member states and had limited their sovereignty and autonomy over welfare and labour market issues (for a similar account see Ferrera 2003, 2005). Most of this process had been driven by decisions of the ECJ and by indirect de facto pressures arising from the common market (also Leibfried 2005). In the area of employment policy, we have a similar picture. For a long time, that policy only consisted of creating a community-wide labour market whereas successful attempts to go beyond such pure market creation were limited to aspects of health and safety as well as gender equality (Streeck 1995). While the member states' semi-sovereignty over their social policy is mostly described in negative terms as a weakening or loss of control, the Union's impact on gender equality, particularly through ECJ rulings, has been greeted positively. At least within the limited focus on labour markets and employment determined by Article 141 (formerly 119), the relevant ECJ decisions can be seen as powerful contestations of national exclusionary practices (see for example, Lewis & Ostner 1995). From the early 1990s on, however, new constellations and changed perceptions about the need to act at the EU level fostered the emergence of a new process. As a result, the EU could expand its activities significantly into the realm of employment policy with gender equality as a core element from the outset.

In the following, the substantive development of the gender equality dimension will be scrutinised in the context of the specific policy process of the EES and its procedural characteristics. While revisions and reformulations of the concrete guidelines are normal in this variable and cyclical process, a number of key events have led to more drastic alterations since 2003. All procedural changes have been clearly linked with substantive aims based on theory and each of these events will be addressed in more detail when the focus is narrowed down to gender equality. Before that, the activation discourse within the EES will be introduced in more general terms.

The activation debate within the EES

At the EU level, two developments were of particular importance for formulating the basic objectives of the EES, and more generally for the move from more traditional social protection to activation. A first step consisted in narrowing down the focus from social policy in general to employment policy in particular. However weak, there have always been voices calling for a stronger EU social policy. Yet, despite the successful inclusion of social policy in the Maastricht Treaty (as a Social Protocol with UK opt out) and in the Amsterdam Treaty (when even the UK agreed), the Commission restrained itself from lobbying for a comprehensive social policy agenda during the 1990s (Ashiagbor 2005). At the same time, efforts were increasingly directed at establishing a 'fully fledged employment policy, which is not parasitical on its social policy' (Ashiagbor 2005: 104). This shift towards a self-contained employment agenda is closely connected with a fundamental reorientation in thinking about the institutions and future of the welfare state. As a result, the second crucial programmatic reorientation consisted in a turn away from employment protection to employment promotion (Rhodes 2005). Employment policy should work towards inclusive and dynamic labour markets with a highly skilled and flexible workforce rather than just the protection of existing jobs. At the EU level these reorientations can be traced back before the launch of the EES, particularly to the so called Delors White Paper (European Commission 1993) and to the 1994 European Council in Essen where an initial coordination process was put in place. The invention of the EES merely elevated those elements to a much more exposed position, leading to a much more comprehensive policy process (see also Goetschy 1999; Jenson & Pochet 2006).

In most general terms, the base line of the Strategy could be summarised as 'bringing as many people into the labour market as possible'. This goal has been promoted through analyses, options, strategies, and objectives. These are formulated in the annual Joint Employment Reports, and the Commission's guidelines, recommendations, and specific communications. Yet the objective of maximal labour market participation should not be achieved only by an unregulated labour market (or a positive universal right to work). Instead, the Strategy recognises that individual chances in the labour market differ considerably and that particular groups, such as women, older workers, low-skilled, or young people may face greater difficulties. Rather than merely suggesting liberalisation, deregulation, or traditional social democratic decommodification, the Strategy regularly makes the business case for most aspects of social and economic citizenship. A key characteristic of this discourse are various attempts to reconcile the notions of flexibility and security within a language of market orientation, economic necessity, and global interdependence. In the process, employment growth and (to some extent) productivity growth through education have become central objectives of contemporary employment and social policy across Europe.

Let us recall that an interest in the exclusionary element of citizenship is a central motivation for our underlying citizenship perspective. Moreover, it is to be expected that the activation discourse will disrupt certain social settlements that were characteristic for post-war Western Europe, especially standard meanings of work and gender relations. Such normative shifts certainly call for critical scrutiny. As a result, the specific focus of the present empirical study is on the gender equality dimension in the EES. This dimension is seen as ideal testing ground for exploring how the EES and the corresponding new paradigm might affect patterns of exclusion and (in)equality.

At this point, it is important to clarify that the EU's role in promoting gender equality more generally lies beyond the immediate focus of this study. Accordingly, important decisions of the European Court of Justice, directives, or broader strategies – such as the Framework Strategy for Gender Equality (see European Commission 2000) or the Roadmap to Gender Equality (see European Commission 2006b) – will be acknowledged as elements of the context but will not be central parts of this investigation.

The EU as promoter of gender equality in Europe

Gender equality has always been a key objective among the different provisions of the EES. However, as its role and its relative weight within the Strategy have not been constant, it is again useful to start by re-examining the initial structure and then address the major turning points. Initially, gender equality was a key objective of the EES, clearly demonstrating the high importance the Union attaches to it in reforming employment policy and labour market institutions (Rubery 2002). On the one hand, family structures, education, and basic gender roles have changed fundamentally over the last decades. This transformation is closely connected with the feminist movement's strong demands for more gender equality but also with increasing female labour market participation. On the other hand, governments have discovered increasing female employment rates as an important instrument for strengthening the fiscal sustainability of social security systems and securing employment growth.

However, this does not fully account for the initial high visibility of gender equality in the EES. In addition, three further aspects have to be considered. First, the 1995 United Nations (UN) Fourth World Conference on Women in Beijing (see United Nations 1995) had placed gender and gender mainstreaming very high on the international agenda, making it difficult to ignore (Interview 10). Second, the 1995 enlargement brought in countries which were not only very vocal in terms of promoting EU employment policy but also gender equality policies. The case of Sweden, which played a crucial role in the early stages of the EES, seems particularly important. In addition to its gender equality record, the Swedish government claimed to have played a key role in including equal opportunities in the Union's main principles in the Amsterdam Treaty and in committing the Union to gender mainstreaming (see Mosesdottir 2001: 39–40). Third, it should not be forgotten that gender equality constitutes (together with health and safety) the very core of successful EU social policy (Lewis & Ostner 1995; Streeck 1995).

Until the mid-term review in 2002, all employment guidelines were grouped under four pillars. 'Strengthening equal opportunities policies for women and men' constituted a whole pillar in its own right. Concerning the operationalisation and promotion of equal opportunities, the individual employment guidelines were quite consistent, at least until 2005. All of them concentrate on three main aspects. First, although not part of the very first set of guidelines (see Council of the EU 1997), gender mainstreaming is defined as the core principle of the EU approach to gender equality and ought to be the basis of every national strategy. While its inclusion is highlighted as a 'major impetus to the integration of equal opportunities issues into the employment framework' (Rubery 2002: 500), the Union also promotes an integrated approach, calling for positive action policies in order to tackle specific disadvantages. Such difficulties are the focus of the second element which highlights three gender gaps. These gaps have been measured statistically and refer to the lower share of women in the overall employment rate (the employment gap), the often higher percentage of women among the unemployed (the unemployment gap), and the structural problem of unequal pay (the gender pay gap). Vertical and horizontal labour market segregation is also consistently mentioned as a key factor contributing to the pay gap. Horizontal labour market segregation refers to the strong concentration of women and men in different sectors and occupations while wages in occupations dominated by women (especially in care-professions) are generally lower than in male-dominated ones (for example, in construction). Vertical labour market segregation describes the concentration of women at lower levels of the professional hierarchy since they often face so-called 'glass ceilings' or 'sticky floors'. Lastly, women are over-represented in atypical forms of employment (such as part-time, fixed-term, agency work, new forms of freelance work, and self-employment). The third regular element consists in family policy objectives for reconciling work and family life, whereby childcare is given particular attention. In addition to these three core elements of the guidelines, the Union did not refrain from issuing related recommendations to specific member states (see Chapters 4, 5 and 6).

Throughout the first five-year period of the EES, there was strong agreement about the relatively high value for the cause of gender equality. Based on the annual analyses of the European Commission's network of experts in the fields of employment, social inclusion, and gender equality,[1] Jill Rubery described the EES as 'by far the most important EU influence on equal opportunities policies' around the turn of the millennium (Rubery 2002: 500; see also European Commission 2002a). Beyond including equal opportunities as fourth pillar, she especially highlights the introduction of gender mainstreaming with the 1999 guidelines (Council of the EU 1999). This view of the EU as a 'catalyst' (Rubery 2002: 503), placing gender mainstreaming high on the agenda, was also expressed by Behning, Foden, and Serrano Pascual who concede that the EES 'can be regarded as the main possibility for pulling the gender mainstreaming approach from the European level towards the EU 15 member states' (2001: 19). In addition, the Lisbon European Council in 2000 formulated a positive vision for a future Union which is significantly based on the modernisation of welfare systems and which goes far beyond the EES. It called on the Union 'to become the most competitive and dynamic knowledge-based economy in the world, capable of sustainable economic growth with more and better jobs and greater social cohesion' (European Council 2000, no. 5). On the one hand, this ambitious goal included the formulation of explicit quantitative targets, among others a female employment rate of 60% by 2010, again strengthening the visibility and relative weight of equal opportunities within the larger reform project (Rubery 2002). On the other hand, the spread of new OMCs in different fields like social inclusion, pensions, or research extended the conceptual debate to neighbouring policy areas and thereby fostered the activation agenda throughout the EU. Instead of reforming labour markets, the project was now to fundamentally reform European economies and European societies as such (see also European Commission 2002b; 2002c; 2003b). Shortly afterwards, the 2002 Barcelona European Council added the target of providing childcare to at least 90% of children between three years and the mandatory school age and to at least 33% of children under three years by 2010 (European Council 2002). As a consequence of both the mainstreaming approach and the emphasis on quantitative targets, the EES is also described as an important instrument providing adequate indicators and statistical tools for analysing inequalities as well as promoting the further development of such tools (Rubery *et al.* 2003; Behning & Serrano Pascual 2001). Furthermore, thanks to its agenda-setting capacities, the EES has the potential to bring specific aspects of inequality to the attention of the member states and other EU institutions. Renewed emphasis on the gender pay gap can be seen as a particularly important example (see Rubery *et al.* 2003; Magnusson, Mosesdottir, & Serrano Pascual 2003b). At this point, it should also be mentioned that the awarding and administration of money from the European Social Fund (ESF) have been aligned with the provisions and objectives of the EES (European Commission 2001c).

However, despite all these positive aspects, the EES fails to explicitly spell out an exact vision of the kind of equality that should be achieved (Rubery 2002). Similarly, it does not provide a precise account of what the meaning of gender mainstreaming is.[2] In this regard, questions about the meaning and the necessary elements of gender mainstreaming were also a key element of all interviews conducted for this research, revealing quite a broad range of different understandings. Consequently, many contributions and reports emphasise the significance of historical and political context within the individual member states in their interactions within EES debates (Behning & Serrano Pascual 2001; European Commission 2002a; Magnusson, Mosesdottir, & Serrano Pascual 2003a). Moreover, despite its initially high status, the issue of gender equality lost much of its visibility over the years. The next subsection takes a closer look at the historical development of the gender equality dimension after the mid-term review in 2002.

Gender equality on the retreat

The non-binding and relatively open regime of the EES has been conducive to the emergence and especially the institutionalisation of a broad transnational discourse surrounding the modernisation of European labour market and welfare practices. Moreover, the procedures and the contents of this process have been repeatedly renegotiated. New objectives have been developed along the way and the process reorganised in accordance with them. However, this general openness has also allowed for significant shifts in the position, the relative weight and the meaning of its gender equality dimension.

While the Lisbon Strategy was launched in a climate of enthusiasm and widespread growth, it soon became clear that the European economy could not maintain its momentum. Moreover, in contrast to the initial hopes, which had also resulted in a rapid extension of policies under the Lisbon roof, actual political change was considered too slow. This tension between a broad and comprehensive strategy and the need to refocus the process on vital priorities constitutes one of the key debates underlying the EES and Lisbon. For the first time, this re-prioritisation became visible in the wake of the 2002 mid-term review, when the Barcelona European Council called for a revised EES based on concerns about its effectiveness (European Council 2002, no. 30–23). In response, the Commission issued a Communication ('Taking Stocks') summarising the conclusions of the review (European Commission 2002d). It asserted that the EES had had an impact on national employment policy and that it contributed to an overall 'shift in national policy formulation and focus – away from managing unemployment, towards managing employment growth' (European Commission 2002d: 2). On the positive side, the review found wide-ranging structural reforms throughout the Union, and convergence of a commitment to the process as such, as well as to certain underlying principles. That review also found that the Strategy had helped to increase policy cooperation among member states. However, structural reforms were far from accomplished. Fundamental reorientations were only in the early stages, still to be developed and implemented. And the process itself was still lagging behind initial expectations. At the same time, the document admitted difficulties in determining causal relationships between shifting national policies and the EES. As a result, the same Communication identified four main challenges for the next phase of the EES:

> (a) the need to set clear objectives in response to the policy challenges (b) the need to simplify the policy guidelines without undermining their effectiveness (c) the need to improve governance and partnership in the execution of the strategy and (d) the need to ensure greater consistency and complementarity with respect to other relevant EU processes, notably the Broad Economic Policy Guidelines. (European Commission 2002d: 3)

The perception that the EES had to be focused on those priorities was taken up by two further Communications. A first one (European Commission 2002c) implemented the call for greater consistency and complementarity by streamlining the different coordination processes. Accordingly, the BEPGs, the EES, the Cardiff Process for Economic Reform, the Internal Market Strategy, the Stability and Growth Pact, and other more recent OMCs were adjusted to the same procedural cycle. Moreover, in order to increase the focus on the implementation of the guidelines, it was agreed to revise the BEPGs and the employment guidelines every three years rather than annually. While the EES initially emerged in a social policy frame and was promoted by proponents of a social Europe, economic aspects had now gained a much stronger weight, and employment issues were moved from social policy to the economic reform agenda. This general move from one context to another has to be seen as a first crucial transformation in the conceptual activation debate.

A second Communication outlined a revised EES in greater detail (European Commission 2003b). Drawing on the challenges defined in 'Taking Stocks' and seeking to simplify the employment guidelines, this document suggested abolishing the pillar structure and replacing it with three new overarching principles and a new generation of guidelines. The overarching objectives – full employment, quality and productivity at work, cohesion and an inclusive labour market – were said to mirror the political balance of the Lisbon agenda. In addition, a much smaller number of guidelines was supposed to advance 'complementary and mutually supportive objectives' (European Commission 2003b: 9) and allow for a much stronger focus on the Strategy's priorities. Hence, the next set of guidelines (Council of the EU 2003a) consisted only of 'ten commandments' (European Commission 2003a: 4) under three overarching objectives. In the process, gender equality was reduced from a pillar of its own into one guideline out of ten.

Nevertheless, gender equality was still relatively high on the agenda. For example, the Commission had identified persisting gender gaps and the lacking implementation of gender mainstreaming among the enduring challenges for the EES and the Lisbon Strategy. Moreover, the new Guideline 6 on gender equality did cover all key aspects that were covered by the fourth pillar in the previous versions of the EES.[3] Overall, there is little evidence that reducing the strong

Table 3.1 Key events in the EES and the Lisbon Strategy

Event	*General description*	*Gender dimension*
Amsterdam Treaty (signed 1997)	• Provides legal basis (Title VIII employment)	• In addition, further constitutionalisation of (gender) equality and gender mainstreaming (esp. Article 2 & Article 3)
Luxembourg Summit (1997)	• Launch of EES	• Pillar in its own right
Lisbon European Council (2000)	• Launch of Lisbon strategy • Launch of other OMCs	• Target: 60% female employment rate
EES Midterm review (2002)	• Strategy is lagging behind expectations	• Commitment still high
Implementation I: Streamlining (European Commission 2002c)	• Streamlining	• *Transformation I:* shift from social policy context to economic policy context
Implementation II: revised EES (European Commission 2003b)	• Three overarching principles • End of pillar structure • Number of guidelines reduced to ten	• *Transformation II:* downgrading from pillar in its own right to one guideline among ten • *Transformation III:* • shift from universal right to aspect of job quality and labour market access
First Kok Report (Employment Taskforce 2003)	• New tone of urgency • Synthesis through social investment • Four priorities	• Gender mainstreaming not mentioned • Consolidation of view on gender as functional requirement for employment growth • Focus on quantitative over qualitative operational-isation of gender equality
Second Kok Report (High Level Group 2004)	• Mid-term review of Lisbon strategy • New: frankness, urgency, blaming, focus on global competition	• Not mentioned
Strategy for Growth and Jobs (Lisbon re-launch, 2005)	• Integration of EES in broader strategy • New NRPs and Community Lisbon Programme • Union refrains from issuing recommendations	• Gender equality guideline disappears

Event (cont.)	General description	Gender dimension
First country specific recommendations after re-launch (2007)	• Recommendations on macro-, micro-economic and employment policy • On basis of more detailed country assessment of European Commission	• New priorities, less attention to qualitative aspects of employment and social security • Gender issues are addressed in country analyses but hardly make it into recommendations

equal opportunities element in the EES had been the main motivation behind those changes. Yet especially when looking at the further historical development of the Strategy, this restructuring should be seen as weakening the gender equality dimension in two ways, both of which must be seen as transformations of the conceptual debate just as fundamental as the previous move from social policy to economic policy. First, the abolishment of the pillar structure certainly decreased the relative weight and, even more important, the visibility of gender equality. Hence, its previous role as one of four basic principles also mirrored the idea of gender mainstreaming that gender issues had to be considered in all other areas as well. During the first period, gender equality was clearly an independent concept which did not serve any other higher cause. Yet having become one among ten other priorities, the mainstreaming idea was no longer visible in this new structure.

Second, the introduction of three overarching objectives simultaneous with the downgrading of the equal opportunities pillar can be seen as another important shift which narrowed down the potential meanings of that pillar. Under the previous structure, equal opportunities were not only a clearly visible and self-contained objective. Given its high status and its independence from other objectives, the gender equality pillar had the quality of a fundamental and unlimited principle in its own right. With the addition of the overarching objectives, this universal status became compromised inasmuch as each question and each action was now interpreted in the much narrower context delineated by the new headings. In short, equal opportunities for women and men shifted from a universal principle – or, indeed, a human right – to an aspect of job quality and labour market access. Their conceptual independence was lost.

Again, there is no evidence that these three major discursive transformations – from social to economic policy, from higher level principle to one priority among others, and from a universal right to a limited and qualified version of equality – were mainly guided by the intention of explicitly limiting the relative weight and conceptual independence of gender equality. Rather, gender equality was subject to interventions in the broader discursive context and in the overall priorities of the activation debate. With regard to gender equality, this shift in contexts was important insofar as neither gender equality nor gender mainstreaming were explicitly defined in the process. Their meanings too were quite fluid and diverse.

Therefore, gender equality was particularly fragile and in danger of falling off the agenda during attempts to refocus the EES and to make it more successful. Moreover, such alterations of the context of a specific discourse did not have to mean that an objective like promoting equal opportunities became meaningless from one day to the other. However, the refocusing of the EES that started after the mid-term review in 2002 developed a certain dynamic, in which its gender equality dimension proved to be particularly susceptible to further losses in weight, scope, and visibility.

Also in the wake of the mid-term review and in addition to the Communications presented thus far, the 2003 Brussels European Council also invited the Commission to establish a

> European Employment Taskforce … to carry out an independent in-depth examination of key employment-related policy challenges and to identify practical reform measures that can have the most direct and immediate impact on the ability of Member States to implement the revised European Employment Strategy and to achieve its objectives and targets. (European Council 2003, no. 44)

This Taskforce was chaired by the former Dutch Prime Minister Wim Kok and its report should prove to have a crucial impact on the further development of the EES. Although the Kok Report (Employment Taskforce 2003) agreed with most of the insights in the mid-term review, it went a step further by adding an extra notion of urgency that was not part of the debate before. The paper supported the need to raise the coherence and consistency of the guidelines as well as to focus them on key priorities. Moreover, it confirmed the global embeddedness of European societies and the general need for political reforms. However, the report was much more straightforward in designating the limited progress of the reform project. The very first sentence reasoned that the 'European Union is at risk of failing in its ambitious goal, set at Lisbon in 2000, of becoming by 2010 the most competitive and dynamic knowledge-based economy in the world' (*ibid.*: 8). This had not been formulated so explicitly before and sent a clear signal. Moreover, besides the threat of failure, the report presented the ageing of European societies in a much more dramatic way than previous documents. Depictions of the 'rapid ageing of the population' (*ibid.*: 8) causing a 'radical demographic shift' (*ibid.*: 12) and resulting in 'severe problems for the sustainability of welfare systems' (*ibid.*) as well as a significant slow-down in average GDP growth per capita clearly contributed to the new degree of urgency. The central conclusion of the report formulates four key priorities in order to refocus the EES, which were immediately taken up by the Commission (Council of the EU 2004b):

- increasing adaptability of workers and enterprises,
- attracting more people to the labour market,
- investing more and more effectively in human capital,
- ensuring effective implementation of reforms through better governance. (Employment Taskforce 2003: 8)

Overall, these priorities constituted a further intervention with the context in how the main goals and individual concepts of the EES were to be defined and interpreted. To begin with, the tone of urgency shifted the initial balance between economic growth (or flexibility) and security in the direction of flexibility alone. Furthermore, the report engaged with both poles of the balance and redefined flexibility and security in a way that investment in human capital was presented as a synthesis (see also Leschke, Schmid, & Griga 2006). Under the premise of social investment, the state purportedly did not need to regulate the economy on a grand scale to ensure the social security of its citizens. Instead, it could invest in their individual skills and competences alongside promoting a flexible economy. And finally, gender equality lost further visibility and status. Most importantly, the overall focus of the EU-wide activation debate was further narrowed down. Qualitative aspects of work – to which gender equality had already been degraded – lost much of their previous relevance due to a new exclusive emphasis on mere labour market participation and (future-oriented) investment in social capital. Moreover, while gender gaps and the need to increase female labour market participation were included, gender mainstreaming was not even mentioned in the report.

Welcoming the work of the Employment Taskforce, the European Council invited the Commission to install another High Level Group to carry out an independent (mid-term) review of the entire Lisbon Strategy in March 2004. And, again, this group was to be chaired by Wim Kok (European Council 2004).[4] The very fact that Kok was put in charge of two reports in such a short period clearly indicated approval of his work. In the employment dimension, the second report did not add many new arguments but rather confirmed previous ones for maximal labour market participation and a shift of perspective towards investment in human capital (High Level Group 2004). However, in its frankness, it increased the sense of urgency even further and proved to be very influential. To begin with it criticised the Lisbon Strategy by stating that

> Lisbon is about everything and thus about nothing. Everybody is responsible and thus no one. The end result of the strategy has sometimes been lost. An ambitious and broad reform agenda needs a clear narrative, in order to be able to communicate effectively about the need for it. So that everybody knows why it is being done and can see the validity of the need to implement sometimes painful reforms. (High Level Group 2004: 16)

Moreover, for the first time, the report explicitly blamed the member states for contributing 'to slow progress by failing to act on much of the Lisbon Strategy with sufficient urgency' (High Level Group 2004: 6). It insisted that '[t]oo much is at stake to respect the sensibilities of those who hinder the pursuit of the common European good' (*ibid.*: 17). This not only contrasted strongly with the consensus-minded language that was hitherto prevalent but also added drastically to the tone of necessity. Furthermore, regarding the challenges for European societies, previous documents normally referred to their global embeddedness in abstract terms. The second Kok report, however, shifted the focus from a general notion of globalisation to a very concrete notion of global competition explicitly naming the US, China, and India as the strongest competitors and noting the gaps that had already opened between them and the Union. At the same time, the High Level Group built on and promoted the new meaning of 'flexibility' that was coined by the Employment Taskforce with its emphasis on social investment:

> The call for more reform is too frequently seen as no more than code for more flexibility which in turn is seen as code for weakening worker rights and protections; this is wrong. The High Level Group understands that flexibility is about agility, adaptability and employability for which the key is the ability for workers constantly to acquire and renew skills, and for a combination of active labour market policies, training and social support to make moving from job to job as easy as possible. (High Level Group 2004: 32)

In the process, flexibility, which used to be seen as positive for entrepreneurs and companies only, was turned into a virtue for every individual. Eventually, the two Kok reports triggered the most fundamental overhaul of the EU's economic and social reform project.

After the publication of the second Kok report and a proposal by the Commission taking up its analysis (European Commission 2005d), the next spring European Council decided to re-launch the Lisbon Strategy in a completely new form (European Council 2005). In particular, the new Strategy for Growth and Jobs integrated the (already streamlined) processes of economic policy coordination through the BEPGs and the EES into a single strategy based on a set of integrated guidelines, organised according to macroeconomic, microeconomic, and employment issues. In accordance with the integrated guidelines and a new streamlined policy coordination cycle (see European Commission 2005b), the member states were only required to submit a single report and the Commission would then synthesise all efforts in one comprehensive report consisting of three parts: an overall report on the developments of the last preceding period, a collection of short reports scrutinising the developments in each member state (and the Eurozone), and a report paying specific attention to the Strategy's three main areas of macroeconomic, microeconomic, and employment issues. Even those elements with an explicit treaty basis were integrated into the new reporting procedures but formally still treated as single documents. For example, each country chapter concluded with draft recommendations based on the Commission's assessment, and the document specifically reporting on employment issues was concurrently the draft Joint Employment Report which then had to be adopted separately by the Council. Moreover, in addition to the member states' NRPs, the Commission published its own Community Lisbon Programme laying out a specific strategy for the EU and its progress (see European Commission 2005a). Furthermore, despite calls for increased naming and shaming of underperforming member states in both Kok reports, the new strategy attempted to increase member states' ownership of the process, emphasising its flexibility and the possibility of adapting its contents to national needs and circumstances (European Commission 2005b, 2005c). Against this background, the EU refrained from its right to issue new country-specific recommendations (European Commission 2005b). The previous recommendations were said to 'remain valid as background references'

(European Commission 2005c: 13). However, the Commission made clear that it could make use of recommendations in the future (European Commission 2005e), which it did in 2007.

The most significant modification regarding gender equality was the disappearance of the specific gender equality guideline. The key contents of previous gender equality provisions could still be found, however, they were now scattered across all the guidelines. Moreover, while gender mainstreaming had been moved to the introductory section, other provisions were shifted under much less explicit, much vaguer headings such as 'life-cycle approach'. Furthermore, the re-launch was intended to refocus the Strategy on certain key priorities but at the same time extended its scope significantly. Hence, when looking at later recommendations covering macro-economic, micro-economic, and employment issues, gender equality was of lower priority and hardly addressed in this context. Often it was only mentioned in the Commission's country assessments but not taken up in the formal recommendations.

In addition, other central documents shifted the language further from promoting equality as a fundamental principle to a language of 'investment' and 'unlocking potentials'. For example, in its report to the Spring European Council proposing the re-launch of the Lisbon Strategy, the Commission argues with regard to gender issues that '[t]he huge potential of women in the labour market remains to be fully exploited' (European Commission 2005d: 26). In the process, it was claimed that the disappearance of an explicit guideline on gender equality would raise 'a new risk that the EU's commitment to advancing gender equality would not survive in this new round of more focused policy' (Fagan, Grimshaw, & Rubery 2006: 572).

Indeed, the picture has been rather ambivalent. On the one hand, some initiatives indicate the continuing political will to promote equality between women and men. Following a joint letter by six heads of state,[5] a European Pact for Gender Equality was adopted at the next European Council under the Austrian Presidency (see European Council 2006, Annex II). The Pact did not introduce any new substantive goals or processes but confirmed the relevance of the gender equality objectives that had been at the centre of the EES, additionally calling on the member states to address gender issues when reporting on the implementation of their NRPs. Furthermore, in 2007 the Commission published a Communication on 'Tackling the pay gap between women and men' (European Commission 2007b), thereby focusing on a key problem of gender inequality in the labour market. On the other hand, this document had to admit that there has been a 'relative lack of change' (European Commission 2007b: 4) since the overall pay gap in the EU in 2005 was just two points below the level of 1995. The picture became even bleaker when taking into account the steady increase of female employment rates in that period. In a way, the European Pact for Gender Equality and the Communication on unequal pay demonstrated well the limitations of promoting gender equality within the framework of the Lisbon Strategy. Gender equality was pushed to the periphery of the conceptual debate. Meanwhile, each intervention to promote it that referred solely to a constitutional or human rights frame, met difficulties and had to make the business case for equality as well. In the context of the narrowly focused employability agenda of the Strategy for Growth and Jobs, very few stronger measures were present while substantive inequalities nonetheless persisted.

Overall, gender equality suffered dramatically in terms of relative weight and visibility in the course of attempts to strengthen other objectives of the Strategy. However, this gradual loss of visibility dramatically minimised the Strategy's potential to capture and to analyse substantive problems of inequality in the context of the broader debate on social and economic modernisation. Moreover, this downsizing has a meaning of its own. Gender equality could now be compromised when 'more important' issues were at stake (Interviews 3, 24). When understanding the EES as a conceptual debate, it seems that something had gone wrong in its gender equality dimension. The next empirical chapters will therefore take a close look at how the gender equality dimension of the EES has been perceived in three member states – Germany, Hungary and the UK – and what can be concluded about transformations of citizenship in this respect.

Notes:

1 Among the main tasks of this network is the annual evaluation of the member states' NAPs with regard to equal opportunities of women and men. The network comprises academics with expertise in gender equality issues from all member states and non-EU states; different networks compete for a tender after which the successful bidders are funded by the Commission for the length of their service contract.

2 For a critical and detailed analysis of the Commission's gender mainstreaming approach, see Beveridge (2006). For a survey on divergent understandings of gender mainstreaming, see OPTEM (2002).

3 The full text of the guideline is: 'Member States will, through an integrated approach combining gender mainstreaming and specific policy actions, encourage female labour market participation and achieve a substantial reduction in gender gaps in employment rates, unemployment rates, and pay by 2010. The role of the social partners is crucial in this respect. In particular, with a view to its elimination, policies will aim to achieve by 2010 a substantial reduction in the gender pay gap in each Member State, through a multi-faceted approach addressing the underlying factors of the gender pay gap, including sectoral and occupational segregation, education and training, job classifications and pay systems, awareness-raising and transparency.

'Particular attention will be given to reconciling work and private life, notably through the provision of care services for children and other dependants, encouraging the sharing of family and professional responsibilities and facilitating return to work after a period of absence. Member States should remove disincentives to female labour force participation and strive, taking into account the demand for childcare facilities and in line with national patterns of childcare provision, to provide childcare by 2010 to at least 90 % of children between three years old and the mandatory school age and at least 33 % of children under three years of age.' (Council of the EU 2003a, Annex).

4 For a criticism of the composition of the High Level Group, see Fagan, Grimshaw, and Rubery (2006).

5 This letter was signed by Göran Persson (Sweden), Jacques Chirac (France), José Luis Zapatero (Spain), Matti Vanhanen (Finland), Jiři Paroubek (Czech Republic), and Anders Fogh Rasmussen (Denmark).

4

Germany – reservations and reforms

Germany is among those countries where a shift from a conservative to a centre-left government coincided with the launch of the EES and its structured discourse on welfare and labour market modernisation. Yet, the characteristics of the German debate have to be understood in the context of recent changes in government and especially of far-reaching reorientations triggered by the German (centre) left. Before their success in the 1998 federal election, the Social Democrats (SPD) had distanced themselves from traditional images of social democracy by portraying themselves as 'Neue Mitte' (new centre). The subsequent change in government also raised expectations of reforming the conservative German approach to gender and family policies, still largely based on an implicit male breadwinner/female caregiver model (Esping-Andersen 1990), to making them match the changed social realities at the end of the millennium. At this point, it is especially important to note that East Germany used to be characterised by a socialist adult worker model, which was still visible when, for example, looking at the childcare infrastructure.[1] In fact, women were hit hardest by the breakdown of the East German economy (Engelbrech & Reinberg 1997); until the mid-1990s, three-quarters of the long-term unemployed in Eastern Germany were women (Vogel 1999). In the national political discourse, however, there was hardly any reference to this different historical legacy. Rather, West German welfare institutions were simply extended to East Germany and the East German Länder are mostly presented as regions with very specific structural problems – especially at the EU level.

Overall, the task of reforming Germany turned out to be rather complicated. Nevertheless, when a grand coalition government consisting of Christian Democrats (CDU and CSU)[2] and SPD took over after Chancellor Gerhard Schröder had announced early elections in 2005, the Federal Republic of Germany was witnessing the most fundamental reforms of employment and social security policies in its history. Even after a full term of that grand coalition under the conservative Chancellor Angela Merkel ongoing welfare reforms could still be seen as adjustments and implementations of the programme initiated in that phase. However, whether these reform debates also strengthened the cause of gender equality is less clear.

Background: debating welfare, activation, and gender

When the SPD/Green coalition government took over in 1998, its plans for reforms were far-reaching and ambitious. In fact, the 1998 coalition agreement promised not only a consolidation of the budget and a modernisation of the welfare state but also a reform of the taxation system based on ecological objectives, new energy policies including an end to nuclear power, new stimuli for education, a pension reform, a new and more inclusive approach to permanently resident migrants and their children (including dual citizenship), and improving the status of same-sex couples. In addition, gender equality featured quite prominently throughout the document (SPD & Bündnis 90/Die Grünen 1998). However, the everyday business of politics and legislation proved to be more difficult – and not only with regard to gender equality.

Uncoupling gender equality from the broader reform agenda
During its first term, the SPD/Green government attempted to negotiate reforms in a consensus-oriented tripartite social pact: the so called Alliance for Jobs (see Germany 2000, 2001, 1999). It is striking that this first cornerstone of the German reform agenda – but also the later more substantial reforms – received only marginal attention in those sections of the German NAPs which dealt with gender equality.

In addition to the Alliance for Jobs, the 1998 coalition agreement had also launched Woman and Work (Frau und Beruf), a programme comprising the gender equality and women's policy measures of the government (SPD & Bündnis 90/Die Grünen 1998: 32). It contained a broad mix of plans for legislative changes, information gathering, awareness raising, and campaigns. Moreover, its activities and objectives were to be closely connected to the negotiations within the Alliance for Jobs (Germany 1999: 63).

However, the history of these programmes also shows the specific problems of integrating a gender equality dimension into the overall modernisation project. First, the Woman and Work programme was based on a rather small budget (Maier 2001). Second, the marginal representation of women in the Alliance for Jobs made it extremely difficult to integrate gender issues (Maier 2001). Neither women nor representatives from the Federal Ministry for Family, Senior Citizens, Women and Youth (BMFSFJ) participated in the central talks (Maier 2000b, 2000a). Third, as the Alliance collapsed in the beginning of the coalition's second term (see Streeck 2003), the missing voice of women within the talks and the overall failure of these talks (unsurprisingly) also translated into very limited results concerning equal opportunities. In fact, the only substantial result in this area consisted in a volun-tary agreement between the federal government, some large employers, and the main employers' associations (BMFSFJ 2001). Given the initial expectations and the promises in the coalition agreement, such a voluntary solution was a disappointment (for example DJB 2001; DGB 2001a, 2001d, 2001b, 2001c; Deutscher Frauenrat 2001a, 2001b) and is contested to this day.

In contrast, the achievements within the public sector outweigh by far the limited voluntary agreement in the private sector. For example, gender mainstreaming was included in the standing orders of all federal ministries (BMFSFJ 2005) and in the policy objectives of the Federal Employment Service (BA). In the process, the Federal Employment Service has especially been highlighted as the most advanced institution practicing the strategy (Maier 2000a). Furthermore, the 2002 JobAQTIV Act, the only significant outcome of the first term with regard to employment policy, which clearly draws on the activation paradigm and explicitly refers to the EES (see Germany 2002, Annex 2), introduced gender equality as a horizontal objective of German employment promotion law. Although the BA did already practice gender mainstreaming, that implied a qualitative change of the legal basis from standing orders and internal policy objectives to federal law. Moreover, in November 2001, the Bundestag passed an Equality Act for the Federal Administration and the Federal Courts, introducing equal opportunities and gender mainstreaming as basic organising principles (see also BMFSFJ 2003). By and large, the government did not hesitate to implement the objectives laid out in the coalition agreement or to initiate new legislation for the (federal) public sector. Yet it was extremely cautious in intervening in the private sector, which it saw as domain of the social partners.

However, even the achievements in the public sector should be treated with some caution. Most of them apply to federal institutions only. After all, key public services such as education are the responsibility of the Länder. Moreover, they have been criticised for slow and problematic implementation (Maier 2001), which in 2004 had not got far beyond the stage of pilot projects, working groups, manuals, or checklists (see BMFSFJ 2005). In addition, the BMFSFJ bore the main responsibility for all questions concerning gender and women, having continuously been building up notable capacities and expertise. However, its budget was rather limited and its standing among other ministries weak. In contrast, ministries such as Labour and Social Affairs, Finance, Interior, or Justice saw little need to implement gender mainstreaming or applied the concept in a rather thin sense as 'affirmative action' for their female employees (Maier 2000b). Generally, the strict division of departmental competences and a strict norm of non-intervention of one ministry in the sphere of another are important aspects of administrative culture in Germany hindering the promotion and implementation of horizontal issues and strategies such as gender mainstreaming.[3] In short, questions concerning equal opportunities were in a difficult position within an ineffective process. The gender equality/women's policy agenda of the Woman and Work programme had become increasingly uncoupled from the labour market and welfare reform agenda.

Efficiency or opportunity?

The situation of gender equality did not change remarkably during the second period of the SPD/Green coalition. As the first term was coming to an end, a new window of opportunity opened up. Following a scandal around forged placement statistics in the BA, Chancellor Schröder installed an expert commission led by Peter Hartz, then a board member of a large German car manufacturer, to make suggestions for reforming that institution. This move proved decisive for the overall reform project, because the commission extended its mandate significantly and suggested much more fundamental reforms (Schmid 2003). In fact, delegating such tasks to an unpolitical body, combined with the timing, was a clever strategic step (Aust 2003; for a critical account Gerntke *et al.* 2002). First, since the commission's work coincided with the federal election campaign of September 2002, Schröder was able to silence internal opposition from the traditionalist wing within his own party and from the trade unions. In fact, the main political conflicts about German labour market reforms were to be found within the German (centre) left rather than between left and right. Second, the CDU/CSU opposition was in an awkward position because it was much more difficult to criticise the work of an independent expert commission. Moreover, the commission granted business quite a strong voice, and its proposals were generally welcomed by CDU/CSU and the Free Democrats (FDP).

At the same time, the recommendations of the Hartz Commission were translated into four pieces of legislation (1st/2nd/3rd/4th Modern Labour Market Services Act/Gesetz für Moderne Dienstleistungen am Arbeitsmarkt), which entered into force between January 2003 and January 2005 (for overview see Germany 2003, Annex 4). The initial uncoupling of gender issues, contained in the Woman and Work programme from the broader welfare reform agenda, was thereby reinforced. Similarly to the Alliance for Jobs, this commission was also criticised for lacking representation of women (one woman out of fifteen members) and resistance towards issues of gender equality (DJB 2002a; Maier 2003). A reference to gender mainstreaming was introduced in the final report but the strategy and concrete measures to promote gender equality were at best patchy and scattered throughout the big project based on the Hartz acts (DJB 2003).

Concerning the promotion of gender equality, the 2002 coalition agreement also features a self-contained section on equality between women and men (SPD & Bündnis 90/Die Grünen 2002, section VII). The language and the substantial contents of this section differ remarkably from the respective section in the previous coalition agreement (SPD & Bündnis 90/Die Grünen 1998, section VIII). First, while the 1998 agreement explicitly framed such issues in terms of women's policy and positive action, the 2002 agreement exhibited a language of gender mainstreaming. For example, actual equality is referred to as a horizontal principle of the federal government (SPD & Bündnis 90/Die Grünen 2002: 61). However, concrete instruments and practices were rare and the Woman and Work programme – previously the main government strategy to promote gender equality – was not mentioned any more in 2002. Accordingly, this agenda was not only uncoupled from the larger reform agenda but completely abandoned as government strategy during the second term.

Moreover, in the wake of those initial steps in 2003, Chancellor Schröder outlined his reform strategy for the second term in the Bundestag. This programme, the Agenda 2010, introduced a new tone of urgency that had been unthinkable when consensus could not be found in the Alliance for Jobs.

> Either we modernise – as a social market economy – or we will be modernised – by the undiminished forces of the market superseding the social. (author's translation)[4]

The labour market reforms explicitly constituted the core element and beginning of the Agenda 2010. In addition, the programme contained plans for further reforms of the federal budget, the taxation system, the social security system, pensions insurance, health insurance and the health care system, education, and research (Deutscher Bundestag 2003). Gender equality, however, was not mentioned at all.

The move of gender equality to the outer fringes of the reform project is also documented in the German NAPs. Subsequently, none of them referred to these cornerstones of the modernisation project in their specific sections on gender equality. Instead, with the programme's increasing urgency (and its initial success), indifference towards the equality agenda resurfaced. On the whole, the government's initial commitment to gender mainstreaming and positive action did not translate systematically into a new regime. However, the reform did have massive gendered effects on social and economic citizenship.

After Schröder had announced early elections in summer 2005 and when a grand coalition of CDU/CSU and SPD came to power later that year, the main direction and contents of the reform project did not change. Rather, while the conservatives had backed Schröder's reform agenda against critics within his own party, they were now also officially in charge of the reform project. In fact, Schröder's successor Angela Merkel positively assessed his Agenda 2010 as a project to be continued. The 2005 coalition agreement also confirmed the commitment of both parties to the aforementioned labour market reforms and the Agenda 2010 (CDU/CSU & SPD 2005). However, the unity of the grand coalition allowed a new party on the left to form and to gain strength: The Linke (The Left) emerged in 2007 from the merger between the Party of Democratic Socialism (the successor of the former East German socialist party) and the Election Alternative Work and Social Justice, a short-lived group of predominantly West German trade unionists and disappointed defectors from the SPD.

Regarding the gender equality dimension, the 2005 NRP only cited measures to reconcile work and family life arguing with the need to counter declining birth rates but not explicitly referencing gender equality measures (Germany 2005). This is important insofar as the document was more or less identical with the 2005 coalition agreement between SPD and Christian Democrats (CDU/CSU & SPD 2005). The 2006 report once more included a general commitment to gender mainstreaming and equal opportunities (Germany 2006). Between 2007 and 2009, the NRPs have been keen to report on new family and childcare policies but specific gender equality activities remain rather half-hearted and mostly restricted to the annexes (Germany 2007, 2008, 2009).

The new conservative Minister for Family, Senior Citizens, Women and Youth, named Ursula von der Leyen emerged in 2005 as a major driving force for equality and family friendliness (she became Minister for Employment and Social affairs in 2009). She initiated a programme according to which 750,000 new childcare places should be established by 2013, catering to about 35% of the children under three. Moreover, in May 2006, the federal government adopted a bill amending the regulations on parental leave and pay. Since January 2007, parents of newborn babies are entitled to take up to three years leave; given the approval of the employer, up to twelve months of this leave can be transferred to the period between the child's third and eighth birthday. In addition, during the child's first year, parents have the right to twelve months of parental pay. The amount can be claimed by the father or the mother, and if the parents split the period between each other it can even be extended to fourteen months (for details, see BMFSFJ 2006a). As of July 2006, a report to the Bundestag maintained there had already been a relatively positive development of childcare places for children under three in western Germany (BMFSFJ 2006b). In addition, the federal government announced that from 2013 onwards each child under three would be legally entitled to a childcare place (Germany 2008). However, this plan was massively criticised by the Länder and municipalities who would be responsible for its implementation and bearing most of the costs.

Activating citizenship?

From a broader perspective on changing citizenship practices, the period of the grand coalition can also be described as a phase in which the changes initiated during Schröder's second term were consolidated. The basic principle of modernised German employment and social policy was already defined as 'support and demand' in 2002. In particular, this implied shifts of responsibilities and legitimate expectations between citizens and the state, which are expressed in most reform measures. The effects on gender equality are rarely addressed by the government but will become better visible once the various contestations of the labour market reforms are taken into consideration (see next section).

The labour market reforms can be grouped under three major themes. First, the reform of the BA aimed at transforming the employment service from an allegedly inefficient bureaucracy into a more business-like organisation based on ideas of 'new public management'. The offices were to be turned into – increasingly efficient – one-stop customer centres dealing with all relevant services and benefits while training measures would increasingly be contracted out to private agencies. In theory, this could lead to better service access for the citizens. But in practice, close attention would have to be paid to the particular circumstances. Hence, it has been argued that the stronger efficiency orientation leads to exclusionary ('creaming') effects against the weakest in the labour market (Hielscher

2006). The second theme included concrete measures to activate unemployed persons and recipients of benefits. In this context, the strategy was twofold. On the one hand, there were measures to support self-employment while granting a certain amount of social security (a monthly allowance and social insurance contributions) as well as new forms of work that should facilitate a new labour market for more flexible low-wage jobs. Yet, again, whether this really added up to increased access to societal resources can only be assessed taking into account potential contestations. On the other hand, activation has to a large extent been pursued through a much tougher sanction regime: the overall benefit levels are drastically decreased with the amalgamation of the former unemployment assistance and the social benefit. Furthermore, the criteria defining what kind of work jobseekers had to accept were redefined on the principle that any job would be suitable, regardless of education, occupation, previous position, or salary. The new salary could even be below local or collectively agreed standards. In addition, the criteria defining reasonable commuting distances were also notably loosened (for details see Oschmiansky 2004). Ultimately, the employment services gained extended options for sanctioning jobseekers for non-cooperation, options that indeed are increasingly used to activate them.

The final theme consisted in reforming the German benefit system. In particular, the former unemployment assistance for the long-term unemployed, which depended on one's previous salary, was abolished and merged with the social benefit. In the case of redundancy, each jobseeker became entitled to an insurance-based unemployment benefit ('Alg I') dependent on his or her previous salary for up to 12 months (up to 24 months for workers over 50). After a jobseeker's right to unemployment benefit has run out, he or she would be entitled to a tax-financed lump sum benefit (plus possible additions for housing, heating, or children) in the same amount as the social benefit ('Alg II'). Moreover, every recipient able to work at least three hours a day would henceforth be treated as unemployed, leading to a sharp increase of the unemployment rate in the first months of 2005 after the new legislation had entered into force (Germany 2006). These changes provoked heated political and public debate as well as fierce criticism. Indeed, the acronym 'Hartz IV' (for the unemployment benefit Alg II) became the colloquial name for the reforms as such. Moreover, while there have been repeated discussions on increasing the unemployment assistance or the duration of 'Alg I' for older jobseekers, the sanction and control regime was tightened even further by subsequent legislation. A law amending the regulations concerning the Alg II (Gesetz zur Fortentwicklung der Grundsicherung für Arbeitsuchende) in 2006 also contains large sections of additional measures against potential benefit fraud including exchange of data between authorities and agencies and new sanctions.

Overall, from a citizenship perspective, there is a new degree of individualisation combining individual responsibility and new options for disciplining individual benefit claimants. Many reforms cut back on social rights that were previously unconditional. The underlying philosophy is very well captured in Germany's second NRP for the period from 2008 to 2010:

> The drawing of benefits and the need for assistance of persons capable of work are to be eliminated … as swiftly and sustainably as possible. On the one hand, job seekers can be offered customized assistance. On the other hand, employable persons drawing benefits can be obliged to actively participate and to undertake every reasonable effort to earn a living for themselves and the persons living together with them in a 'community of need' from their own resources. (Germany 2008: 30–31)

The concept of people living together in such a community of need crucially shifts responsibility from the state to individuals, their partners, and family members. For example, the estimation of individual benefits also takes into account the financial situation of the partner (who also has to disclose it to the case manager at the employment agency). At the same time, it is worth noting that the new legislation neither differentiates between married and unmarried nor between heterosexual and same-sex partnerships, in stark contrast to most other German laws. The gradual extension of the statutory retirement age from 65 to 67 is another good example of this new emphasis on economic activity as citizen's duty (see Germany 2008). These measures are based on a quite rigidly defined duty to work, combined with concrete sanctions which can also translate into decreasing access to societal resources. However, while these reforms imply a re-pooling of risks and responsibilities, they hardly imply new citizenship rights.

The German labour market reforms clearly intervene in the nexus between flexibility and security. The current balance between the two was massively contested as hampering flexibility – and therefore economic growth and necessary change. The main aim of the reformers was to break up the old nexus and to push all social security and labour market institutions towards more flexibility. However, there have hardly been any efforts to resolve this binary opposition and to achieve a synthesis by interfering with the meaning of both concepts, comparably to the shift towards social investment visible at the EU level. Against the background of such a strong flexibilisation discourse, equality found itself in a difficult position. While gender issues are not very visible in the context of the mentioned labour market reforms, they have been fiercely contested (see next section).

The childcare and family policies initiated by von der Leyen can be seen as those exceptions where new rights were created and where gender plays a central role. Most important in this respect are the new rights to parental leave and pay. In addition, public investment in childcare is a crucial societal resource that can increase parents' and especially women's autonomy and thereby contribute to the equality of their actual life chances. In addition to family policies, a new right to receive support to obtain a lower secondary school leaving certificate granted to unemployed early school leavers was granted by legislation in 2009 (Germany 2009). However, even those new rights and resources have to be seen in the broader context before a positive impact on gender equality can be assessed. Given the essential contestedness of citizenship, it should be possible to locate the interventions discussed in the previous sections within a web of contestations. This should also allow for better understanding the connections between the German and the EU-wide activation debate.

Contested trajectories – tracing influence and ambivalence

The previous sections have shown that the objective of gender equality became uncoupled from the broader reform agenda despite initial high expectations. Yet, the role of the EES in relation to the German reform debate was not addressed. Given the EU's track record in gender equality issues and the EES's guidelines (at least in the early years), it is a relevant question what kind of role the Strategy played. Therefore, the second part of this section addresses contestations from within German society.

Contestations from above
Since the second set of guidelines issued in 2001, Germany always received recommendations on gender equality. At least until 2006, these are quite consistent in their content and the problems they address. The excessively high gender pay gap, the negative impact of the tax and benefits system on women's employment, the lack of childcare places – and how the few available do not always correspond with working hours or school schedules – were raised each year between 2001 and 2004. Another recurring issue was the need for Germany to provide adequate statistics and data broken down according to gender, in correspondence with EES indicators. This issue was already present in the first set of recommendations, which were formulated in much broader terms (Council of the EU 2000d). However, in the first round of recommendations made within the restructured framework of the Strategy for Growth and Jobs in 2007, gender issues were treated much more benignly. Thus, the Commission's specific country report on Germany's progress in 2006 describes the lower participation of women in the labour market and the number of childcare places as problematic. It also strongly criticises that little action had been taken to tackle the pay gap (European Commission 2006c). However, none of these assessments were taken up in the following year's recommendations (Council of the EU 2007) or the Commission draft (European Commission 2006d). From then on, the Commission's country assessments and recommendations did not criticise any further aspects of gender inequality, instead repeatedly praising Germany's response with regard to childcare (Council of the EU 2008, 2009). Germany's rather lax reporting on gender relevant issues beyond childcare in more recent times has not affected the Commission's positive views.

Despite this (at least initially) consistent and explicit advice, the responses found in the German NAPs have been limited – similarly to the low profile of gender in the context of the broader welfare reform project. The pay gap remains largely unaddressed. Instead the government consistently referred to the constitutional equality between women and men and the wage-setting autonomy of the social partners. Regarding concrete actions, the federal government mainly produced a report on unequal pay and the economic situation of women and men in 2002 (Bundesregierung 2002). The gender pay gap in Germany had been constantly between 19% and 22% from 1995 to 2001. Because the problem was known before (see, for example, SPD & Bündnis 90/Die Grünen 1998), this move was criticised as a strategic attempt to evade negative claims (DJB 2002c; Maier

2001: 14). Moreover, based on the NAPs, it took the German government until 2003 to collect pertinent data on unequal pay. Yet even in a more recent compilation there is not much information about the German gender pay gap beyond that 2002 income survey (European Commission 2006a). And while the Commission had still criticised explicitly the absent approach to tackling the gender pay gap in 2006 (European Commission 2006d), this problem was not mentioned in subsequent employment recommendations under the renewed Strategy for Growth and Jobs (Council of the EU 2007, 2008, 2009).

Despite the initial reluctance, one can identify an increasing synchronisation of language and detail between Germany and the EES over the years. Thus, the German reports increasingly adopted the terms of the EU-wide conceptual debate. In addition, EU provisions paid more attention to the characteristics of the German context. For example, while the German government has started to accept partial responsibility for the gender pay gap (for example, provision of data, awareness raising, addressing unequal pay in the public sector), later EU recommendations also respected the autonomy of the social partners. Hence, they suggest the government should 'encourage the social partners to take their responsibility to considerably reduce the gender pay gap' (Council of the EU 2003b: 24). Generally, it is important to note that the recommendations are not explicitly used to apply external pressure to member states but rather as part of a communicative process.

In addressing criticisms of inadequate childcare provision, the German NAPs usually pointed to the legal entitlement of such care for all children from the age of three until school age. Concerning the *de facto* lack of childcare places, however, the government has usually referred to the responsibility of the Länder and municipalities (see Germany 2001: 66, 2002: 24). Yet another reorientation was evident when the federal government switched from simply denying responsibility to admitting that it 'attaches huge importance to expanding and maintaining a supply of childcare facilities' (Germany 2004: 32) and that it, along with the Länder and local authorities would, 'shoulder responsibility for ensuring this requirement is met' (*ibid.*). More recently, however, the issue has received new attention due to the initiatives of Ursula von der Leyen to reconcile work and family through extending childcare. Her plans resonated well with previous criticisms of the EU and significantly changed the tone of the debate. As a result, the Commission started to describe the German childcare programme as making substantial progress (European Commission 2007a: 2) and the subsequent recommendations laud it as decisive response to previous recommendations (especially Council of the EU 2008).

Lastly, responses concerning the impact of income tax regulations on female employment came rather late (see Germany 2003) and remained very hesitant. For a long time, the German tax system has been criticised because married couples are given the possibility to split their taxable income. Moreover, the incomes are taxed according to two different tax codes while the smaller income is taxed at a higher rate ('Tax Code V'). Individual taxation and the abolition of Tax Code V is an old concern (not only) of German feminists, and a revision of the taxation system was already among the promises of the first Schröder government (for feminist interventions, see DJB 2006b, 2006a, 2006c, 2002b). However, the issue quietly slipped off the agenda in the very early years (Maier 2001). A later response to the EU recommendation reads:

> The regulation of the German Tax Law (Recommendation no. 4) shows no gender-specific differences per se. Effects on the employment rate of women are possible, however, in connection with the perception of values in society or other political sectors, e.g. regulations on the labour market, provision of child care facilities. Some consider it a definite disadvantage that 94% of women who earn an additional income belong to tax class V with a comparably high tax burden. (Germany 2003: 23)

In general, the way Germany responded to the employment recommendations corroborates our initial impression that the significance of such recommendations as direct contestations with relevance to citizenship was only minor. Nevertheless, it is possible to identify a two-way synchronisation of language and practices. Germany does not seem to be entirely indifferent to recommendations, yet while certainly not silently complying, it has entered a critical dialogue about them. In fact, the EES does not seem to be about compliance but rather a structured dialogue organised around specific issues. However, Germany only engaged positively in such dialogue after a national activation discourse had taken hold.

Contestations from within

In addition to transnational contestations, which do not have much direct influence, there is a further way in which the EES debate could be significant. For example, it could enhance the position of third actors and empower them in contesting national practices – for example, by providing information and discursive resources. In theory, this could be the strength of the EES as it is a rich source of data, political guidance, and expertise. Accordingly, national trade unions or women's organisations could draw on the guidelines and recommendations, on the comparability of member states produced by common targets and indicators, but also on the specific expertise provided by the different expert networks of the Commission as resources for applying pressure on the national government.

As already indicated, the labour market and benefit reforms raised massive debates and criticism within Germany. They were criticised as blaming the unemployed for their joblessness (Oschmiansky 2003), for a strong bias towards negative incentives, for disciplining benefits recipients and the unemployed (Hickel 2003), and for lacking a balance between flexibility, security and new forms of insecurity (Engelen-Kefer 2005; Gransee 2005; Trube 2005). An early critique from the German Trade Union Federation (DGB) commenting on the initial legislation can be taken as exemplary inasmuch as it targeted the benefit cuts and the strong imbalance towards disciplining and sanctioning (DGB-Bundesvorstand 2003; see also Engelen-Kefer 2005). The amalgamation of unemployment assistance and social benefit was criticised as a massive loss of income and thought to raise the risk of poverty from long-term unemployment. While jobseekers might get better access to childcare, the new regulation of social security was deemed to aggravate existing forms of gendered risk and exclusion rather than correcting them (Betzelt 2007, 2008).

Taking a broader perspective on the political landscape in Germany, the constantly decreasing political weight of the SPD since 2005 and the growing success of the Linke as an established (albeit extremely controversial) new force regularly gaining access to regional governments can only be fully understood in light of the contested activation discourse and the related labour market reforms. Similar to many trade unions, the Linke is fundamentally opposed to most aspects of the debate on welfare modernisation at the EU level. In contrast, it has successfully mobilised more traditional leftist ideas based on strong state responsibility, redistributive justice, and material security rather than investment in social capital. In this context, the SPD and the conservative parties (especially the CSU) have at least partially rediscovered social justice and public responsibility as political topics. The SPD especially is still searching for ways to emancipate itself from Agenda 2010 without losing its modernisation credentials. At the same time, it had constantly to redefine its relationship with the Linke, which is luring away voters. Yet while the Linke could be an important political partner, it has been maligned as communist or anti-constitutional by conservatives.

However, the EES is not perceived as very helpful in this political debate. The DGB, for instance, sees itself as well embedded in a network of national institutions such as the wage-setting autonomy of the social partners, the tripartite control of the federal employment service (albeit weakened in the course of the reforms), or its established routes of access to the Ministry of Labour and Social Affairs, the government, and the SPD – routes it prefers in everyday political business. At the same time, the contents of the EES and the Lisbon Strategy, especially the strict supply-side approach, were repeatedly criticised in my interviews with DGB representatives (Interviews 11, 17, 14). They raised general objections against activating strategies without a focus on job creation – especially in light of the structural problems in Germany – and against sanctions as a main activating instrument. This general critique is shared by all critical voices on the German left.

In more focused debates about equal opportunities in German social policy, women and gender experts within the trade unions have played a crucial role. However, other women's organisations face crucial problems in getting access to the relevant policy-making discourses. In interviews with members of the steering committee of the German Women's Council, it was repeatedly mentioned that the strict separation of departmental responsibilities constituted a critical barrier. As already indicated, women's issues and gender mainstreaming are within the responsibility of the BMFSFJ. As a result, women's organisations have experienced tremendous difficulties accessing, for example, the Ministry of Labour and Social Affairs (part of an even larger Ministry of Economics and Labour between 2002 and 2005), thus precluding them from having an effective role in the national activation debate (Interviews 13, 18). In addition, explicitly feminist voices have expressed stronger disapproval of the regressive character of the reforms as reproducing reactionary gender roles and family models based on the male breadwinner model (BAG 2002; Reihs 2005). A particular target of criticism is the extremely high proportion of women in so-called minijobs or receiving a small self-employment grant, for neither produces enough income to fully sustain a person, let alone a family (Leschke, Schmid, & Griga 2006; Brandt 2006). Moreover, people employed in minijobs are not covered by social insurance and there is evidence that this construct fails to provide a bridge into regular employment. Some 85.5% of minijob holders are women (see Kalina & Voss-Dahm 2005) while the share of women in the low wage sector in the wider sense has been 69.9% (Kalina & Weinkopf 2006). Trade unions and women's organisations have called for more rigid legislation based on rights and prohibitions of certain practices as an alternative to the still existing voluntary agreement in order to promote gender equality in the private sector. But these have had little success in this general flexibility-oriented context (see Deutscher Frauenrat 2009b; Deutscher Frauenrat 2009a; also Kohaut & Möller 2009).

Looking at the broader discursive context of the different contestations, it seems that the German version of an optimistic modernisation discourse led by ideas of modernised social democracy and the possibility of a Third Way has acquired a much stricter tone mainly aiming for flexibility and competitiveness after the stalemate of the Alliance for Jobs. On the one hand, most important positions surrounding the reforms could be summarised as a social exclusion discourse, focusing on new risks of poverty and the exclusion of those who lost out amid fundamental structural changes (for example Bäcker 2006; Brandt 2006; Dörre 2005; LAG AzuP 2005; Taux 2005). The main actors in this debate are the Linke, trade unions, anti-poverty and unemployment NGOs, and parts of the SPD. This discourse emphasises social rights in terms of redistributive justice and collective responsibility. On the other hand, there is a strong debate about 'free riders' or benefits abusers legitimating arguments for sanctions and restrictive measures (for an academic justification of such arguments, see Boss, Christensen, & Schrader 2005). In this context, flexibility and individual responsibility are the conceptual key features with the result that unemployed people are often blamed for being unwilling to work. While even some conservatives have meanwhile rediscovered social justice and withdrawn from extreme positions in this direction, the former discourse is still being advocated, especially by the FDP.

In contrast, even despite the initially ambitious objectives of the SPD/Green government, a specific gender equality discourse could not be established within the debate about reforming labour markets and social security systems. The new programmes then set up by von der Leyen (CDU) triggered new debates about family policy with a special focus on reconciling work and family and a more equal division of labour between parents. While central documents of the federal government are still strongly framed in terms of demographic change and low birth rates, the recent debates and initiatives point to a substantive change of family and gender norms within the conservative camp. However, this process is still heavily contested, especially by other Christian Democrats and the Catholic Church. Hence, at the beginning of Merkel's second term – now heading a CDU/

CSU/FDP coalition government – the CSU proposed a bill granting a financial bonus to those parents who stay at home with their children and do not take up a childcare place (labelled 'stove bonus' or *Herdprämie* by their critics).

Conclusion: a limited frame of gender equality?

Given the broader discursive and specific political developments presented in this chapter, what can be said about the reception of the (EU) activation discourse in Germany in general? Overall, the exchanges within the EES raise the impression that Germany has long been unreceptive if not resistant – at least to its gender equality provisions. The aforementioned synchronisation could only be identified after the EES had been in place for a considerable period. Throughout the interviews, reports, and complementary texts consulted for the present study, two basic conditions are quite consistent. The first refers to Germany's general reception of the EES and its interaction within it. In general, the EES is met with some reservation in Germany (Interviews 9, 5, 7). This tendency was expressed by public officials in direct criticisms of the non-binding procedures as well as in defensive references to German federalism and to the wage-setting autonomy of the social partners. While such fragmented power structures certainly compromise the effectiveness of the Strategy it can, however, be argued that such reservations have to be understood as expression of a specific administrative culture. German policies are more or less exclusively formulated in terms of law while softer, more fluid processes seem to be somehow suspect to its officials. Moreover, such processes might require different skills, perceptions, and procedures. Such basic reservations are also shared by German women's organisations, the Linke, and trade unions who do not spend much energy on using the EES as a political resource. Women's organisations complained about a lack of access and institutional hurdles due to the strict distinction between departmental competences. Trade unions preferred the existing national institutional channels. Together with the Linke, many trade unionists display more fundamental scepticism towards the employability-centred activation discourse, especially towards its rigid supply-side orientation, soft alternatives to employment protection law, and the shift in the direction of individual responsibility and more flexibility.

However, despite these basic reservations, Germany's interactions within and responsiveness to the EES/Lisbon Strategy (as reflected in both national and EU debates) have increased the more deeply the activation discourse became embedded in the national context. Moreover, some of the basic concepts in the current debate about employment policy did enter the German context via the EES (Büchs & Friedrich 2005). Even more significantly, the reform of the BA and the merging of unemployment benefits and social benefits were clearly informed by experiences from abroad. In particular, the German and British members of the European Employment Committee (EMCO)[5] played a crucial role by actively facilitating intensive bilateral exchanges up to the ministerial level. German officials highlighted how this extensive bilateral cooperation was crucially enhanced by regular and friendly contacts with their British colleagues in Brussels. On a more general level, much reference was made to the importance of the European level for the emergence of some form of 'mainstream' debate on employment policy, a debate said to be furthered by EMCO discussions, peer review sessions, thematic seminars, and numerous bi- or trilateral events (Interviews 16, 19, 9). Overall, only after the substantive activation discourse had taken hold in Germany (and after the structural reforms had started to pay off) did the federal government discover the Lisbon Strategy as a space for fruitful political engagement. This discovery may have been assisted by the restructuring of the Strategy in 2005 which included the discursive transformations discussed in Chapter 3, inasmuch as the German government seems to be much more prepared to talk about economic issues than about social policy at the EU level.

The second basic condition found to be generally consistent is in the context of gender equality in Germany. At least in the area of employment policy, equality between women and men is never portrayed as a fundamental right but rather as an 'indispensable factor for job quality' (Germany 2004: 10) or increasingly linked with demographic concerns (Germany 2005: 50). The low visibility of gender equality in the labour market reforms is probably the most significant expression. Moreover, the history of gender equality since the SPD/Green government came into office shows that the issue is not as embedded in everyday political processes on the ground. Despite the high expectations and the political commitment in the beginning, gender equality lost visibility and momentum. The concept of gender mainstreaming was taken up quite enthusiastically but its integration into actual practice did not proceed too far. As a result, the narrow and employability-centred gender equality frame that developed in the more recent EU conceptual debate fits much better with recent trends in German politics than a more fundamental human rights frame.

At the same time, the German NAPs contain – sometimes fragmented – signs of awareness about how complex gender issues are. For example, they make reference to the objective that men should take on more responsibilities in care, as promoted by new regulations allowing parents to split parental leave between them. Moreover, the new parental leave and pay regulations as well as investments in childcare are also driven by the objective of improving the sharing of work and care between parents. It remains to be seen how these family policies will develop and whether they will have any substantive consequences in relationships between women and men (for potential problems, see Verloo *et al.* 2005). These limited signs of gender awareness might be seen as evidence that there are some institutions and individuals who generate knowledge and promote the cause for equality between men and women within the German government and administration (more generally, see Naumann 2005).

Lastly, although in a slightly varied form, the combination of both these conditions can also be observed in the area of equal treatment more broadly. An anti-discrimination bill transposing a set of equality directives – most of them based on Article 13 of the EC Treaty – got stalled in the legislative process until August 2006. Despite repeated announcements, the deadlines for the majority of the directives had expired in 2002 (Directive 2002/73/EC) and 2003 (Directives 2000/43/EC and 2000/78/EC) without legislative action. Indeed, Germany even received a negative ECJ ruling, noting its failure to comply with the directives.[6] This was just further evidence of reservations against EU processes and against interfering in the private sector, on the one hand, and the difficult standing of issues of equality, on the other. The debates about this legislation, especially the contestations by the conservative parties, demonstrate these conditions most clearly. Moreover, the legislation ultimately approved a new Federal Anti-Discrimination Agency, which is formally independent but not very strong or visible. Nor does it have any legal powers to prosecute and to sanction cases of discrimination.

To conclude, the activation discourse is gaining ground and increasingly informing the welfare modernisation project in Germany. This process is deeply political, characterised by opposing attitudes and perceptions, political conflicts, and unequal power relations (in terms of access to and influence on policy debates). Concerning citizenship, the specific German version of the activation paradigm as it has materialised in the labour market reforms makes cuts to previously unconditional social rights while introducing strong individualised citizenship duties to work, supported by an increasingly strict regime. The gender dimension of these welfare reform debates, however, remains largely neglected and indifferent to existing and new forms of exclusion. Contrary to the new logic of maximal labour market participation, traditional gender models endure and continue to inform social and employment policy in Germany. The only progress has occurred very recently when a conservative minister introduced childcare measures with a high potential for achieving greater equality. While the German debate did feed on the content of the broader transnational debate about active social policy, the evidence of any direct impact by the EES is very limited.

Notes

1   For accounts on gender relations in Germany including a focus on the different situations in East and West Germany, see Beckmann and Kempf (1996), Bothfeld, Schmidt and Tobsch (2005), Bothfeld *et al.* (2005), or Rosenfeld, Trappe and Gornick (2004).
2   The German Christian Democrats consist of two parties: the CSU (Christian Social Union), which exists only in the state of Bavaria, and the CDU (Christian Democratic Union) standing for elections in all other federal states. Since both parties are not in direct competition with each other, they form a Union at the federal level.
3   This issue came up in many interviews with German bureaucrats and external observers (Interviews 18, 16, 19, 5, 7).
4   Original: 'Entweder wir modernisieren, und zwar als soziale Marktwirtschaft, oder wir werden modernisiert, und zwar von den ungebremsten Kräften des Marktes, die das Soziale beiseite drängen würden.' (Deutscher Bundestag 2003: 2481 A)
5   EMCO consists of two members (and two alternates) from each member state and the Commission. It plays a key role in the EES since all discussions and formal decisions are prepared here or have to pass through the committee at some stage.
6   Case C-43/05: *Commission v. Federal Republic of Germany*; see also Case C-329/04: *Commission v. Federal Republic of Germany*.

5

The United Kingdom – teaching activation

Compared to Germany, where welfare reforms were first initiated by a centre-left government, the Conservative governments under Margaret Thatcher and John Major had already intervened quite radically in the British welfare settlement. While Labour was responsible for a number of substantive changes, it could nevertheless build on these developments. Moreover, in contrast to the German SPD, where Schröder and his co-modernisers met fierce resistance, the modernisers around Tony Blair and Gordon Brown had already accomplished the transformation of their party to 'New Labour' when they came to power in 1997 (King & Wickham-Jones 1999; Taylor-Gooby, Larsen, & Kananen 2004).

Concerning gender equality, UK policies have been described as expressing the norms of a male breadwinner/female caregiver model. At the same time, there is evidence that these underlying gender norms are currently changing towards an adult worker model. Hence, it is an interesting question to pursue, whether this normative change can also be identified in the UK's interactions within the EES and how such basic assumptions are related to social realities from the perspective of its citizens.

Background: debating welfare, activation, and gender

The following section reconstructs the development of UK social policy since the mid-1990s. Welfare reforms can be seen as continuing a process that started under the Conservative government of Margaret Thatcher but were decisively shaped by the last Labour governments.

From negative to proactive activation

Before Labour came into power in 1997, the Conservatives had for some time declared a lack of flexibility in the UK economy, wide-ranging welfare dependency, and the need to liberate the forces of the market. Their corresponding approach to unemployment presented work as the central way towards independence and has been described as 'negative activation' (Taylor-Gooby & Daguerre 2002: 20). It stressed individual responsibilities, by cutting back on social rights and benefits, thereby creating financial pressures and increasing labour market participation. The most important development in this respect was the introduction of the Jobseeker's Allowance (JSA) in 1996 as a benefit containing sanctions in case of non-compliance (see overview in Larsen & Daguerre 2003).

However, some also realised that labour market participation alone might not be sufficient to sustain a competitive UK economy. Hence, both the government and the Confederation of British Industry (CBI) increasingly promoted the importance of education and the need for a skilled workforce (Ainley 1998). In a rapidly changing world, the UK was called upon to undergo a 'skills revolution' (CBI 1989) and become a 'learning society' (see Ainley 1998).

When Tony Blair became Prime Minister in 1997, his party had renamed itself 'New Labour' promoting a 'Third Way' or a modernised version of social democracy (see Blair 1997, 1998; Giddens 1998). As a result, the government's approach to social and employment policy was also based on the trinity of the market, labour market participation, and education/skills. The welfare state was supposed to be rebuilt around work, according to the principle of 'work for those who can, security for those who cannot' (DSS 1998: 23). The claim was made that

> [u]nemployment damages lives and causes poverty and ill health. The deprivation it brings can affect the next generation, imposing low expectations and denying opportunities for achievement. (United Kingdom 1999, Foreword)

Gordon Brown, especially, the Chancellor of the Exchequer (who became Prime Minister in summer 2007) has put a strong emphasis on the work ethic as a core value (see HM Treasury 2000, 2001, 2005b). Work has been reaffirmed as a normative principle with regard to more recent plans for further welfare reform:

> For individuals and families, the benefits of work are clear. Work is the best route out of poverty. It strengthens independence and dignity. It builds family aspirations, fosters greater social inclusion and can improve an individual's health and well-being. Furthermore, there is a clear link between benefits dependency and hardship. (DWP 2006a: 2)

However, present social and economic conditions are seen as so unpredictable and competitive that the individual's working life would also have to become more flexible. The main challenge for the government is said to be creating

> a flexible labour market where enterprises and workers are both able not only to adopt working practices which most suit their individual needs and circumstances, but also to continually adjust those choices to reflect the economic and social changes that inevitably take place. (United Kingdom 2000: 3–4)

Against this background, employability and adaptability – key concepts of the EES as well – have become central virtues for individuals and organisations (see, for example, DWP 2005a; HM Treasury 2004a). In addition, a strong emphasis on education has continually gained momentum and moved to the core of the UK approach to employment and welfare (DWP 2007a; Leitch 2006; United Kingdom 2007). Today, even childcare is framed as early childhood education and the UK government has set itself the goal of becoming 'world leader in skills by 2020' (United Kingdom 2009: 25).

Thus far, the differences between New Labour and its Conservative predecessors seem rather insignificant. In particular, the strict sanction regime introduced with the JSA remained unchanged, with education emphasised as key priority. However, in other respects Labour's strategy has differed. First of all, Labour added a strong proactive element to its activation strategy, derived from the insight that some social groups face specific problems regarding the labour market. While education should help to eradicate such disadvantages in the future, specific programmes were designed to assist those currently at risk: for example, the long-term unemployed, older workers, the disabled, young people, or lone mothers.

Therefore, the government launched different 'New Deal' programmes in 1998 representing a 'manifestation of a new contract between the citizens and the state' (Taylor-Gooby & Daguerre 2002: 20). At that point, the state accepted the obligation of providing opportunities for specific claimants of benefits to actively participate in the labour market or training while concurrently being required to actively seek work as well as to accept offered work or training (Taylor-Gooby & Daguerre 2002). All such schemes followed a basic pattern of targeted assistance but differed in their compulsory elements. The New Deal for the long-term unemployed (New Deal 25 Plus) and the New Deal for Young People are mandatory schemes offering a period of personal assistance and counselling followed by a second period of work experience/work placement, training, or other measures to develop reading, writing, and other basic skills (see, for example, United Kingdom 1998: 9). In case the claimant did not cooperate with the employment service, benefit cutbacks or timely withdrawals would be imposed (for example United Kingdom 2002; see also HM Treasury 2005a).

In addition, there were New Deals for older workers, disabled people, 'inactive' partners of benefit claimants (encouraging them to earn an additional income), and the New Deal for Lone Parents. The latter was most important with regard to gender issues. It involved a specific childcare element, based on the insight that single parents – the majority of whom are women – faced specific barriers to entering the job market. In fact, the unemployment rate of single parents is extremely high, placing them among the poorest groups within the UK (EOC 2003; United Kingdom 1999). The fact that in the UK about 1.75 million families are single-parent families, which is equivalent to one-quarter of all families (Evans *et al.* 2003) and the highest percentage of single-parent families in Europe, just adds to the significance of the problem. In 1998, 1.1 million of such families were claiming state benefits (United Kingdom 1998: 39). Moreover, over two-thirds of children in workless households lived in lone parent families (DWP 2006b).

While this programme is generally presented as successful, the rate of single parents on benefits is still perceived as too high (DWP 2006a; United Kingdom 2006). Therefore, starting in November 2008, even lone parents on income support are increasingly being required to actively seek work (United Kingdom 2009). As an intermediate political goal, the entitlement to income support was limited from October 2010 to lone parents whose youngest child is below seven. The majority will then be moved into the more restrictive JSA regime. In addition, the New Deal for Partners has also been repeatedly referenced in discussions since the majority of recipients are women and as the programme supports them to move out of economic dependency (Rubery 2000, 2001).

Two further developments are worth mentioning: first, so called 'make-work-pay' policies (see Peters *et al.* 2004; for a particular gender perspective see Fagan & Hebson 2004), particularly the National Minimum Wage (introduced in 1999) and the Working Tax Credit (for details, see United Kingdom 2004). In the most general terms, both instruments are supposed to ensure that families receive more income from work than they would from benefits. From a gender equality perspective, the National Minimum Wage was said to be especially helpful for women, who comprise 70% of the beneficiaries (see DWP 2002), while the tax credits as such have been criticised as contradictory, reproducing the male breadwinner model (Bellamy & Rake 2005).

Second, New Labour initiated institutional reforms in order to reinforce the reorientation towards activation. To begin with, the Department for Work and Pensions (DWP) was newly created from the Department for Social Security (DSS) and parts of the former Department for Education and Employment (DfEE) in June 2001. The new ministry became the key institution in charge of delivering the government's welfare to work agenda, administering around 20% of total government expenditures and employing about 25% of all civil servants (Prime Minister's Delivery Unit 2006). Moreover, through new analyses and proposals, the DWP has sustained a strong reform dynamic even after the government's main attention had to be drawn to other issues (for example, with the change from Blair to Brown as Prime Ministers). While its headquarters are rather small, most of its work is carried out by executive agencies, particularly Jobcentre Plus, the outcome of another key institutional reform.

The launching of Jobcentre Plus in April 2002 was presented as a crucial step in the 'transformation of what was essentially a passive benefit payment system into an active welfare state' (United Kingdom 2002: 16). It was created by merging the Employment Service and the Benefits Agency into a single integrated organisation dealing with all benefits. In particular, this move extended the activation agenda to a whole range of 'inactive' groups, such as lone parents or disabled people who had not previously been targeted because they were not receiving JSA (Karagiannaki 2007). While Jobcentre Plus has mostly been presented as a success, it was also heavily criticised by a report produced by the House of Commons Work and Pensions Committee early in 2006. The report stated that organisational, technical, and financial problems as well as poor staffing had 'contributed to truly appalling service levels' (Work and Pensions Committee 2006: 5) and might also threaten especially vulnerable parts of the society (for the government's response, see Work and Pensions Committee 2006a, 2006b).

Thus far, the political trajectory can be characterised as a continuous and gradual mobilisation of the activation agenda, with the Labour government adding specific proactive parts. The next section addresses a genuinely new element.

Family and childcare policies

Not so long ago, the UK was described as a country with no family policy and no public provision of childcare at all (Hantrais & Letablier 1996). This situation implied significantly gendered consequences, especially for lone parents whose particular risks have already been mentioned. However, the Labour government launched a comprehensive national childcare strategy which was intended to address three key problems of the traditional UK approach of leaving childcare entirely to the market and the family: the variable quality, the high cost, and the dearth of childcare places, a problem aggravated by regional disparities and insufficient information (DfEE 1998).[1] This childcare strategy was politically justified by arguments about (present and future) opportunities for children and parents as well as genuine choice. Moreover, the government argued that the 'economy will prosper if more skilled and capable people are able to take up job opportunities because they have access to good quality, affordable and accessible childcare' (DfEE 1998: 5). In addition, the government launched the Sure Start programme in 1998 to deliver these objectives. For example, Sure Start Children's Centres should provide services for pre-school children in the 20% poorest wards by March 2006 (HM Treasury 2003b). The new ten-year childcare strategy formulated in 2004 set the targets of establishing Children's Centres in 2,500 communities by 2008 and in 3,500 communities by 2010 (HM Treasury 2004b: 63). These centres are intended to be one-stop access points providing childcare and nursery education, family support and counselling as well as health services under one roof.

Evaluating the initial period, the 2004 Pre-Budget Report formulated the childcare strategy for the next ten years (HM Treasury 2004b). This document kept previous analyses, goals, and measures intact but introduced a new emphasis on the quality of childcare reflecting the government's stress on education. While childcare had long been understood as a measure to help parents balance work and family responsibilities, it was now being redefined as early childhood education and seen as a crucial productive factor in the social investment state. Only those children receiving education of the highest quality from the earliest possible age would be able to sustain the competitiveness and welfare of the UK economy in the future.

> What happens in the early years of a child's life is critical for later life development. Poverty, low income, social class and parental education all impact on children's life chances from very early in life. Good quality childcare and early education can have a positive effect on child outcomes, boosting cognitive development and improving social skills and confidence. (HM Treasury 2004b: 65)

Furthermore, the document also established a connection between the positive development of children and their parents' employment situation. Poverty was said to constitute the major barrier to children's development and future opportunities

(HM Treasury 2004b: 68). Yet the claims about the benefits to working parents went much further:

> Parental employment can bring benefits to the adults involved through increased self-esteem, extended social networks and a greater sense of control and reduced mental health problems all resulting in knock-on benefits for children. Maternal employment in particular can be an important protection against future hardship. (HM Treasury 2004b: 68)

In other words, working parents were presented as good if not better parents – a clear departure from the traditional male breadwinner/female carer model. Finally, especially mothers' employment was presented as crucial and leading to 'important economic benefits, impacting on productivity and gender equality' (HM Treasury 2004b: 68).

These childcare policies were complemented by changes in employment law, in which new parental leave and pay regulations are most relevant for gender relations. However, once again, the new legislation was not explicitly rooted in a gender equality agenda but was instead intended to ensure children's future opportunities and parents' continuing connection to the labour market (HM Treasury 2004b; see also Bellamy & Rake 2005). Since the first introduction of the Maternity and Parental Leave etc. Regulations (1999), the government repeatedly extended the periods for maternal leave (up to 52 weeks in 2010) and the provisions concerning statutory maternal pay (up to 39 weeks in 2010). Even more interesting with a view to equality, these regulations are also increasingly being extended to fathers. First, the Maternity and Parental Leave (Amendment) Regulations (2002) granted them the (limited) right to two weeks of statutory paternity leave. Second, mothers now had the right to transfer parts of their maternity leave and pay to their partner (HM Treasury 2004b; see also HM Treasury 2005a). While this move was justified with changed social realities and the increasing will of fathers to participate in the upbringing of children (HM Treasury 2004b), it has to be seen as a first step rather than fundamental change of gender relations in the UK (see Thompson, Vinter, & Young 2005; Yaxley, Vinter, & Young 2005).

In general, New Labour's childcare and family policies were clearly embedded in the activation agenda. Moreover, while the labour market instruments of the New Deal are more directly targeted at immediate activation of inactive citizens, the Childcare strategy is characterised by future orientation and a remarkably strong emphasis on social investment. However, as Lister (2006) among others makes clear, these measures are not without contradictions, especially when looking at them from a gender equality perspective.

What about a specific gender equality agenda?

Most of the activities discussed thus far were not primarily designed to target institutionalised relationships between men and women. Nevertheless, they are consistently mentioned throughout the NAPs under the equal opportunities dimension. In searching for an explicit gender equality agenda, the UK NAPs offer rather little information. At the same time, however, they express the consciousness that legal provisions and institutions in the equality field are quite advanced, especially when compared to other EU member states. For example, this is evident in the earliest response to the first inclusion of gender mainstreaming in the employment guidelines:

> The UK has a long tradition of encouraging women's access to the employment market and into all careers. Our policies are already in line with the objectives set out in this Guideline. (United Kingdom 1999: 42)

Such self-confidence can be found throughout all subsequent NAPs which restrict themselves to discussing only issues perceived to be of particular importance.

When looking at activities with an explicit focus on gender equality in employment and welfare, two institutional reforms have to be mentioned. First, in November 1998 the government introduced new mainstreaming guidelines to all its departments and agencies (Women and Equality Unit 1998). These Guidelines on Policy Appraisal apply to all policies, programmes, and services and were intended to prevent 'differential impact on disadvantaged groups' (United Kingdom 1999: 43). Accordingly, this is not specifically gender mainstreaming but targets a broader range of inequalities (especially concerning gender, ethnicity or disability). While they can still be criticised (for example Rubery 2000), the UK NAPs all display greater awareness and a more advanced approach to mainstreaming than other NAPs. Under most guidelines, they contain data differentiated according to gender and the particular problems of women/mothers are also consistently addressed beyond the specific gender equality guidelines.

The second institutional change worth mentioning is the creation of the Women and Equality Unit as a central government institution responsible for all questions of women's policies and gender equality, supporting the work of the Ministers for Women. Many topics on its agenda such as unequal pay, childcare, balancing work and family life have been consistently addressed in the NAPs. Since October 2007, the Unit belongs to the Government Equalities Office, a newly established department responsible for a broader range of equality issues. Among its responsibilities have been to lead action with regard to the Government's Public Service Agreement on Equality and to prepare an Equality Bill, something only introduced in the House of Commons in April 2009.

Besides these institutions, a Gender Equality Duty came into force in April 2007, requiring public authorities to promote gender equality and eliminate sex discrimination. It complements the legal rights based on the Sex Discrimination Act and the Equal Pay Act and can be understood as a form of 'legally enforceable gender mainstreaming' (EOC 2006a: 7). While such a step was of limited impact in the German case (also due to federal complexities), the situation in the UK could be different due to stronger equality institutions with legal powers. However, although it is of a broader scope, the Gender Equality Duty does not seem to have become a very strong reference point in the UK debate on welfare modernisation. Hence, it remains to be seen how this duty of gender mainstreaming affects issues of employment and welfare in the future.

Finally, the government commissioned and published research on particular aspects of inequality between women and men, particularly, the Kingsmill Report (2001) and the reports of the Women and Work Commission (2005, 2006) on the problem of unequal pay. By and large, the activities exclusively targeting gender inequality were limited to changes in the institutional set up and to research and could thus be criticised for not aiming at substantive change (Bellamy & Rake 2005).

Activating citizenship?

Crucially, most of the activities surveyed have been formulated in terms of policies rather than in terms of formal rights and duties. While the German reforms were initiated through parliamentary acts, the reforms in the UK have been developing more gradually based on government strategy papers, pilot schemes, evaluations, and gradual extensions. A Welfare Reform Act only became law in November 2009 and did not set up an entirely new system. For example, the Childcare strategy is chiefly about defining objectives and resources for the delivery of services, rather than legally formulated individual rights and duties. In general, recent employment policies in the UK affect citizenship practices mainly in terms of access to societal resources. In particular, access to employment is the societal resource at the basis of most programmes and policies discussed thus far, especially the New Deal. More recently, education and skills have become increasingly prominent in UK discourses on welfare reform. For example, the 2009 NRP describes a high skills level as key requirement for greater social mobility, quality of life, health, and well-being – with regard to both individuals and communities (United Kingdom 2009: 25).

In addition to this strong access orientation, shifts in rights and duties can also be identified (albeit to very different degrees). To begin with, the developments display a tendency towards duties and disciplinary elements. The intervention regime of the JSA and the New Deal were rationalised as balancing excessive rights which had caused lethargy and welfare dependence. The more rigid duties and conditionalities of the JSA were introduced by the Conservatives but New Labour did little to match them with a new generation of general social or economic rights. Moreover, many of those new duties are of a more differentiated nature. For example, the Building on New Deal report (DWP 2004) outlines two different '[n]ational intervention regimes based on core rights and responsibilities' (DWP 2004: 45). As a result, JSA recipients are subject to the Core Intervention Regime, while claimants of other benefits are subject to the 'Core Work-Focused Interview … Regime' (DWP 2004: 45). In contrast, inactive people who do not receive any benefits but would like to get a job are not entitled to any of these activating measures – and many of them are women (Rubery 2000). Similar to Germany, then, current developments in the UK have been accompanied by a differentiation and individualisation of citizenship. In addition, in the UK the formerly vague duty to work has also acquired a much stricter meaning and is applied in a much more differentiated way to different parts of society. Theoretically, this approach might have advantages as particular citizens could profit from programmes tackling specific disadvantages they are experiencing. However, particular groups have faced tougher disciplining than others, and yet other groups might be completely excluded from the benefits of such differentiated rights. Over recent years, this dynamic has gathered new momentum. For example, the obligations of workless lone parents were increasingly tightened (United Kingdom 2007, 2008), while the strongest call for increased conditionality was probably made by the Freud review (Freud 2007). Moreover, this tendency towards discipline and surveillance has been further intensified by recent reforms of the Incapacity Benefit, which was replaced by the Employment and Support Allowance in October 2008 with the goal of reducing the number of people on incapacity benefits by one million (DWP 2007b). In particular, the new regime introduced a mandatory Work Capability Assessment undertaken by a general practitioner to establish what kind of work a claimant is able to do (DWP 2007b, 2008). This triggers the question of the extent to which even health(care) is now also being reframed as a functional requirement for employment rather than a fundamental right in itself. In this respect the Gregg Review was particularly instrumental in indicating the high number of Incapacity Benefit claimants as a major obstacle to employment growth and suggesting a more restrictive system with tighter controls (Gregg 2008).

The government has always emphasised the importance of balancing rights and responsibilities (HM Treasury 2002a: 67; see also HM Treasury 2003a, 2004a, 2005a) and claimed that '[o]nly by extending rights and responsibilities together can the welfare system be made more fair and efficient' (HM Treasury 2004a: 79). Yet on closer examination, new rights remain the exception. Most significant in this context were the (few and sometimes soft) rights in the context of parental leave and childcare, such as the right to two weeks paternity leave, the right for mothers to transfer parts of their maternity leave to their partner, or the right to request more flexible working hours to care for children. Beyond rights for parents and families, the 2009 NAP announced plans for a 'right to request time to train' (United Kingdom 2009: 28), modelled after the right to request flexible working hours for parents and intended to increase the skills of the UK workforce.

Regarding gender equality, the New Deal for Lone Parents and the New Deal for Partners can have a positive impact on the disadvantages of women. Doubtless, the massive childcare programme is also crucially important. However, gender equality is not the main aim of these agendas but at best an indirect beneficiary. In fact, given the fact that explicit action aiming for equal opportunities only contained changes in the institutional machinery and research, it can be argued that the welfare to work agenda did not create new citizenship practices explicitly aimed at realising gender equality. For instance, lone parenthood has increasingly been framed in terms of child poverty rather than an inequality problem (for example, United Kingdom 2007, 2008). As important as this issue may be, this specific framing also implies that the gendered patterns of disadvantage and exclusion, which especially affect lone mothers, have become sidelined within the conceptual debate and social policy practice. The Gender Equality Duty mentioned above is a special case in this regard since it was introduced to complement existing individual rights based on the Equal Pay Act of 1970 and the Sex Discrimination Act of 1975 – but with stronger rules for public action.

Nevertheless, there is some evidence that – during all these renegotiations of rights, responsibilities and access – the fundamental rights to equality in general, and to gender equality in particular, are very strong frames of reference informing and structuring the debates at a higher (constitutional) level. However, this evidence cannot be definitely assessed without examining closely the different processes of contestation taking place around the current restructuring of UK employment and social policy.

Ultimately, while the reforms clearly embrace the activation paradigm and while the UK NAPs report all these activities in the communication process of the EES, it is still unclear what influence the EU-level debate has on the reforms in the UK.

Contested trajectories – tracing influence and ambivalence

Thus far, this chapter looked at historical developments on the basis of government activities. This section complements the narrative by taking into account some of the contestations surrounding welfare reforms in the UK. This broader perspective allows for insights about the workings of the EES but also criticisms and alternative views on the UK's welfare to work agenda and on its gender equality dimension.

Contestations from above

Similar to Germany, the UK has received quite consistent employment recommendations concerning gender equality over the years. These have addressed the lack of childcare facilities (2000–2007), the vulnerability of lone parents (2000–2004), and the central problem of unequal pay, which had not featured very prominently thus far. Since the first set of recommendations, the gender pay gap in the UK has consistently been criticised as one of the highest in all the member states (2000–2004, see also European Commission 2009b). Closely related were the recommendations that mention occupational and sectoral segregation of the UK labour market as a problem requiring more action (2002–2004). However, with the new round of recommendations (since 2007), there has been much less detail with regard to employment in general and to gender inequalities in particular. While childcare was cited as a 'point to watch' in 2007, other gender-related issues hardly received any attention. Unequal pay and labour market segregation were mentioned in the Commission's annual country assessments but not taken up as recommendations. Moreover, according to the EU country assessments and recommendations, the UK labour market suffered from two key problems: low skills undermining productivity, and specific disadvantages of certain groups. In this context, the problems of lone parents are regularly subsumed under the latter and little detailed attention is paid to gendered disadvantages in general.

Responding in its NAPs, the UK admitted the failure of the traditional approach to childcare (United Kingdom 2000: 10) and basically accepted the childcare-related recommendations as justified. At the same time, the ongoing government programmes targeting childcare and lone parents were presented as highly ambitious and very successful (for example, United Kingdom 2005, 2003, 2002). According to the 2005 NRP, the employment rate of lone parents had risen by 11.3 percentage points to 56.6% since 1997 (United Kingdom 2005: 41). In addition, the extended requirement for lone parents to actively seek work has been presented as an appropriate and equality-oriented response.

However, the gender pay gap has remained stubbornly high through all these years. Moreover, the government's actions in this respect have lagged considerably behind the scope and intensity of activities regarding childcare or lone parents. The main government activity reported was the introduction of the National Minimum Wage in 1998, which helped to confine the problem and proved especially beneficial for women, who represent around 70% of those working in low wage employment (DWP 2001: 84; see also TUC 2006). Nevertheless, actual research thirty years after the Equal Pay Act shows that women still earn around 15% less than men. The gap is even wider when including differences between full-time and part-time employment, in which case it can rise to 41% (Women and Work Commission 2006; see also Harkness 2002; Rubery & Grimshaw 2001). The gender pay gap was addressed in all NAPs but the approach, such as that outlined in the 2005 report of the DWP (2005b), remains patchy and much less ambitious. Programmes and campaigns to tackle gender stereotypes, and especially to encourage girls and women to take up education and careers where women are in the minority, constitute a key element of the strategies against labour market segregation. Previous activities, particularly the Kingsmill review (Kingsmill 2001), did have limited effects (see HM Treasury 2002a; United Kingdom 2002). In addition to the EU, national actors have also been involved in contestations of current transformations of citizenship. But how do they relate to the UK welfare reform and the communicative process of the EES?

Contestations from within

To begin with, welfare reforms and transformations of social and economic citizenship are not the top priority of women's organisations in the UK (Interview 22). Moreover, the potentially critical voices contributing to the UK debate on gender equality in employment and social policy are more approving than outright challenging of Labour's approach. Many are also of a more specialist nature, and the boundaries between civil society organisations and activist academics are often indistinct.

For instance, the limited approval of Labour's policies can be illustrated by contributions from the Fawcett Society, one of the oldest women's NGOs in the UK (Bellamy & Rake 2005). In a comprehensive report of 2005, it analysed the main factors influencing and reproducing gender inequalities in the UK: specifically, social norms and attitudes, constraints in the micro-economy of the household and in the macro-economy, and the institutions of the welfare state. The authors identify a contradiction at the state level. For while the government's welfare to work agenda would promote a citizen-worker model based on individual rights and duties and maximal employment (Bellamy & Rake 2005: 7; also Lister 2003b), many welfare institutions would still take for granted a gendered division of labour based on marriage (especially pensions and tax credits). In its conclusions, the report lauded the government for many of its activities in this domain. However, the state was also criticised for being unable to intervene in gender relations on a more sustainable base because it lacked an explicit gender equality agenda. Such an agenda would have to address men and women, their institutionalised relationships and their relative position in society.

The only voice which directly refers to the EES comes from the UK members of the European Commission's Expert Group on Gender and Employment who have held senior posts within the group for most of the time. In addition, they have directed it for two periods and regularly distributed their assessments through academic channels as well as in policy reports for the Commission's Employment DG. In general, they also supported many activities of the Labour government. However, they also continuously criticised the government for lacking that perspective on the situations and roles of men which would be necessary for abolishing persisting gender inequalities in the labour market. In addition to the symptoms of the pay gap and horizontal segregation, these reports describe the long hours culture in the UK contributing to the entrapment of many women in low-paid, part-time jobs (Rubery 2004, 2003; Fagan 2002; Rubery 2001, 2000). This neglect of the other side of gender relations has been explained as the government's 'defensive' (Rubery 2000: 3) approach to gender mainstreaming, intended to ensure that new legislation or policies did not create new discrimination (and therefore, a risk of litigation). In contrast, the Expert Group called for more 'proactive' (Rubery 2000: 18) gender mainstreaming aimed at transforming existing unequal gender relationships.

A third example of a rather cooperative strategy based on limited approval of Labour was the Changing Times campaign of the Trade Union Congress (TUC). In this project, the TUC highlighted the diversity of employees' needs and especially the importance of working time. For many, especially those with caring responsibilities, control over and flexible working time might be even more important than pay. In the process, the campaign aims to renegotiate the meaning of flexibility in a way that benefits both employers and employees. As part of the programme, the TUC also offers a specific methodology to negotiate changes within companies in order to 'achieve changes that are win-win-win for staff-employers-customers'.[2] This alternative positive meaning of flexibility is not related to social capital and future investment but to empowering individuals to balance their private and working life in a self-reliant and cooperative way according to their needs. Moreover, and even more importantly, such a new meaning of flexibility and the resulting control over personal life-time would be a crucial requirement for a new redistribution of caring responsibilities.

A final voice that has to be mentioned is the Equal Opportunities Commission (EOC), which existed until autumn 2007 as an independent non-departmental public body. The Commission was the central institution responsible for gender equality and combating related discrimination. In October 2007 it was merged with the Commission for Racial Equality and the Disability Rights Commission into a comprehensive Equality and Human Rights Commission (EHRC) which additionally assumed responsibility for matters of sexual orientation, age, religion and faith, and human rights. The EOC and the gender-related activities of the EHRC have also focused on the pay gap, market segregation, and the promotion of new male roles. Their approach is also factual and cooperative, concentrating on research, advice to employers, and contributing to government consultations. Thanks to its privileged institutionalised position, however, this body also exercises specific leverage, especially the competence to investigate individual discrimination complaints and the capacity to support lawsuits of general significance such as equality between women and men (for details see EHRC 2008, 2009).

With the exception of the members of the EU Commission's UK gender equality experts, who are institutionally linked to the Strategy, most voices in the UK do not even try to draw on its communicative processes. Given their limited approval and cooperative approaches in combination with quite a strong institutional machinery, the soft procedures of the EES are not perceived as value added (Interviews 20, 22, 21). References to EU processes are normally limited to directives and ECJ case law. Thus, contestations of government policies refer to the UK's opt out from the Working Time Directive (Rubery 2003; 2004) or ECJ case law intervening in the UK pay system.[3] Moreover, against the UK's good performance on most indicators, the Strategy provides little leverage.

From a more general perspective, all issues of equality in the UK are embedded in a comparably strong fundamental rights frame, which is visible in most government rhetoric and especially enacted through the formal equality institutions. Especially in the context of the fading of gender equality in the EES, this comparably strong rights frame – in combination with a relatively strong equality machinery – is a much more powerful resource (Interviews 23, 21).

Conclusion: policy teaching

Given the activities and progress which are regularly reported by the UK in response to most recommendations, does this mean that the UK is particularly amenable to the European modernisation debate? UK officials certainly have far fewer reservations towards the policy-making style of the EES than, for example, their German colleagues (Interview 6, 2, 7). On the one hand, there is little risk that new European legal (especially labour law) norms could be imposed on the UK. On the other hand, UK administrators are much more familiar with policy formulation in terms of benchmarks and targets or with designing pilots in order to create best practices. However, the story should not end here.

Many patterns and policies that are considered best practices across Europe originated in the UK. In fact, German as well as Hungarian officials repeatedly mentioned that they had a strong interest in the British case, in particular the introduction of Jobcentre Plus as well as the New Deals. This assessment, combined with the good performance, puts the UK in a favourable position. And indeed, when its behaviour is examined more closely, the UK rather seems interested in presenting its success and in teaching how it was achieved along with the underlying strategic and conceptual knowledge. Hence, the UK government uses the EU activation debate to promote its own ideas about 'modern' economic and social policy throughout Europe. At the core lies the fundamental argument that flexibility and security, competitiveness and social justice are not only reconcilable but mutually reinforce each other based on a social investment approach:

> The Lisbon declaration was not only ambitious; it also flew in the face of the often-heard argument that higher productivity and higher employment are incompatible objectives … Whatever the labour market model, key elements for successful reform are the same. (HM Treasury 2002b: 3–4)

Moreover, the UK government greeted the Kok Report with praise since it brought the European approach more in line with national priorities (DTI 2004; HM Treasury 2003a; United Kingdom 2004). As a result, the work of the Employment Taskforce was not presented as some external EU activity. Instead the UK's contribution was emphasised as crucial to keeping the European reform project on track (HM Treasury 2003a, no. 4.8). The integration of the EES into the re-launched Lisbon Strategy was also welcomed as necessary and the Strategy's new emphasis on competitiveness and growth constituted a key priority of the UK presidency in the first half of 2006 (FCO 2005). Thus, in an address to the European Parliament, Tony Blair used rather frank language to call for a new policy agenda at the EU level:

> Now, almost 50 years on, we have to renew. There is no shame in that. All institutions must do it. And we can. But only if we remarry the European ideals we believe in with the modern world we live in. The purpose of our social model should be to enhance our ability to compete, to help our people cope with globalisation, to let them embrace its opportunities and avoid its dangers. Of course we need a social Europe. But it must be a social Europe that works.
>
> And we've been told how to do it. The Kok report in 2004 shows the way … This is modern social policy, not regulation and job protection that may save some jobs for a time at the expense of many jobs in the future.
>
> And since this is a day for demolishing caricatures, let me demolish one other: the idea that Britain is in the grip of some extreme Anglo-Saxon market philosophy that tramples on the poor and disadvantaged. The present British Government has introduced … the largest jobs programme in Europe that has seen long-term youth unemployment virtually abolished. It has increased investment in our public services more than any other European country in the past five years. We needed to, it is true, but we did it. We have introduced Britain's first minimum wage. We have regenerated our cities. We have lifted almost one million children out of poverty and two million pensioners out of acute hardship and are embarked on the most radical expansion of childcare, maternity and paternity rights in our country's history. It is just that we have done it on the basis of and not at the expense of a strong economy. (FCO 2005: 41–42)

In addition to such instructive statements, the government is sometimes quite clever in presenting its own practices as evidence. Examples can be found when looking at the use of favourable OECD quotations (for example, United Kingdom 2003: 6). Moreover, all NAPs refer to the (over-)achieved Lisbon targets and draw comparisons to the lower-performing EU average. A similar example is how some NAP sections on the UK approach to gender mainstreaming note that the strategy has been reliably practiced for some time (especially United Kingdom 1999; see also Rubery 2004).[4] In the same manner, referring to UK parental leave legislation, the 2009 NRP update states that 'rights, which already compare well with the rest of the EU, are being extended' (United Kingdom 2009: 38). The 2006 update on the UK NRP emphasises the government's wide consultations with stakeholders and claims that '[t]he International Monetary Fund (IMF) has praised the high degree of transparency in the UK policy-making process' (United Kingdom 2006: 2). While German officials only gradually adopted the language of the EES, UK officials have spoken the activation idiom rather fluently from the beginning. Thus equipped with important discursive resources, Labour has generally to a lesser extent deliberated its views with a group of European equals, instead attempting to establish its intellectual authority over the activation discourse and related practices. Or as one respondent put it in 2006: 'Lisbon is Tony Blair reforming Europe' (Interview 23). Nonetheless, the UK's approach to gender equality and mainstreaming is still criticised as unjustifiably complacent (Rubery 2000; Rubery *et al.* 2005), and the remaining pay gap shows that there still are major problems.

Overall, this chapter has shown that the activation paradigm is much more deeply embedded in political discourses and institutions in the UK. The foundations already laid by the Conservatives were built upon by Labour – mainly by concentrating on proactive activation of specific groups and childcare. Some of the adopted measures have had positive consequences for equality between women and men. However, an explicit gender equality agenda is not part of the larger welfare reform project. In comparison to the German case, it is striking that the UK hardly features conservative voices calling for traditional images of the family or for maintaining a male breadwinner model – even as popularity has shifted between Brown and the Conservative leader David Cameron. Rather, it seems that the underlying gender contract in the UK is moving towards an adult worker model – without intervening substantially in the corresponding social realities. Concerning citizenship, the active approach to social policy also implies a shift towards individualised and differentiated duties. In contrast to Germany, the UK emphasises more strongly access-oriented programmes such as the national Childcare strategy.

Notes

1   While the initial Green Paper (DfEE 1998) indicates which sums will be invested, it does not include a target of how many childcare places shall be created in total (perhaps hoping that employers would voluntarily contribute a substantial amount of childcare places). Later, the Budget sets the interim target at 1 million new childcare places by March 2004

for all parents who want such care for their children ages three to fourteen by March 2010 (HM Treasury 2002a).

2　See www.tuc.org.uk/work_life/index.cfm?mins=466, accessed 9 December 2009.

3　See, for example, statements by the EOC (2006b) and the trade union Prospect (2006b, 2006a) about *Case C-17/05: Cadman v Health & Safety Executive.*

4　In contrast, one respondent in the EU Commission criticised the UK NRP for strong gender equality rhetoric but little strategic action (Interview 2).

6

Hungary – openness and rights without access

This chapter extends the empirical investigation to a new post-socialist EU member state. Diversity of its members had always been a key feature of the EU and has of course massively increased with the latest Eastern enlargements. Therefore, Hungary is included as a country with an entirely different legacy in terms of economic organisation and performance, welfare provision, and gender norms. Furthermore, it is still facing a process of economic and social transformation that goes far beyond the scale of even the more substantive structural reforms in Germany or the UK. In addition to the themes discussed in Chapters 4 and 5, here we will be examining how activation resonates in a post-socialist context with its very specific problems.

Overall, the case of Hungary is characterised by extensive ideological shifts as well as by much larger budgetary and labour market problems. On the one hand, citizenship practices in Hungary have been in turmoil, particularly with respect to the changed situation of women in the labour market. On the other hand, against the background of institutional restructuring and normative reorientation, the disappearance of gender equality from the conceptual debate at the EU level has had the most serious effects.

Background: debating welfare, activation, and gender

Regarding the distinct characteristics of the Hungarian context, there is first the complex transformation from a socialist system into a market economy and multi-party democracy with all its political, social, economic, and cultural consequences. Second, Hungary has only recently become an EU member state. Both processes are crucial conditions with respect to transformations of citizenship, the relationship between women and men, and Hungary's participation in the EES.

For all their differences, the stories of Germany and the UK are similar in one crucial aspect. In both countries, the reforms of the last decades departed from an institutional settlement consolidated after the Second World War. This settlement was increasingly questioned and undermined by economic recession, unemployment, and far-reaching structural change. Yet these systems were not entirely abolished but rather reformed gradually – albeit extensively – on the basis of the activation agenda. In Hungary, in contrast, many institutions, norms, and practices have been disrupted in a much more fundamental manner over the last two decades. Moreover, some of these disruptions seem to have much stronger exogenous qualities. Therefore, this chapter will also require a somewhat more extensive first section on the political-historical context. Hence it extends its scope beyond the institutional boundaries of the welfare state and looks further back in time.

Post-socialist transformation and conservative backlash

Before the regime change, male and female activity was nearly equally high with employment rates of 90.8% for men, 85.5% for women, and 88.2% in total. In its first stage, however, the economic transformation not only led to extensive privatisation of formerly state-owned companies but also to a massive drop in employment. Although Hungary has suffered immensely in the financial crisis since 2008, the most difficult phase was the early and mid-1990s with extremely negative effects on employment, especially among women and older workers. In fact, between 1989 and 1992, Hungary lost around 1.1 million jobs (within a total population of just over 10 million) and the overall employment rate (again, of 88.2%) fell by 21.4 percentage points (Hungary 2001: 5). This is even more dramatic when considering that unemployment officially did not exist at all in any socialist state. Moreover, the decline in female labour market activity from 76% to 50% between 1990 and 1995 was the largest throughout the (at that time) new applicant states (Pollert 2005). Although employment rates rose again in 1998 (Hungary 2001), Hungary's employment rate still was the third lowest in the EU in 2007 (European Council 2009).

In contrast to most other Central and Eastern European countries, and also in contrast to the average of the EU member states before the 2004 enlargement, the unemployment rate of women in Hungary has long been lower than that of men.[1] Moreover, the Hungarian NAPs hardly count women among those groups facing particular disadvantages or risk in the labour market (Hungary 2004, 2005b, 2006). However, the relatively low female unemployment rates should not be misinterpreted as indicating that women were in a better position in the labour market. Instead, while many men and women lost their jobs in the course of the capitalist restructuring, men became mostly unemployed while many women completely left the labour market (Nagy 2004) or moved into informal work (Hungary 2006; Pollert 2005).

The capitalist transformation was accompanied by a drastic deregulation not only of prices for products but also of wages and working conditions (Kollonay Lehoczky 2005b; Pollert & Fodor 2005). Most of these developments were based on a radical liberal discourse emphasising the free market and the reduction of state intervention in the economy as the core strategy for achieving economic transformation. This strategy was in turn promoted by key government actors, such as former Finance Minister Lajos Bokros (1995/1996) but also by the World Bank or the International Monetary Fund, which played a central role in this first phase of post-socialism (Goven 2001; Haney 2002; on Central Europe in general, see Deacon & Hulse 1997; Ferge & Juhász 2004). Many Hungarians lost their previously secure jobs, the cost of living increased while wages remained low, and employers were able to demand much more flexibility from their employees, in particular longer and more flexible working time (Pollert 2005). However, well in line with the socialist legacy, full-time employment of women and men persisted as the general norm. At the same time, while employment conditions worsened and working hours increased, it became increasingly difficult for many women to stay in the labour market.

While men and women were equally affected by early retirement schemes from 1989 (Pollert & Fodor 2005), the statutory retirement age of women remains lower than that of men and many women have left the labour market at a very early stage (Nagy 2004). Until 1997, the statutory retirement age for women was 55 (60 for men) but has been gradually raised to 59 years in 2004 and to 62 (for women and men) in 2009. Moreover, it became much more difficult to reconcile work and care (Szabo 2003). Until the late 1980s, in order to enable universally high labour market participation and state-led emancipation, Hungary – like all communist states – offered a wide range of childcare, specific protection for mothers, and other forms of family support. Among the benefits and services were nurseries provided by (state-owned) employers. After privatisation and in face of the immensely difficult restructuring of the economy, employers axed most services that had ensured women's employment. Hungary witnessed a massive decline in childcare for children under the age of three, especially in rural areas, and much more dramatic cutbacks of other state provisions for families (Fodor *et al.* 2002; Fultz, Ruck, & Steinhilber 2003; Szabo 2003). Moreover, while the situation in public kindergartens (for children aged three to six) seems not to have worsened and might still be better than in many Western European member states, the demand is certainly not being met (Korintus & Vajda 2002). In the process, mothers have been competing under the same conditions as men, which has further contributed to pushing women with caring responsibilities out of the labour market. This trend has been furthered by a system of generous childcare leaves which has come to constitute a major path out of employment (Fodor 2005; Nagy 2004; Szabo 2003).

Changing social attitudes towards gender roles are a final factor to be considered here. Despite all emancipatory state-socialist activities, most central and eastern European societies remained very conservative regarding the relationship between women and men; Hungary has even been described as the most conservative among them (Eberhardt 2005). Thus, promoting gender equality outside the workplace was never on the agenda under the socialist adult worker model. Women participated equally in employment and other public activities (for example, in meetings or socialist organisations) but were left with the additional weight of household and care-work. Therefore, not all women experienced socialist state-led emancipation as entirely liberating.[2] Moreover, socialist labour markets also featured pay gaps, occupational and sectoral labour market segregation as well as glass ceilings and sticky floors (Klement & Rudolph 2006; Pollert 2003). After the fall of communism, Hungarian society experienced a fundamental shift of social norms and attitudes against everything associated with the old authoritarian order and in the direction of conservative or 'traditional' values. This conservative shift resulted in a decisive backlash against gender equality in Hungary (Fodor 2005; Kollonay Lehoczky 2005a, 2005b; Szabo 2003). In fact, this change of attitudes has also been noted in government documents:

> In the 1990s, the decrease of female employment was also followed by a conservative shift in attitudes, even among women themselves, towards the employment of women. (Hungary 2004: 29)

This last development is crucial in understanding the gendered effects of the capitalist transformation on the Hungarian labour market. In particular, the conservative party FIDESZ has since then emphasised the return to traditional values and family roles, arguing that women finally had the choice to stay at home and care for their children (Kollonay Lehoczky 2002). Family policies, a field that was key to socialist emancipation and high female labour market participation, 'can be seen as perhaps the most divisive issue between left- and right-wing governments' (Krizsán & Zentai 2003: 10; see also Szabo 2003). This potential for divisiveness was particularly visible between 1998 and 2002 under Prime Minister Viktor Orbán (FIDESZ) who immediately reinstalled the previous generous childcare allowances that had been abolished in the course of an austerity package under the predecessor government in 1995 and 1996. Although Hungarian parental leave schemes are generally available for both women and men, they are nearly exclusively taken up by women, with some arguing such schemes would promote an ideal mother who 'sacrifices herself for the family' (Krizsán & Zentai 2003: 10). And indeed, women who have left the labour market to care for children constitute a large share of the inactive population and find it extremely difficult to return to the labour market afterwards.

Moreover, debates about family policies replaced direct debates on gender issues, weakening arguments for gender equality based on fundamental rights (Krizsán & Zentai 2003; see also IHF 2000b). Women's rights, especially the kind of social and economic protection under socialism, were often seen as inadequate and outdated both by conservatives emphasising alleged pre-socialist 'traditional' values as well as by liberal modernisers emphasising civic freedoms from state intervention (Einhorn 1996). While the traditionalist discourse might have peaked between 1998 and 2002, it is nevertheless still present (Fodor 2005). Against this background, women's inactivity is not perceived as a particular problem of inequality.

However, neither the recent history of gender equality nor that of social and economic citizenship in Hungary is merely the result of deregulation plus conservatism. Rather, the corresponding approach has been fragmented and unstable, shifting at least with each change in government. Moreover, issues of anti-discrimination and (gender) equality were kept on the Hungarian political agenda, particularly from the outside – even before EU membership became certain.

Promotion from outside – balancing backlash and transformation

On the whole, compared to Germany and the UK, Hungary seems to have been much more open to external influences during its most recent history. In this context, processes originating in the UN and the EU have kept gender issues on the political agenda in Hungary despite the conservative backlash (for example, Krizsán & Zentai 2006).

A first international key event for Hungarian gender equality policies was the UN Fourth World Conference on Women in 1995 (Krizsán & Zentai 2006). To implement the Beijing Declaration and Platform for Action (see United Nations 1995), the government set up an action plan described as the only comprehensive strategic document addressing gender inequalities in Hungary thus far (Krizsán & Zentai 2006). The action plan adopted seven out of twelve policy areas and fields for action identified at Beijing: women's rights, implementing equal opportunities, improving women's social equality, gender education in public schools, violence against women, involvement of women NGOs, and the establishment of an information system for women on women (for a detailed assessment, see Biró & Szabó 1999). However, no follow-up document was prepared by the then reigning FIDESZ government and no further action was taken (Eberhardt 2005; NANE & HCWG 2002). Nevertheless, the period between 1995 and 1998 also witnessed the creation of the Secretariat for Women's Policy within the Ministry of Labour, the first Hungarian institution responsible for promoting equal opportunities.

Another important international process has been the Convention on the Elimination of Discrimination against Women (CEDAW) and the monitoring procedures of the Committee established under it. Hungary had signed and ratified the Convention in 1980 and transposed it into national law without reservations. From the 1990s on, the reports submitted by the Hungarian government and the corresponding CEDAW conclusions provide a comprehensive and critical picture of Hungarian gender equality policies. Of particular importance were the CEDAW conclusions on Hungary's combined fifth and fourth report (United Nations 2002). In fact, CEDAW raised concerns and criticism in each area relevant for equality between women and men under the Convention (Krizsán & Zentai 2006): the lack of appropriate legal definitions and procedures to tackle discrimination against women; a weak and inadequately resourced gender equality machinery; entrenched traditional stereotypes; the low proportion of women in high-level elected and appointed public positions, and women's disadvantages in the labour market (see United Nations 2002, no. 313–338). Moreover, the Convention has remained the most important reference point for Hungarian women's NGOs and feminists in national political struggles (Dombos, Horváth, & Krizsán 2007; see also NANE & HCWG 2002). However, the potential of these processes should not be over-estimated. Despite all international commitments and even some embarrassing criticism, the Hungarian approach to gender equality has remained fragmented and vulnerable to relapse.

This fact is best illustrated by the history of the national equal opportunities machinery. Even taking into account the limits of its competences, the Secretariat for Women's Policy (1995–1996), which shortly afterwards became the Office of Equal Opportunities (1996–1998), was described as 'a very progressive and effective organ' (IHF 2000a: 18) which launched 'revolutionary programmes and formed an unusually intense relationship with the media' (IHF 2000b: 191). However, in 1998 the Orbán government replaced it with a Secretariat of the Representation of Women 'at the lowest possible level of the Ministerial hierarchy' (IHF 2000a: 18). While the new secretariat continued to implement the agenda of its predecessor, the downward shift had seriously diminished its visibility, voice, and capacities (all of which had already been limited before) (Eberhardt 2005; Krizsán & Zentai 2003; more generally NANE & HCWG 2002). In addition, the FIDESZ-led government created the Council for the Representation of Women (Government Decree 1059/1999), a consultative body consisting of government officials, representatives of women's NGOs, and academics, intended to advise the government in questions of equal opportunities between women and men. In practice, however, this body never gained acceptance and was only convened rarely, with breaks of several years between meetings. In general, the national equal opportunities machinery changed at least with every change in government. Its more recent history will need to be addressed again below in the context of EU enlargement.

A further characteristic of Hungary's fragmented and unstable approach to gender equality relates to gender mainstreaming. Despite the push the strategy received from the Fourth World Conference on Women and from its adoption by the EU (see European Commission 1996), it never gained ground in Hungary. This circumstance was then criticised by the 2002 CEDAW conclusions (United Nations 2002, no. 316). In addition, Hungary's 2005 report on the implementation of the Beijing Platform for Action – one year after its EU accession – admits that gender mainstreaming has not yet been established (Hungary 2005a: 4). Besides these UN-based processes which intervened to some extent in the fragmented approach to gender equality, the next section will address a further development which raised high hopes among feminists and other promoters of equality in Hungary: its accession to the EU.

Turning the outside in? – EU accession and hopes for a more coherent approach

Hungary's EU accession was a central moment for its participation in European debates about modern social policy and an activating welfare state. In addition, the accession process also constitutes a contextual condition in a much more substantive sense. The 1993 Copenhagen European Council decided that all formerly communist countries in Central and Eastern Europe (European Council 1993) should eventually be given the prospect of joining the Union. Therefore, it defined certain conditions (the so called Copenhagen Criteria) each candidate had to meet in order to qualify for accession.

> Membership requires that the candidate country has achieved stability of institutions guaranteeing democracy, the rule of law, human rights and respect for and protection of minorities, the existence of a functioning market economy as well as the capacity to cope with competitive pressure and market forces within the Union. Membership presupposes the candidate's ability to take on the obligations of membership including adherence to the aims of political, economic and monetary union. (European Council 1993: 13)

In addition, the 1995 Madrid European Council specifically emphasised the importance of the *acquis communautaire* and the administrative capacities to transpose and to implement it (European Council 1995). The *acquis* is the cumulative body of EU laws including the treaties, regulations, and directives passed by the European institutions, as well as ECJ judgements. Not surprisingly, these conditions produced enormous legislative and administrative activities in all the applicant states. When Hungary entered the EU on 1 May 2004, these requirements would also have decisive influence on Hungary's interaction within the communicative processes of the EES and on its national institutional framework concerning all issues of equality.

Since it was a condition of EU membership that the entire *acquis communautaire* be transposed, it is also easy to understand why many Hungarian feminists had such high expectations regarding their country's EU accession (Szabo 2003; Sloat 2004). These hopes were mainly fuelled by the Union's role as a key promoter of gender equality and gender mainstreaming, by the extension of the anti-discrimination agenda with the inclusion of Article 13 in the Amsterdam Treaty, and by the Union's uncompromising insistence on and monitoring of the transposition of all legal provisions without exception. Exploring how the conditions were put in practice, it is useful to look again at the legal and institutional framework for (gender) equality.

After the first period of the relatively progressive Secretariat for Women's Policy (1995–1996) as well as the Office of Equal Opportunities (1996–1998), and after its downgrading under Viktor Orbán the next government under Prime Minister Péter Medgyessy from the socialists (MSZP) changed the equal opportunities machinery yet again in 2002. The low-level Secretariat for the Representation of Women was replaced by the Directorate for Equal Opportunities, within the newly created Ministry for Employment and Labour. The new directorate was responsible for three groups facing particular disadvantages: women, disabled people, and the Roma community (EIRO online 2003). Furthermore, the directorate drew up another National Action Plan on ensuring equality between men and women for the period between 2003 and 2006. The plan claimed to be in line with all EU regulations, laying down wide-ranging activities for different ministries and government agencies, all the way from reviewing legislation to producing data disaggregated by gender. The EU contributed 3.9 million Euros through its PHARE programme (EIRO online 2003), the main financial instrument for supporting Central and Eastern European countries who have applied for EU membership. In May 2003, the head of the Directorate, Katalin Levai (who had also headed the previous Secretariat of the Representation of Women) was even promoted to a Minister without Portfolio for Equal Opportunities. This move was rather surprising to many observers and has been greeted with acclaim, although Levai's work was also criticised as a politics of minimal steps combined with rhetoric (Eberhardt 2005; Krizsán & Zentai 2006).

The most important condition behind this reorganisation was certainly the change of government. In fact, the MSZP had consistently framed equal opportunities in terms of human rights rather than as some attempt of external intervention (Dombos, Horváth, & Krizsán 2007). However, external events contributing to this reorganisation should not be completely overlooked. On the one hand, in 2002 the CEDAW report had heavily criticised Hungary's approach to gender equality (United Nations 2002). On the other hand, a number of EU initiatives in the areas of gender equality and anti-discrimination had raised awareness and visibility of these issues in addition to the regular monitoring of the applicant states (EIRO online 2003). In this context, it is important to mention the equal treatment directives based on Article 13 (Council of the EU 2000c, 2000b) and the amended gender equality directive (Council of the EU 2002). Moreover, in connection with the Community Framework Strategy on Gender Equality (2001–2005) formulated by the Commission (European Commission 2000), the European Council adopted a Community Action Programme to fund and to support it (Council of the EU 2001). Furthermore, in 2000 the Council had adopted a Community Action Programme to combat discrimination in general (Council of the EU 2000a).

However, even this significant reorganisation and elevation of equal opportunities should not have a long-lasting impact. In 2004, Katalin Levai, the new Minister for Equal Opportunities, stood as a candidate for the first Hungarian elections to the European Parliament heading the list of the MSZP. After her move to Brussels, no new minister was appointed. Instead, the Government Office for Equal Opportunities was integrated into the Ministry of Youth, Family, Social Affairs, and Equal Opportunities, which was established in 2004. Although Hungary's 2006 report to CEDAW claimed that the promotion of gender mainstreaming was among the main tasks of the minister heading the new Ministry (CEDAW 2006), gender equality had certainly suffered from this reorganisation. At that point, the office then became just one single piece within quite a large apparatus concerned with a broad range of policies. Moreover, apart from rhetoric and a few implicit references in the era of Katalin Levai and some references in documents addressing external actors, there is still no evidence that any gender mainstreaming has been practiced within the national government and administration. In fact, Levai's sudden move to Brussels was criticised for signalling that the promotion of equal opportunities, in which she was the main government figure was not that important anymore (Interviews 28, 38). Finally, in the course of a drastic reduction of the public service following the elections in summer 2006, the Hungarian Government Office for Equal Opportunities was further reduced and the substantive expertise of the office was criticised in different interviews (Interviews 28, 24, 25).

In addition to these changes in the ministerial bureaucracy, a comprehensive legal framework for equal opportunities and anti-discrimination was established with the Act on Equal Treatment and Promotion of Equal Opportunities, which entered into force on 27 January 2004, shortly before the accession date. Its main intention has been prohibiting and sanctioning of discrimination while proactive promotion of equality has had much less weight. According to one lawyer involved in the drafting, it was a key aim to create a sound legal foundation for anti-discrimination in order to shield it from political disputes (Interview 30). Therefore, legal protection of equal treatment and the political promotion of equal opportunities should be clearly distinguished. With regard to more proactive measures, the new Act demanded that the government presents a National Equal Opportunities Programme and that all employers in which the Hungarian state has a share of more than 50% would draw up Equal Opportunities Plans as well (for the rest of the private sector, this was voluntary). However, the national programme did not create much further activity since the compulsory equality plans were simply ignored by most employers – partly because the act did not contain sanctions for non-compliance and partly because there was a lack of awareness. Most of all, the act did not mention gender mainstreaming.

The Equal Treatment Act also created an independent Equal Treatment Authority (2005) with the capacity to investigate violations and impose fines of up to 20,000 Euros. Theoretically, its competences include more general activities to raise awareness and promote equality through research and campaigns. In practice, however, due to its limited resources, it is struggling to keep up with several hundred individual complaints per year (however, for example, in 2010 only 42 cases led to a decision). Yet, generally speaking, the work of the authority has been evaluated quite positively (Interviews 30, 28, 29). Yet it is interesting that the first decision on gender-related discrimination only came in November 2007 while the vast majority of cases are about ethnic discrimination, mostly of Roma. Nevertheless, over the years, the Authority has become an important source of expertise and practical guidance with regard to gender equality and especially gender mainstreaming (Kakucs 2009).

Considering the influence of the EU, it should not be assumed that the content or the very existence of the Equal Treatment Act resulted somehow automatically from EU accession (see also Sedelmeier 2009). Previously, the FIDESZ government had argued that the transposition of the social policy and equality *acquis* had already been completed with some minor amendments of the Labour Code in 2001 (Szabo 2003; Dombos, Horváth, & Krizsán 2007). Yet to achieve this goal, there still had to be a change in government (in 2002) as well as a great deal of effort by a network of equality advocates in Hungarian politics and academia. On the one hand, the composition, preferences, and strategic considerations of this network provide the best account of the specific form of the Act at present. In fact, members of that network pointed out that a single comprehensive act had been the only way to get legislation on equal opportunities through parliament (Interviews 30, 37). Moreover, the act could draw on two previous bills, which the MSZP had (unsuccessfully) introduced in opposition (for details, see Dombos, Horváth, & Krizsán 2007). On the other hand, respondents also emphasised the weight of references to EU accession as a crucial discursive resource during debates on the Act. In addition, it was argued that the general presentation of EU requirements in those debates shifted from being framed as externally imposed pressures (by the FIDESZ government) to a presentation of the EU as community of shared normative standards (by the MSZP government) (Dombos, Horváth, & Krizsán 2007). However, while previous equal opportunities bills as well as the initial draft of the present Act put much more stress on gender issues, the Act in its final version was much less sensitive about specific inequalities between men and women.

Since the Hungarian Equal Treatment Act does not include a notion of gender mainstreaming, there were strong hopes that it would be introduced later on once Hungary had participated in European governance processes. As already suggested, the EES in particular was seen as the important instrument for transferring gender mainstreaming from the EU to the national level (Behning, Foden, & Serrano Pascual 2001). In other words, while the Equal Treatment Act was interpreted as part of the formal transposition of EU law, hopes were raised that EU policy processes like the EES would provide actual practices for promoting equal opportunities and especially gender mainstreaming (Krizsán & Zentai 2006). Against this background, it makes sense to address Hungary's interaction within the EES as part of the broader political context.

Looking at this issue from a more general perspective, the Strategy was received with much more openness, and the obligation to adopt the entire *acquis* has been crucial to this reception. Because the Strategy is based on the employment title in the Amsterdam Treaty, it has much more solid foundations in this new member state than in the UK or Germany. Of course, guidelines and recommendations do retain their soft and non-binding quality. However, because the process as such was introduced in the course of the accession to the EU and its introduction was based on instruments similar to the adoption of the hard parts of the *acquis*, it seems to have a much stronger quality affecting its reception and institutional traction. For example, Hungarian officials argued that differences between hard and soft EU law did not matter much and that the EES was perceived as equally important (Interviews 30, 3). Moreover, this difference is reflected in the greater significance of EU funds for Hungarian employment policies. While ESF money represents a rather marginal share of the overall budgets for employment policy in the UK and in Germany, it is essential for Hungary, especially for active labour market policies (Hungary 2006, Statistical Annex; also Interviews 3, 27). In addition, Hungary had participated in EU employment policy even before its formal accession, for example through a Joint Assessment (Hungary 2001; see also European Commission 2003c; European Commission 2003d) and through participation in EMCO. Furthermore, the Hungarian NAPs have much more weight as genuine strategy papers. In contrast to the UK and German NAPs, which document activities in retrospect, the Hungarian NAPs lay out the actual national employment strategy for the next three years. Hence, the re-launch of the Lisbon Strategy in 2005 came more as a shock for Hungarian officials as designing the strategy required more resources than the respective unit could provide on an annual basis. Then suddenly in 2005, the guidelines and procedures were changed again (Interviews 3, 27, 24). However, the revised 2006 NRP, created after the re-election of Ferenc Gyurcsány (MSZP) in April 2006, displays another major reshuffle of political strategies. In addition, it describes major changes of the institutional framework at the highest political level with respect to responsibility for the programme's implementation. Consequently, this 2006 NRP has indeed become the central strategic document bringing together 23 different national strategies. This increase in significance follows the integration of economic and employment policy into one strategy at the EU level. However, despite all these efforts, it seems that Hungary lacked the capacities to maintain consistently high quality with regard to this strategic planning and reporting enterprise. In 2009, the European Commission concluded that '[t]he National Reform Programme (NRP) for 2008–2010 does not reflect a clear coherent strategy for the medium-long term' (European Commission 2009a: 66). Nonetheless, it was the 2008/2009 financial crisis which also made it extremely difficult to react with a consistent and forward-looking strategy.

The different reception of the EES was also substantiated in interviews with Hungarian officials. They claimed that the Strategy was seen as a welcome tool providing knowledge and assistance in restructuring Hungarian employment policy and labour market institutions, at least at the more technical levels of policy-making (Interviews 3, 27). This was again particularly evident in the 2006 NRP (Hungary 2006). This document embraced activation language emphasising the reconciliation of flexibility and security, the need for specific assistance to groups facing disadvantages in the labour market, individual responsibility, the role of the state as provider for the economy and the citizens, and the importance of knowledge and skills. Moreover, in terms of concrete measures, Hungary has merged unemployment and social benefits in the same manner as Germany and the UK. It has even borrowed some of the names for its own programmes. Thus, the English version of its NRP includes policies named 'Sure Start' or 'Pathways to Work'. The Public Employment Service introduced individual job search agreements with its unemployed clients. Similarly, integration programmes have been introduced for recipients of social benefits. However, these affirmative expressions of the activation agenda also have to be looked at carefully. To begin with Hungary is facing financial problems that far exceed those of Western European welfare states and seriously undermine the adoption of a substantive activation approach beyond the core norm of maximal labour market participation. The seriousness of these budgetary problems only became fully visible after the 2006 parliamentary elections leading to dramatic austerity measures by the re-elected government. Since then, Hungary has not been able to recover financially and the political climate has become rather rough, especially due to a strengthening and radicalisation of the extreme right. In addition, the strict supply-side approach of the Strategy has its limitations for Hungary due to massive structural problems causing low labour demand. In other words, the Hungarian state is lacking the resources to pursue many of the more access-oriented elements of the activation agenda. Moreover, these structural difficulties hit some Hungarian regions (especially in the north-east and the south-west) much harder (Hungary 2001; 2004; 2005b). At the same time, the greater openness towards the EES should not be misunderstood as automatic compliance or even internalisation of external EU norms. In contrast, the Hungarian government has been self-confident enough to adjust the Lisbon targets with reference to the specific problems of the post-socialist states. The national targets for 2010 as defined by the Hungarian 2004 NAP were an overall employment rate of 63% (EU target: 70%), a female employment rate of 57% (60%), and an employment rate for older workers of 37% (50%) (Hungary 2004, Table 1). In this context, it is important to note that such a strong formulation of the activation agenda (despite the ongoing fiscal restraints) is a very recent development. While raising overall activity has always been identified as the main challenge, there were fewer references to further reaching characteristic elements of the activation paradigm such as social investment. Previous reports contained only some specific measures and policies clearly based on the activation. Moreover, given the problems and the reorientation between the poles of post-socialist transformation and EU accession, finding a new balance between flexibility and security is an essential part of the current process. As a result, activation certainly contributes some important elements such as the revision of previous early retirement and maternal leave policies, tailor-made advice for jobseekers, and active benefits. However, in contrast to the historical developments in Germany and the UK, this paradigm is not the dominant discourse informing all transformations of the economy and the welfare system.

However, despite this specific openness towards EU processes and despite the high hopes that practices of gender mainstreaming would be introduced, there is no evidence that the national equal opportunities framework and the EES have been combined. Almost none of the Hungarian employment-related reports to the EU (from 2001 on) addressed gender issues beyond the explicit gender equality guideline. Furthermore, none of the documents submitted since Hungary's accession within the EES and the integrated Strategy for Growth and Jobs contained any explicit or implicit references to gender mainstreaming (Hungary 2004; 2005b; 2006). The 2006 document treated gender issues only with regard to quantitative targets for female employment. In addition, young mothers who have left the labour market to care for children and who have problems returning afterwards are the only group facing substantive gender-related problems, according to the national reports. Yet potential solutions have remained limited, aiming at maximising overall employment figures rather than minimising exclusion. The 2009 NRP thus suggested restricting childcare allowances and eligibility to increase the employment of young mothers while only promising more childcare places. More substantive structural inequalities such as labour market segregation or job quality are completely ignored.

Overall, through the Equal Treatment Act and the related Equal Treatment Authority, the fragmented and unstable history of gender equality and equal opportunities seemed to have come to a preliminary end. However, participation in EU governance did not contribute the practices of gender mainstreaming which advocates of gender equality had hoped for. At the same time, the promotion of equality will face new obstacles since the economy and public finances received a massive blow from the economic crisis after 2008 and as Hungarian politics became increasingly conflictive including ultra-conservative populism as well as the strengthening of nationalist, racist, and sometimes violent groups. The next section translates these developments in terms of citizenship practices.

Activating citizenship?

The previous chapters on Germany and the UK displayed a general trend from unconditional social rights to increasing duties and individualisation in the course of the activation agenda. In contrast, the legacy of state socialism constitutes an entirely different starting point. On the one hand, this period was characterised by equal labour market participation of men and women as well as by a wide range of measures, supporting families and protecting women in order to ensure such high employment rates. On the other hand, it is debatable whether one can speak about citizenship in state socialist regimes at all since the social services, provisions, and benefits were not based on entitlements but rather granted by a paternalistic state from above (Fodor *et al.* 2002). Nevertheless, even before 1989 Hungarians enjoyed several public provisions and services that were quite important in their everyday life and could be described as elements of citizenship. In addition, despite many specific inequalities women were better off in some respects. However, these rudimentary elements of citizenship certainly did not qualify as democratic citizenship, especially because essential citizenship practices in terms of rights and democratic participation were lacking.[3] By and large, the Hungarian citizenship regime has been in constant turmoil and a clear trajectory is hard to identify. Rather than being driven by a project of large-scale welfare reform, the recent development of Hungarian social and economic citizenship consists in two parallel processes of de-structuring and re-structuring (borrowing from Ferrera 2003, 2005). Between these two major poles, the activation agenda is less significant.

Especially recalling the gendered effects of the transformation towards capitalism that were mentioned, the first period after 1989 is best described as de-structuring of social and economic citizenship. The massive rise and, indeed, the very first appearance of unemployment combined with extensive reductions of state expenses on social benefits and services came not only as a shock but also as an existential threat for many Hungarians (for a concise overview see Ferge & Juhász 2004). Moreover, working conditions deteriorated, forcing employees to work more and more flexibly for stagnating wages (see Szabo 2003). In addition, the reduction of family support and benefits made it much harder to combine work and care and added to the gendered effects of the transformation. Concerning its gendered implications, the de-structuring was particularly promoted by a strong conservative discourse emphasising 'traditional' gender and family roles and by a liberal discourse emphasising the market (and civic freedoms). Overall, these developments constitute a fundamental unsettling of political institutions and historical legacies but also of citizens' everyday practices. Such practices involve new freedoms and opportunities (such as real choice between political parties), but also substantive losses in terms of public goods and social security.

At the same time, this process of de-structuring was accompanied by a process of re-structuring of social and economic citizenship – especially influenced by EU accession and UN-led processes promoting gender equality. The transposition of the equality *acquis* constituted a key element in this regard. In particular, the Equal Treatment Act installed a range of new citizenship rights to equality and freedom from discrimination. While legal protection of equality was fragmented and scattered across sectoral laws (in particular the Labour Code), and while its promotion in the policy-making process was vulnerable to party political interventions, the new act introduced a new form of stability and visibility. To begin with the creation of the act can be seen as re-contextualisation of equality, which (if legally codified at all) was limited to specific fields such as employment. Now equality was constituted as a field in its own right – quite contrary to the development of the gender equality dimension in the activation debates discussed thus far. Moreover, the comprehensive nature of the act, covering all sorts of discrimination and all types of legal relationships theoretically added further visibility and significance. Finally, for the first time in Hungary, the act created a relatively strong institution (the Equal Treatment Authority) independent from political intervention, endowed with the real competence to enforce its provisions. However, the act only concentrates on anti-discrimination and has weaknesses in addressing gender inequalities. Most importantly, it does not include gender mainstreaming. While its handling of indirect discrimination and sexual harassment (Nagy 2004) are also criticised, the act is certainly an essential leap in terms of citizens' rights to equal treatment. In fact, this major introduction of citizenship rights constitutes a key characteristic of the Hungarian case.

Contested trajectories – tracing influence and ambivalence

Against the background of this fundamental reorganisation and reorientation, this section looks at the contestations surrounding the gender equality dimension and Hungary's interaction within the EES, allowing us to draw a much more subtle and reliable picture of the new configuration of citizenship in Hungary.

Contestations from above
The general reception of the EES in Hungary was already discussed in the first section of this chapter. At this point, particular attention will be paid to recommendations as crucial instruments for criticising concepts and practices of the Hungarian welfare economy. Due to Hungary's very recent accession to the Union and the Commission's memorandum on new recommendations after the re-launch of the Lisbon Strategy in 2005, the list of employment recommendations has been limited. In 2004, the first recommendations to Hungary after its accession merely noted the low employment rate for women but were neither particularly strong nor particularly helpful with regard to gender equality. The EU only calls for 'more flexible and family-friendly working arrangements including attractive part-time' as part of a very general activation strategy (Council of the EU 2004a).

However, this advice seemed to be unaware of the fact that part-time work in Hungary is not only entirely unusual but also not an option due to extremely low wages (Hungary 2004; Nagy 2004). For even recent Hungarian NRPs report that the majority of part-time work is done by elderly women, which suggests more their existential hardships than the growing acceptance of part-time work. Later recommendations and country assessments have been sometimes quite critical of Hungary's performance, even though in most cases of macro- and microeconomic policy rather than employment (European Commission 2006d). However, gender issues have rarely been among the top priorities; if any, the Council only sporadically recommends to ensure that work and private life be reconciled (Council of the EU 2008). However, even these suggestions have been heavily dominated by the extraordinary emphasis the EU puts on fiscal consolidation and structural reforms, which outweigh all other substantive aspects. In this context of macroeconomic crisis, especially since the international financial crisis after 2008 hit Hungary extremely hard, the recommendations clearly favour raising employment in quantitative terms over realising individual human rights to equality. Therefore, more specific advice, which might include substantial comments about existing Hungarian family policies or affect the relationship between women and men, is missing.

In addition, the EU did also monitor the transposition of the *acquis* in Hungary before accession. Yet, although equal opportunities between women and men were listed as mid-term priorities, issues of social, employment, and equality policies did not feature very prominently in these reports. The overall tone was rather friendly, acknowledging Hungary's progress and suggesting adjustments. For example, in 1999 it was acknowledged that '[l]abour law is already largely aligned with the Community acquis' (European Commission 1999). Another document even gave the impression that the equality *acquis* was more or less in place (European Commission 2001a). In general, the reports seem to suggest that transposing the equality and social policy *acquis* in Hungary was more a question of minor adjustments. Against this background especially the FIDESZ government stressed that Hungarian law was more or less in line with EU law and, if anything, just needed some minor adjustments (see Dombos, Horváth, & Krizsán 2007).

Contestations from within

Several contestations from within could be identified in interviews with Hungarian activists and critical academics. Parallel to the fundamental shifts within the Hungarian citizenship regime, these actors have mainly been struggling to promote gender equality as a basic norm generally. At the same time, there has been a major emphasis on the promotion of gender mainstreaming to ensure greater equality on a grand scale. However, Hungarian feminists are facing some serious difficulties in this regard. The first problem is related to the government's comprehensive approach towards equality and anti-discrimination. Although it was meant to maximise the visibility and effectiveness of equal opportunities in the Hungarian context, it left feminists and women's organisations with some problems. For instance, feminists were among the very few contesting the Equal Treatment Act as such, arguing that gender inequalities should be treated differently than other 'minority' issues and calling for gender mainstreaming (Interviews 25, 24, 28). In fact, the only other organisation opposing the Act was the Hungarian Catholic Church. Moreover, the Equal Treatment Authority could be a potential target of feminist struggles (for example by pursuing strategic litigation) or an ally by raising awareness and campaigning for gender equality. However, the authority's resources are very limited. It is also struggling with the number of individual complaints and often unable to pursue its further-reaching tasks. Lawyers at the Authority admitted that they were sometimes faced with the dilemma between widely publicising their cases and risking an increased case load they could not manage (Interviews 35, 36). Hence, the situation in Hungary could be generally described as a competition of inequalities, in which different civil society organisations compete for attention and resources. Especially *vis-à-vis* the massive problems of the Hungarian Roma, gender issues are often seen as less serious.

At the level of political discourses and divisions, the Hungarian women's movement is relatively weak and fragmented, and gender issues are not high on the agenda of other civil society organisations. At the same time, members of women's organisations quite consistently and explicitly criticised the Government Office for Equal Opportunities for lacking leadership, intellectual leadership, and cooperation. In general, feminists and women's organisations put more emphasis on CEDAW and its broader human rights approach than on EU gender equality norms. Similarly, in most post-socialist countries feminism generally lacks popularity since it is discredited as a rejection of socialist norms (Fodor 2005; Gal & Kligman 2000; Montgomery 2003). In an increasingly radical political climate, Hungarian feminism was challenged even more. In the same period, women's organisations in Hungary were engaged in more specific debates within the field of social policy. Particularly significant was a conflict regarding domestic violence between feminists and promoters of child and family welfare. Many respondents claimed that this conflict had a negative impact on the treatment of gender issues up to the ministerial level, maintaining that the Minister for Youth, Family and Equal Opportunities (until summer 2006) was a strong proponent of family issues with little understanding for feminist views.

Generally speaking, the case of gender equality in Hungary has only a very weak voice and is lacking a specific face (Open Society Institute 2005: 75). Against this background, it is hardly surprising that the high expectations that the EES would implement gender mainstreaming were not fulfilled.

Conclusion: rights without access – the missed opportunity in Hungary

While Germany and the UK have demonstrated gradual and more specifically welfare-oriented reforms guided by the activation agenda, the Hungarian case is characterised by much greater variability as well as more frequent and more extensive shifts. The post-socialist transformation is the central contextual condition in this respect. It involves much more fundamental social and economic challenges as well as more extensive ideological shifts between neo-liberalism, 'new traditionalism' (Einhorn 1996: 73) and activation. Activation is a more recent ingredient in the massive Hungarian reform project which was only taken up in the course of Hungary's EU membership. Moreover, since it can only offer limited solutions and guidance in response to Hungary's specific problems, the specific Hungarian version of activation can only be described as premature.

From a citizenship perspective, the developments can be described as a process of de-structuring and re-structuring of citizenship practices. While, in the early period especially, much of the old non-democratic citizenship regime was abolished and basic civil and political rights were installed, recent years have seen a specific re-structuring of new citizenship practices with regard to substantive equality. A highly important step concerning the gender equality dimension was the introduction of the Equal Treatment Act in 2004, which brought a comprehensive set of new rights to equal treatment. However, given the limited resources of the institutional equality framework, the weak voice of the feminist movement, and the general conservative climate, gender issues were facing serious problems. Moreover, the Act is largely unable to proactively tackle socially reproduced structural inequalities. In short, inasmuch as gender relations seemed to profit rather little from the framework, it can be argued that the re-structuring of citizenship in Hungary brought important rights but no citizenship practices in terms of access to these rights.

With regard to this lack of access, many hoped that EU policies like the EES would introduce gender mainstreaming practices. However, the EES has had no linkage with the Hungarian equality framework, its main actors and practices. At this point, the consequences of the disappearance of gender equality from the EES become visible to the full extent. It is clear that the EES has been received quite well in Hungary, which is very open to engage with its communicative processes. Therefore, the rhetorical question has to be posed: how would the situation look if strong and consistent promotion of gender equality and gender mainstreaming would have remained key elements of the Strategy?

Besides the limited value of the activation paradigm itself for the specific problems of a post-socialist society, the relationship between the activation agenda and the EES is also quite specific in the Hungarian case. The present study has shown that in Germany as well as in the UK national welfare reforms are strongly informed by a substantial activation discourse while the formal role of the EES as regulatory process is rather marginal. In Hungary, in contrast, it is mostly the openness to the EES and its perception as an important governance mechanism that helped to initiate a (still very basic) version of the activation agenda. Moreover, in Germany and the UK it was possible to delineate specific gender equality dimensions within the larger welfare reform projects (regardless of their success). Against the more fundamental destructuring and restructuring of citizenship in Hungary, however, gender issues have mainly been addressed in the context of general equal opportunity or anti-discrimination policies but are not an inherent element of labour market and social security reforms. Due to the disappearance of gender equality from the EES, it could be claimed that the Strategy has deprived itself of its potentially positive influence. In the process, gender issues are mostly treated as statistical problems (i.e. unequal employment rates) but not as problems of inequality and exclusion within the integrated national project of economic and welfare reforms.

Notes

1 In 2003, the unemployment rate for women was 5.6% and 6.1% for men (Hungary 2004). In 2004 the unemployment rate for women (6.3%) did exceed that of men (6.0%) for the first time since the early 1990s (Hungary 2005b); this trend continued in 2005 with 7.4% female unemployment and 7.0% male unemployment while the rise of overall unemployment is explained by an increase of the statutory retirement age and other measures to move citizens off benefits (Hungary 2006).
2 For accounts of women's exclusion from citizenship under socialism, see Einhorn (1996, 1993), Chamberlayne (1990), and Rosenberg (1991).
3 In this context, Tilly (1999) claims that citizenship is a necessary but certainly not a sufficient condition for democracy.

7

Conclusion: the activation of citizenship – transnationally negotiated

This chapter draws together the insights from the previous chapters in order to obtain a more comprehensive picture. The activation agenda has gained momentum as a central conceptual framework guiding reforms of welfare in the broadest sense in all cases discussed. However, in addition to the EU-wide debate actual transformations of citizenship mostly rely on specific national activation debates, closely intertwined with but not identical with the Europe-wide debate. The first part addresses how our concepts and practices of citizenship are entangled with the activation agenda. In particular, that agenda's increasing dominance implies new differentiated and individualised duties, a massive promise of access to societal resources, and some limited rights. Moreover, the activation agenda vitally contributes to a broader tendency of imagining citizens as rational individuals living in a market environment, where they are linked by contractual relationships and are active in an entrepreneurial way, maximising social capital. This broader epistemic context also contributes to more concrete transformations of citizenship including its exclusionary element.

The second part of this chapter concentrates on the specific role of the EU-level activation debate. In this respect, the EES can be seen as a specific process of political knowledge production where the concepts and conditions of adequate welfare reforms – and thereby citizenship – have been renegotiated in a transnational conceptual debate. This analysis of the EES demonstrates that we should think of politics not only in terms of redistribution or regulation but also in terms of meaning making at the level of concepts and categories. Such meaning making has had rather negative outcomes in its gender equality dimension. The chapter closes reflecting on the broader political and normative implications of the present study.

The activation of citizenship

In all three member states examined in this study, we can observe a large-scale restructuring of welfare states. The activation agenda has been visible in each single process but differs across contexts in terms of its composition, degree of embeddedness, primary focus and meanings. Nevertheless, some similar patterns can be identified. The following presentation of the comparative insights concentrates on the similarities rather than the differences in the cases analysed. At the same time, it underscores the wide-ranging diversity of emphasis, meanings, and practices as well as different forms of political contestation within this broader field.

To begin with each of the reform projects has made activation its core political objective in its narrow sense as maximising citizens' economic activity in order to produce employment growth. In addition, this fundamental reorientation towards employment growth implies a more general reorganisation of the conceptual foundations of the welfare state. In the process, a wide range of formerly independent policy fields and objectives is now treated as employment-related and subordinated under the main objective of maximal labour market participation (Figure 7.1). Social benefits, gender equality, and family policies as well as more recently health care are being reformulated on a large scale. Each system had previously been organised in a largely independent way and directed towards very specific goals – social citizenship (women's) personal autonomy, and individual health. Now, however, they are being merged or coordinated more narrowly with employment-related institutions and activities. This reorganisation should ensure more efficient public services and sustainable finances but also intervenes in the larger epistemic context of citizenship. Generally, most labour market and welfare state reforms actively intervene in notions of flexibility and security and of individual and public responsibility.

However, in the context of this larger trend, the concepts which are created and redefined do not have the same weight and meaning in all debates. For example, in Germany and Hungary, flexibility and security have remained largely opposing concepts and the balance has shifted more towards the former – though to quite different degrees and following quite different paths. In the UK and at the EU level, the two concepts are presented as reconciled and supportive of each other. Unsurprisingly, these transformations have been deeply contested and involve political and social conflicts as illustrated in each of the case studies. Finally, the different manifestations of the activation agenda are clearly gendered. It is a paradigm that promotes new gender norms based on general activity of women and men in the formal labour market. However, this fundamental programmatic change only partially reflects changed social realities since many substantive inequalities, such as an unequal division of (especially care) responsibilities and chances in the labour market, still persist. At the same time, the political objective of realising emancipation and equality has become increasingly subordinated to the priority of employment growth. In particular, equality has been increasingly framed in purely quantitative terms while many other aspects of substantive equality and inequality are neglected.

Figure 7.1: Activation as reorganisation of policy spheres

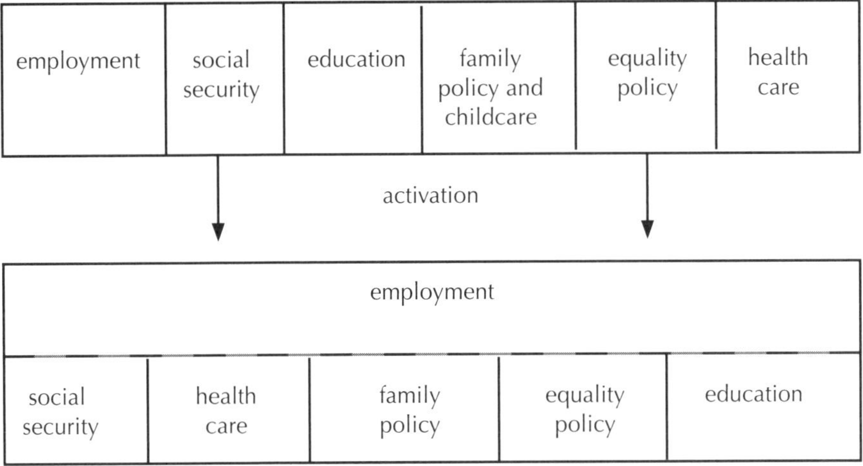

Among the three countries investigated, the activation agenda is certainly most deeply embedded in the UK as demonstrated by its early spread from employment policy to other areas like education and childcare. Moreover, the programmatic synthesis between flexibility and security is remarkable inasmuch as it contributes not only the solution to a core conceptual tension in employment and social policy but also significantly tones down some key social and political conflicts. Similar to the developments at the level of the EES, this synthesis has been facilitated through a strong social investment perspective. Moreover, the UK is the case in which legislation and policies most clearly express the gender norms of an adult worker model. However, persisting inequalities between men and women and the gendered effects of reforms are only implicitly addressed in different neighbouring contexts. Given the stubbornly high pay gap, persisting labour market segregation, and polarisation of various kinds, the costs and benefits of the new paradigm are distributed quite differently among women and men. Moreover, due to the strict public–private distinction and state non-intervention, many women are still facing the double burden of doing the major part of childcare and household work while being trapped in low(er) paid part-time employment. Nonetheless, equality is generally embedded in a much stronger human rights frame and scrutinised by relatively strong equality institutions. Moreover, the recent Gender Equality Duty significantly underscores this frame while its specific impact has yet to be assessed.

In Germany, the activation discourse took much longer to become translated into actual institutional practices. Nevertheless, the welfare reforms starting in 2004 constituted a major leap in the materialisation of the activation paradigm. They have dominated concrete policies as well as political debates on employment and social policy since then. However, there is hardly any evidence of a social investment approach and very few attempts to overcome the opposition between flexibility and security. Rather, the balance has been tilted towards the flexibility end of the continuum. In fact, the rhetorical and theoretical synthesis that can be observed in the UK has been vehemently impeded by massive social and political conflict and contestation in Germany, especially from the left. From the perspective of German gender norms – in contrast to the UK – the shift from the male bread-winner to an adult worker model has not yet progressed as far. While the promotion of gender equality was initially high on the reform agenda of the SPD/Green government, it was limited to the public sector, became increasingly uncoupled from the major reform project, and did not play a role in the subsequent reforms of labour market social security institutions. In the process, especially women have been trapped within the newly created low pay labour market. Accordingly, if activation pushes large groups of citizens into jobs where they cannot sustain a living, it creates a massive disruption of citizens' everyday practices and a major risk of being excluded from equal citizenship. However, recent debates in the realm of family policies show that traditional gender norms are increasingly being questioned – even among the Christian Democrats.

While the developments in Germany and the UK can be described as gradual processes of welfare reform informed by a broader activation discourse, the situation in Hungary is characterised by much more elementary social, cultural, political, economic, and institutional shifts. Against this background, a move towards a rhetoric and politics of pragmatism and problem-solving that is characteristic for the activation agenda is very difficult. In contrast, Hungarian politics is polarised and adversarial while not all the conflicts are specifically about social policy or gender roles. On the one hand, there is the capitalist transformation from a system of all-embracing paternalist security to radical privatisation and neo-liberal deregulation. On the other hand, this massive shift has been mitigated – at least partially – by external influences, especially Hungary's EU accession. In this regard, the activation paradigm was taken up late, in a rather fragmented manner, and it is of limited use as a grand strategy beyond the main focus on maximal activity and employment growth. In light of these fundamental problems the relationships between women and men have also been much more fundamentally affected. It is therefore much harder to identify and trace interrelations between the rudimentary activation paradigm and the gender equality dimension of the project of reforming labour markets and social security systems. Questions of gender equality have become rather marginal and been reduced instead to problems of mothers with small children returning to the labour market after a childcare break. The Equal Treatment Act in 2004 created a number of new citizenship rights with regard to equality. However, the specific project of welfare reform has not been combined with this aspect of re-structuring. The governance process of the EES did not introduce gender mainstreaming practices to the Hungarian context as many had initially hoped. In the current political and social situation, issues of gender equality do not feature prominently and suffer from a lack of access to these new rights. Finally, the Equal Treatment Act has failed to conceptualise more complex forms of inequality, which is best illustrated by the missing notion of gender mainstreaming. In general, the Act can be described as a missed opportunity to highlight gender equality in employment and social policy and to influence the implementation of the activation paradigm from the early stage.

By and large, most of the characteristics of activation were discussed in the first chapter of this study. However, in some respects, the elements of the paradigm are much less pronounced than suggested. For example, investment, future orientation and related shifting patterns of equality play a role in the UK and at the EU level but are hardly observable in Germany and Hungary. Other elements are simply more complex than suggested by the contributions cited in the introduction, as will be shown in the more detailed discussion in this chapter. The gender focus clearly demonstrated that the underlying gender norms as well as the actual relationships between women and men have undergone change. However, measures explicitly promoting gender equality are rather weak in each of the three cases. Overall, this study has demonstrated that the broader activation debate has gained strength as a central programmatic agenda which informs current transformations of citizenship. Moreover, besides some larger trends, the details of this programme as well as related political reforms can differ significantly across contexts with regard to their combination, relative weight, and meaning. Simply explaining variations by referring to different implementations of shared norms would ignore the fact that much of the content of these debates is highly contextualised and local. Each of the four activation debates discussed in this study displays a different constellation of key concepts surrounding the core norm of employment growth. At the abstract-conceptual level, the EES is particularly important since it is where the member states – and hence the national activation debates – come together to negotiate analyses, problem definitions, categories, fundamental goals, priorities, and strategies (Figure 7.2). Moreover, it is important not to restrict the notion of discourse to political talk. In contrast, political and administrative practices – for example, with regard to parental leave and pay – are crucial for the production and consolidation of meaning. Therefore, new practices can also be contributions to the conceptual debate.

The activation discourse implies shifting citizenship practices in all cases. In particular, the activation agenda does not promote an entirely new vision of citizenship. Rather, it reframes and reorganises the conceptual landscape of citizenship. In general, the move towards the activating welfare state involves a re-pooling of risks and a redistribution of responsibilities, which also affect the relationships between individual citizens, groups of citizens, and the state. The main driving force behind this transformation is the paramount emphasis on economic activity in the labour market as a key way to growth. A somewhat weaker focus on education and skills adds the further objective of productivity growth to the goal of merely raising employment in numbers. To begin with, the redistribution of responsibilities contains a new and much stricter responsibility to work and to enter the formal labour market when inactive. However, this shift of responsibilities has not been implemented in terms of new universally formulated citizenship duties applying equally to all citizens as in the case of Marshall's (1992) vague and implicit duty to work. Rather, it is operationalised in terms of diverse additional

Figure 7.2: Overlapping activation debates

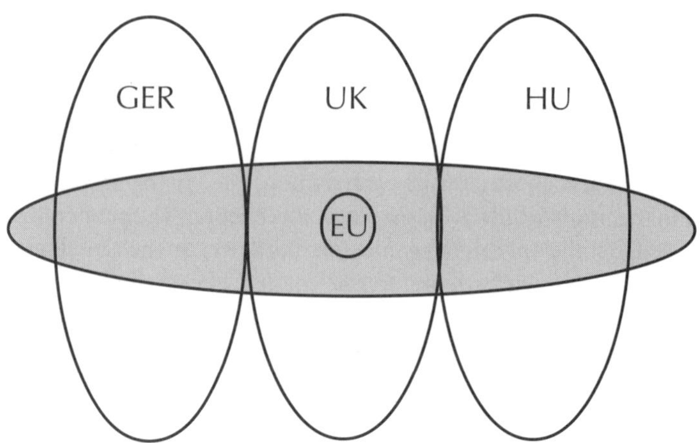

duties, administrative practices, and normative as well as objectified analytical arguments about the value of work for the individual and the society, all of which contribute to this primary objective. Moreover, these new specific duties do not apply to all citizens equally but are created for particular groups of citizens – either according to their individual situation (for example, as a lone mother or a disabled person) or according to their relationship with the state or its agencies (mostly as a recipient of a specific benefit). For example, unemployed people are required to actively seek work or to comply with the employment services in all cases. In addition, these duties are expressed by different disciplinary regimes which can be quite robust. Failure to meet these expectations can lead to punishment in the form of a reduction or withdrawal of benefits. Not surprisingly, new duties, increased individual responsibility, and discipline are the most contested elements of the activation agenda.

The fundamental reorientation towards a newly defined duty to work is a primary reason for changes in gender norms, as discussed in each of the cases studied. However, in contrast to bottom-up struggles for an equal distribution of care, women's economic autonomy, and equity in further gains from employment, this intervention in the underlying gender norms is rather indifferent towards substantive gender inequalities that have existed before or might be implied by the new circumstances. The primary goals are macro-economic rather than at the micro-level of personal self-realisation.

Yet, as mentioned in Chapter 1, the activation discourse is not only about duties and discipline. In addition, the vision of the activating welfare state is based on the insight that some people face particular difficulties and require specific assistance in order to get into and remain in the labour market. With regard to citizenship, access to societal resources has certainly been the main emphasis in the context of activation. In all countries studied, specific programmes are supposed to help people who face specific obstacles to find work. In particular, active labour market policies such as the UK's New Deals are at the core of employment policy in the activating welfare state. They should ensure that currently unemployed people get the opportunity to earn their livelihood and be included in the labour market. In addition to the aforementioned disciplining elements, these policies represent the promise that each citizen will get the support he or she needs. Beyond these rather short-term activities targeted at very specific groups, education is the other key element of the activation agenda. In this domain the state takes up new responsibilities to provide access – not only to employment but to social capital and future opportunities. Education and skills are now seen as an essential comparative advantage of Western societies for ensuring growth, competitiveness, and high employment in a globalised economy. Nevertheless, the emphasis on education is more recent than targeted active labour market policies. Moreover, it is much stronger in those contexts where the notion of social investment has been fully embraced. For example, productivity growth through better skills and education has become a core objective in the UK while modernisation debates concerning schools and higher education in Germany are not as closely tied to the national activation debate. An emphasis on childcare, understood as early childhood education, setting the foundations for children's future opportunities, can be identified in all contexts.

Regarding the gender equality dimension of these wide-ranging reform debates, we can also observe specific ambivalence in the promises of increased access. It was mentioned that the transformation towards activation also implies transformations of the underlying gender models towards an adult worker model based on the economic activity of all citizens. Moreover, all the cases in this study display at least some awareness that women are facing particular problems under these conditions. Therefore, various programmes such as the UK New Deal for Lone Parents, reorganisations of Hungarian maternal leave rules, or large-scale childcare programmes should ensure that women do not lose contact with the labour market, thus becoming entrapped in long-term unemployment and poverty. However, these programmes mainly aim at providing access to the societal resource of formal participation in the labour market (with a special focus on mothers), while access to other societal resources within and beyond employment is increasingly ignored. Such access could refer to societal resources within employment, such as equal pay, equal career opportunities, or recognition and self-respect from a consistent and successful career. In addition, access to societal resources beyond the labour market, especially the opportunity to balance work and private life through an equal share of caring responsibilities, would be another essential requirement for an adult worker model which minimises gendered patterns of exclusion and disadvantage (see Fraser 1994). This central ambivalence inherent in the current activation debate has been identified in various forms by this study, most important as large-scale reframing of gender equality from a human right to a quantitative measure and the resulting inability of the conceptual activation debate to address qualitatively substantial problems of inequality. The persisting problem of unequal pay for women and men is another example of significant substantial inequalities that remain neglected by the activation debate.

In most cases, these promises of tailor-made support for individual citizens are closely connected with institutional reforms aiming at more efficient and customer-oriented services. For instance, reforms of public employment services and the merging of unemployment benefits and social assistance are at the core of the activation strategies in all three countries. With regard to gender, large programmes to provide childcare are the most relevant examples. However, this study demonstrated that the activation agenda is about promising access rather than actually guaranteeing it in practice. Equally important, it was shown that in most cases access only refers to employment without considering societal resources that are related to qualitative aspects of work or to aspects beyond the labour market but closely intertwined with working life.

In contrast to large-scale promises for increased access to societal resources, rights play only a minor role in the activation context. Family policies, especially parental leave and pay, are among the few areas where the activation discourse consistently promotes new rights (especially in Germany and the UK). Rights to parental leave and pay could theoretically respond better to the social realities of European societies and rights could make a much stronger contribution to the personal autonomy of citizens with caring responsibilities. For example, the two weeks paternal leave in the UK are rather symbolic. Nevertheless, especially in their potential to break up existing stereotypes about care, rights to parental leave and pay play an important role. In addition to parental leave and pay, further rights seem to have emerged in some contexts with regard to childcare and training. For example, the German federal government has announced a right to childcare for all children under three years as of 2013. However, this plan has met heavy criticism from municipalities and Länder, who would be responsible for putting it into practice. Yet it is far from being realised. Moreover, Germany and the UK have introduced minor rights to education and training so that the unemployed might obtain basic school leaving certificates in the context of active labour market policies.

At this point, it is useful to return to a classic text on citizenship in searching for the bigger picture. Marshall presented the emergence of social citizenship as the large-scale response to the massive inequalities resulting from a society where citizenship was nothing more than a status of equal civil rights and where intra-societal relationships were merely based on (especially work) contracts between individual citizens (Marshall 1992). Similarly, Charles Tilly (1999) describes citizenship as a special contract distinguished by the fact that it does not bind individuals but the collective of the citizenry as such. Against this background, however, the individualisation and differentiation of duties imply that this imagination of citizenship has been weakened. In this context, Gerhard, Knijn, and Lewis identify a broader trend towards 'contractualisation':

> [C]ontract has been used more and more freely, and has been invoked as the mechanism of choice by which to regulate relationships that are addressed by social policy

and family law, and that had not previously been subject to this form of thinking. (Gerhard, Knijn, & Lewis 2002: 106; see also White 2004)

The term contractualisation (describing a process) implies that new applications as well as new meanings of the contract are proliferating. It involves traditional references to a symbolic social contract at the foundations of a particular polity but also to formal agreements, for example, between a government and public agencies or between a benefit claimant and the employment service. Moreover, while contractualisation certainly undermines the universality of citizenship, it does not have to mean its complete dissolution. Although it certainly originates in attempts to raise the efficiency of public institutions and services, it could theoretically also enhance the situation of citizens to receive specific targeted support and have a say on the conditions of the contract (Yeatman 1995, 1997; for criticism see Vincent-Jones 2000; Freedland & King 2003). Of course, this general trend is broad and contested and its implications are difficult to grasp without consideration of the particular context (Jayasuriya 2001, 2002).

Generally speaking, the trend towards contractualisation is strongest in the UK. For example, New Labour embedded its project of welfare reform in a very explicit rhetoric of the social contract. Thus, the key government document outlining the vision of a modernised welfare state had the title 'New Ambitions for Our Country: A New Contract for Welfare' (DSS 1998). Moreover, beyond this symbolic dimension, the following has been said about Labour's approach to contractualisation:

> The whole hierarchy of public service relationships has been re-constructed as a series of contractual or contract-like arrangements … So it fits squarely into this logic to complete the process by contractualising the relationships at the base of the pyramid, namely those between the public service professionals who deal directly with citizen-clients and those citizen-clients themselves. (Freedland & King 2003: 469)

In Germany, neither the governments under Gerhard Schröder nor Angela Merkel have deployed social contract rhetoric to frame their political agenda. However, the new individualised duties implied in the labour market reforms discussed are based on contractualist arrangements between benefit claimants and the employment service. The fact that politics in Germany is mainly formulated in terms of law adds visibility to these duties but also demonstrates the character of these contractual arrangements as instruments for managing individual (mis)behaviour rather than as voluntary contracts between free agents. Despite a counter-discourse accusing the reforms of increasing social exclusion and poverty, the reform agenda is well embedded in rhetoric of individual responsibility. On the one hand, this objective is framed as a necessary reduction of overly extensive state responsibilities. On the other hand, such framings go hand in hand with analyses explaining unemployment with reference to individual behaviour and misconduct.

The trend towards contract-like arrangements and individualised duties is least pronounced in Hungary due to the limited and very recent strengthening of the activation agenda. The most significant development has been the activation of the Hungarian benefit system. With the introduction of job search agreements for people on unemployment benefits and integration agreements for people on social benefits in 2005, Hungary has certainly joined the trend.

These new meanings and uses of contractual relationships point to a further key characteristic of the activation agenda that must be discussed before its significance with regard to transformations of citizenship can be fully understood. In general, all activation discourses and policies discussed address a very specific subject, which is the foundation of all problem definitions and strategies. We have already indicated that the activating welfare state emphasises individual responsibility over public risk protection. This further implies a worldview in which individuals willingly accept this responsibility and are essentially capable of coping with most problems by intellectually comprehending them and developing their own appropriate strategies. In contrast, the emergence of post-war welfare states was driven by the aim to overcome structural risks and power inequalities while individual citizens were perceived to be more or less defenceless against them. Furthermore, the growing focus on social investment and social capital implies a human world which basically consists of markets where citizens' biographies are mainly subject to economic operations such as allocating resources, producing, investing, or innovating. Such an environment requires the individual subject to behave as an economic actor while other needs, motivations, identities, and practices recede into the background. Certainly, this tendency to imagine human beings as rationally interacting in a market environment is an idea that is much older and much more deeply embedded than the activation agenda.[1] However, that agenda has added a very specific twist, acknowledging that individual citizens might be in different need of assistance to access for thriving in that market environment. This economistic element of the activation discourse thereby draws on narratives about sustainability, productivity, and self-enhancement rather than about the survival of the fittest.

The abovementioned trend towards contractualisation is probably the clearest crystallisation of the political imagining of citizens as entrepreneurial subjects individually striving for social capital in a market environment. Individualised duties based on contractualist arrangements put special pressure on the affected citizens to adopt the epistemic outlook of the activating welfare state and to behave accordingly, as independent social capital maximisers. Moreover, such practices communicate those notions of the entrepreneurial subject, social capital, and the market to others who are not immediately affected by them. Imagining the citizenry as rational and self-responsible individuals is very different from conceptualising it as social classes who have to be protected from structural risks on the basis of that social citizenship prevalent under most welfare regimes of the post-war era. In particular, the previous points demonstrate that the conceptual activation debate is not only about concrete problems, policies, or best practices but also about fundamental ontological and constitutional issues.

On the whole, the emerging activation paradigm affects the boundaries and relationships between different dimensions of citizenship. In contrast to the socialist adult worker model in Hungary and East Germany, under the male breadwinner/female carer model prevalent in the UK and western Germany, economic citizenship was a highly exclusive dimension primarily reserved for (skilled) working men (and trade unions representing their interests). Social citizenship, in contrast, despite serious inequalities (for example, with respect to pensions of women and men) was more inclusive. Today the boundary between those dimensions is blurred because every citizen is treated as citizen-worker and because other policy areas are being activated and merged. Moreover, this study has shown how the traditional elements of social citizenship – more or less unconditional rights, negligible duties, and the unconditional provision of public services – are increasingly being modified and revised in the context of activation becoming the dominant programme for political reform. In particular, individual-ised duties and conditionalities have been added to the general rights. At least rhetorically, these new duties should be balanced by better access to societal resources through individualised and enhanced provision of services. Looking at gender, however, demonstrates that this trend is imbalanced and that it involves old and new forms of exclusion in all three cases. While it would be premature to reject duties and contractualisation as such, they pose a risk to the balance of citizenship.

This blurring of those substantive or 'vertical' boundaries between different dimensions of citizenship within the welfare states examined adds to the tran-snational transformation of citizenship blurring and its spatial boundaries (see Chapter 2). Therefore, the transnational activation discourse contributes to the large-scale process of a hybridisation challenging our theoretical understanding of citizenship. Academic debates have long acknowledged that our understanding of citizenship is being conceptually challenged by people's mobility, the changing nature of national borders, international law and human rights, and by internal contestations uncovering inequalities among diverse citizens despite their formal equality. In addition, the activation agenda implies that the imagination of an equal citizenry is actively undermined by the state itself introducing conditional duties, disciplinary regimes, and diversifying categories of citizens.

However, some further considerations are necessary before the relationship between activation and citizenship can be completely understood. Therefore, the next section discusses how exactly the activation agenda is linked to current transformations of citizenship with a particular focus on the activation debate at the EU level.

Negotiating citizenship in a transnational conceptual debate

Throughout the present study, it has become clear that the EES – even where recommendations have been consistently issued over many years – does not have the power to successfully contest national citizenship practices. In contrast, this study finds, it can be generalised that the effects of the EES are much more com-plex, mediated, and at a higher discursive level rather than at the level of national policy-making.

As outlined in the introduction, the EES is best understood as a specifically structured conceptual debate where member states and the Commission exchange their views on social and employment policy. The overall substance of the debate consists in negotiating a far-reaching programme for adequately governing welfare and labour markets in a globalised world. The contents of the EES can be described as a collection of analyses and definitions (including their operationalisation as indicators) of certain problems, risks, and their broader implications. In addition, they consist of specific solutions and strategies for achieving a maximum of activity in a balanced way as the main route to competitiveness, growth, and a modernised European social model. The scope of the negotiations thereby covers a whole epistemic world reaching from practical questions about concrete policies to basic ontological issues. With a view to the formal aspects, since the member states are quite clearly committed to the process as such (Jacobsson 2004), its procedures provide a specific framework for the debate through which its contents are pre-structured. In fact, the close linkage and co-constitution of contents and procedures, political means and ends, is a key feature of this conceptual debate.

The protagonists in this narrative are agents from the member states (primarily from the ministerial bureaucracy) and the Commission, which plays a particular strong role as agenda setter and epistemic (rather than just normative) entrepreneur. In addition, single member states – in this study especially the UK – massively try to influence the course of the debate. In fact, it is not a process of top-down discussion from the EU to the member states, for those states formally have the final word at the EU level. Finally, the Strategy triggers a great deal of bilateral and multilateral exchange between the member states about concrete practices related to the contents of the Strategy. However, links to national policy-making are rather indirect and mediated. What is discussed, are the epistemic foundations and frameworks within which national processes are embedded. Moreover, this study also found that not all actors have access to the debate and that not all voices have the same weight within it.

In addition to these phenomenological insights about the programmatic nature of activation as developed in the conceptual debates of the EES, this study has found some general conditions characterising the interaction of Germany, Hungary, and the UK with regard to the Strategy in general and its gender equality dimension in particular. Accordingly, German cooperation was characterised by initially very broad reservations against the process as such but also by later strengthening of the activation agenda and an increasing synchronisation of the discursive exchanges within the debate. Moreover, gender equality is often not framed as a human right but rather subordinated to other objectives. For its part, the UK values the EU activation debate as close to its own approach, and using the EES as well as the broader Lisbon Strategy to promote these contents throughout Europe. At the same time, gender equality is also not at the top of the British agenda but can nevertheless draw on a strong foundation of equality and non-discrimination as fundamental rights and promoted by a strong machinery. Finally, the Hungarian case is characterised by a comparably higher receptiveness towards the EES, but at the same time, cooperation in the gender equality dimension is hindered by the contentiousness of that theme between major shifts in citizenship practices. Nevertheless, given the structural problems in Hungary, the substance of the activation paradigm is often unable to provide adequate solutions beyond the central goal of maximising employment rates.

Before we pay further attention to the specific characteristics of the EES as a conceptual debate, it is useful to relate this idea to other theoretical contributions on the EES, the OMC, and so-called new modes of governance. In the process, it is especially important to distinguish this idea from theoretical assessments viewing the EES as encouraging learning and/or deliberative problem-solving (for the most important assessments, see Sabel & Zeitlin 2007; Trubek & Zeitlin 2003; Zeitlin 2005b, 2005a). Understanding the EES as political knowledge production through a process of conceptual debate is preferred to such often overly optimistic notions for a number of reasons (for a more detailed discussion, see Pfister 2009). First, it makes it clear that procedures and content cannot be separated from each other. In contrast, many positive assessments of the OMC present it as a deliberative learning tool that could be applied in principle to any political field. Its success would only depend on the proper application of a method rather than on the respective substance, in a sense, suggesting that the OMC (and the EES) could transform every issue into a positive outcome. Second and closely connected, the term 'conceptual debate' does not suggest that the outcomes will necessarily be positive whereas terms like 'learning' or 'deliberation' clearly do. Such a notion might therefore lead to indifference against inequality or even increased exclusion. Finally, the notion of a conceptual debate does not reproduce that implicit view of a politics of pragmatism and problem-solving which underlies recent debates on governance and especially on the virtues of open coordination. Instead, a conceptual debate can be about highly political topics, including fundamental conflicts and unequal power-relations. The outcomes of this conceptual debate might not be directly linked to political struggles about redistribution of resources or concrete regulations. Instead they might be tied to conceptual parameters and categories of modern social and employment policy as well as the epistemic authority to define them. Power thereby becomes manifest as capacity to create knowledge that is 'socially robust' (Nowotny, Gibbons, & Scott 2001: 166) rather than the ability to influence others' behaviour. In short, the transnational activation debate of the EES is political in terms of meaning making.

Against this background, a first and vital aspect of the conceptual debate is constituted by decisions about the Strategy's composition – which concepts are included, how they are defined, operationalised, and which problems and suggestions they combine. Furthermore, the relationship between these concepts is extremely important since they will support, confine, explain, and sometimes even contradict each other. Accordingly, not only their inclusion or non-inclusion in the process is relevant but also their interplay and relative weighting. Finally, especially since the concepts of the EES are intentionally defined rather broadly and since the Strategy does not intend to prescribe specific policies – instead identifying problems, useful approaches and common targets – the particular meaning of each concept is a further crucial aspect of the debate. This does not have to mean that actors actually agree on common meanings but that the discursive contexts and practices in which they use a concept outline a specific range of its potential meanings. At the same time, the concepts as such cannot determine the reception of the EES in national context. Besides the general relationships between concepts, this study has also uncovered certain discursive mechanisms allowing for a better understanding of the dynamics behind the debate. These mechanisms are highly contingent, and it is impossible to provide a complete list. Therefore, some specific examples from the gender equality dimension will be used as illustrations.

More generally, concept formation and concept innovation are the first main examples of the discursive operations within the conceptual debate. If we look at how the contents of the EES are formulated and structured, the many elements and sub-elements are amalgamated into a much smaller number of key concepts such as 'employability', 'adaptability', 'life-long learning', 'active' (as opposed to passive) instruments, or 'gender mainstreaming'. Such major concepts reduce complexity by always combining specific analyses and problem definitions with certain solutions and strategies. In particular, specific conceptual innovations, such as 'social capital' have often also been coined to evade previous political conflicts and conceptual blockades. Indeed, the central role played by these broad key concepts was confirmed in different interviews (Interviews 12, 6, 11, 5, 7). The Strategy's gender equality dimension has also been characterised by specific key concepts like reconciling work and family life, gender gaps, labour market segregation, childcare, and – most importantly – gender equality and gender mainstreaming. In fact, the notion of gender mainstreaming makes it more of a master concept listed alongside others while at the same time encompassing them. All these concepts involve some more or less clearly defined problematisation. Often, concepts are also quite clearly linked to specific solutions: for example, the reconciliation of work and family is clearly linked to childcare as a vital strategy. In other cases, such as the gender pay gap, responses have been less clear since that term did not receive much attention in the process of the conceptual debate. Hence, we can see how potential political actions to address specific problems as well as the related problem-solving capacities are already pre-structured at the conceptual level.

To discuss a further characteristic discursive operation, this conceptual debate produces certain social categories of citizens who require particular attention or who should be targeted by the same instruments. In the preceding case studies, hence, the central gender-related categories were – only to a minor extent – women in general or women and men in relation to each other. Women in relation to men in general would be the main social category for most theoretical accounts of gender mainstreaming. In contrast, the debates focused on women as mothers of small children (for example, those on childcare leave) and particularly single mothers as disadvantaged groups, who are particularly likely to be inactive. These categorisations can then be connected with specific administrative practices, such as mandatory job search interviews and childcare offers to complement active labour market policies in the case of single mothers. In many cases, categories are not purely based on empirical features but also involve more fundamental normative-ontological assumptions. For example, it is symptomatic for the activation agenda that unemployed people are now widely categorised as 'jobseekers'. This is not just a case of glossy political rhetoric but expresses the underlying notion of an entrepreneurial subject who is far too productive and flexible to become a victim to structural risks.

Beyond the formation and innovation of concepts and categories, the conceptual activation debate is also about the relationships between them and their meanings. The dynamic aspects of these cannot be fully understood by merely looking at the definition of a particular concept in a policy document inasmuch as it may have been intentionally left rather open in the course of the debate. For example, the third chapter uncovered how the conceptual relationships of gender equality within the activation debate changed in the course of different steps of (re)prioritisation. At the same time, gender equality has been narrowed down, subordinated to other concepts and lost visibility in the process. As already demonstrated, it was degraded from a pillar in its own right to a matter of job quality, from a higher order principle into one priority out of ten. As a result, conceptualisations of gender equality were increasingly unavailable for analysing substantive issues of inequality beyond quantitative employment rates. However, it was also shown that these processes should not (mainly) be understood as intentional, direct interventions in the priority and meaning of the concept gender equality. Rather, gender equality suffered from prioritisations of other elements and interventions in the broader context – in combination with a certain readiness to (at least to some extent) sacrifice qualitative objectives such as gender equality to the top priority of growth. In general, prioritisations play a key role in these debates – not only with regard to the relative weight of particular concepts but also with regard to their meaning, as the present study corroborates. Prioritisations of problems, objectives and strategies have to be analysed in relation to each other rather than looking at objectives alone.

Moreover, the specific fragility and susceptibility of the notions of gender equality and gender mainstreaming to changes in the wider context of the Strategy was also based on their initial conceptual vagueness as well as on the strong reliance of the gender equality dimension on gender mainstreaming. The complexity and imprecision of gender mainstreaming is addressed in a number of feminist evaluations (for example Beveridge 2007; Beveridge & Nott 2002; Squires 2005). The majority of these contributions also make it clear that gender mainstreaming is not a goal in itself but a strategy for promoting gender equality. However, in the course of the decreasing capacity to analyse substantive gender inequalities within the ongoing activation debate, the objective of gender equality and the strategy of gender mainstreaming became increasingly lumped together and used interchangeably. Both were, increasingly hollowed out in an environment lacking specific information about concrete problems, underlying causes and possible solutions. Such an approach, seen generally, could trigger interpretations that inequality and exclusion are mainly caused by ignorance or error rather than being structural and deeply embedded in the societal fabric. In fact, some respondents seemed to interpret the spread of gender mainstreaming as a shift away from previous positive action policies, which would be justified by previous successes in promoting gender equality. However, we have also seen that equality can be embedded in a stronger human rights frame at the national level, as in the case of the UK. At the same time, the Hungarian case demonstrates that a strong legal framework requires adequate practices in order to realise equality. Where any of these elements is weak, gender equality is more likely to undergo renegotiations in the course of the conceptual debate outlined.

Beyond these shifts in context, the study also found examples for direct negotiations about specific concepts although not always surrounding the gender equality dimension. For example, the UK regularly tried to determine definitions of particular concepts and insert its own notions of flexibility and security into the EU debate in order to promote its specific version of a growth-oriented and competitive social policy based on individual responsibility. These attempts were labelled as 'policy teaching', as a constant attempt to influence others by establishing a certain cognitive authority. Moreover, the increasing synchronisation within the exchanges between Germany and the Commission can be seen as resulting from negotiations about the definition and operationalisation of specific concepts. For example, by repeatedly pointing to the wage-setting autonomy of the social partners, the German government successfully promoted a more complex understanding of the problem of unequal pay and its potential solutions, which was accepted by the Commission. Similarly, with regard to specifying responsibilities and adequate strategies concerning childcare and education, Germany brought the Commission to respect its more complex federal organisation but also accepted a new notion of federal competence in issues where previously only Länder and municipalities were held responsible.

It is difficult to say how the situation with regard to gender equality would look if the EES had maintained its initial momentum in this dimension. However, there was widespread agreement that the EES was vital for the promotion of gender equality – at least until 2003. Because it was a conceptual debate it could have provided a further EU process, which would clearly name problems of inequality, keep gender equality on the agenda and promote adequate practices of mainstreaming. Despite the EES's limitations, we have also seen that the EES had the potential to raise the awareness of certain problems and to promote certain practices, such as the collection of adequate data. Even in the German case which was characterised by fundamental reservations, the conceptual debate at the EU level had some impact on the perceptions and especially the language of the national actors. At the same time, this study demonstrated that the contextual conditions in a member state can make it more receptive to the EES. Accordingly, perhaps the most interesting – though unanswerable – question in this context is what might have happened in Hungary if the EES would have really been able to deliver the actual policy practices of gender mainstreaming that were so eagerly awaited by Hungarian feminists.

Once we accept the nature of the EES as a conceptual debate, we also have to accept that it is not able to have direct impact on national policy-making as well as on transformations of citizenship in general, and on shifting patterns of inclusion and exclusion in particular. However, this study has also demonstrated the importance of these secondary conceptual discourses in developing the epistemic foundations of welfare and citizenship. As a result, while the EES does not create any specific practices of EU nor national citizenship, it can nonetheless be understood as further blurring the distinction between national and EU citizenship.[2] In other words, terms and conditions of national political membership (i.e. national citizenship) are no longer determined by national politics alone but also renegotiated in transnational conceptual debates. Citizenship as such is becoming increasingly hybrid.

Given the significance as well as the inherent ambivalence of that debate, the final section will therefore engage in a reflection on the broader political and normative implications of the present study as well as on how to raise the significance of tackling inequality and exclusion within a conceptual debate such as the EES.

Political and normative implications: political citizenship and participation in political knowledge construction

On the whole, the present study has substantiated that each historical citizenship formation is a complex composite of many different citizenship practices. Depending on how the activation discourse is interpreted and translated into citizenship practices, this study has also demonstrated that activation has significant effects on the institutionalised relationship between citizens and the state as well as on citizens' everyday life. In fact, some of them are experiencing existential changes in their living conditions. The focus on the gender equality dimension has allowed for significant insights in the exclusionary potentials of the activation agenda. In this context, we have also seen that the reorientation towards activation has generated significant effects on the overall balance of citizenship across Europe.

Moreover, beyond the need to balance rights, duties, access, and participation, this study has also shown that these practices are always embedded in (and contribute to) a much broader conceptual environment. Most important in this context, each historical citizenship formation is not only the result of certain social struggles cementing specific institutionalised relationships between the state and its citizens. In addition, the resulting relationship is essentially based on specific notions of how exactly both parties to it are constituted. The activation agenda contributes to the broader tendency of imagining the world as a marketplace and citizens as rational and independent actors inhabiting it. Of course, this perspective is not exclusive to the activation discourse. Yet it significantly shifts the attention from markets as self-help systems to the possibility of growth based on productive social capital. At this point, some problematic aspects of this conceptual framework should be addressed.

To begin with, the dominance of the *homo oeconomicus* as a guiding idea of subjectivity might not reflect the experiences and needs of many citizens; secondly, the aforementioned perspectives on subjectivity and on the human world as a globalised market crucially limit the scope of the conceptual debate about social policy and ultimately about citizenship. In particular, the dominant view on society as a market excludes all alternative ideas of meaningful human activities and relationships. For example, the meaning of care can go far beyond any notion of social capital and future opportunity (see Fraser 1994; Lewis & Giullari 2005). Furthermore, in the course of the activation debates studied here, formal participation in the labour market has come to be seen as the most important societal resource by far. In contrast to this very limited notion of social inclusion – and although economic autonomy might in fact be an important objective for numerous people – many might aim for completely different forms of inclusion or draw on very different societal resources in their everyday life. Especially by scrutinising the gender dimension, many substantive instances of exclusion and disadvantage within and beyond the labour market have been uncovered in this book – while they hardly would have been visible from a perspective viewing the world as market.

Looking for possible reactions to the problems uncovered, a first important question concerns whether restrictions of rights can be adequately balanced by elements of access only. In this regard, Lister emphasises the importance of rights as a requirement for meaningful participation in society – despite the critique of purely rights-based liberal accounts – because 'citizenship as rights enables people to act as agents' (Lister 2003a: 37). At the same time, she uses the notion of a 'relational self' (Lister 2003a: 38) whose embeddedness within social relationships and contexts is constituted by rights. Moreover, rights claims provide a key resource, especially for the excluded, to achieve and demand full citizenship (Lister 2003a, see also Mehta 2005 #1777). Law is the crucial medium for formulating and communicating such rights.[3] Therefore, rights are much more effective guarantees that responsibilities are being translated into practices – especially when contrasted to mere promises. However, if social policy is primarily being defined in terms of (individualised) contractual relationships, on the one hand, and in terms of quantitative targets, on the other, social policy practices run the risk of becoming uncoupled from rights (drawing on Armstrong 2005). And ultimately this could lead to a social policy which increasingly uses disciplinary and surveillance measures to reach quantitative targets or benchmarks instead of realising citizenship. In other words, it is insufficient to balance an intervention in the realm of rights with practices of increased access because there are hardly any guarantees that responsibilities are actually realised. Hence, one important question is which new citizenship rights might be required under the activation paradigm.

However, the contested nature of citizenship as well as the essential diversity of citizens' living situations and needs make it impossible to come to a definite answer in a book like this. Moreover – for the obvious reasons uncovered in this book with regard to conceptual debates – such issues should not be determined by academics (just another form of exclusive conceptual debate). Instead, proposals for new rights have to be scrutinised in the public and decided in a democratic process. Suggestions for alternative rights are quite likely to be already out there but out of sight, for example within the CEDAW framework or the discourses of affected citizens and their civil society organisations. Yet, the problematic exclusive character of the conceptual debate remains and constitutes the most significant obstacle to such an open democratic process. The transnational conceptual debate about activation in general and its gender equality dimension in particular is far removed from public influence and oversight. At the same time, it is highly important that any proposal for new rights be strictly based on the actual needs of the citizens. Therefore – rather than reflecting on potential social, economic or gender-related rights – this book emphasises the political element of citizenship. Since the activation debate is itself a deeply political process, it requires a strengthened element of *political citizenship* with regard to *meaning making and conceptual debates*. At the core of such an element, a *right to participate in political knowledge production* as well as the *participatory citizenship practices* for realising this right would be absolutely essential. In particular, the empirical study tracing the interaction between activation and different types of citizenship practices did not come across many significant practices of participation. Yet participation has to be seen as an equally important requirement of political membership from the citizenship perspective of this study. Political citizenship understood as political participation is a necessary condition for contesting existing practices, institutions, and conceptual frames of citizenship as well as for contributing one's own alternative ideas, concerns, or needs to the conceptual debate.

This claim is based on the insight that in the case of the EES's gender equality dimension an initial key principle became gradually hollowed out in the course of the conceptual debate. Using Carmel's terminology, gender equality certainly did not become 'unthinkable' or 'impracticable' (see Carmel 2005: 42). However, it was no longer presented as political priority. By contrast, as long as gender equality was clearly viewed as a fundamental principle in its own right (i.e. until 2002), any policy neglecting its gendered implications or even producing new inequalities between women and men would have been viewed as illegitimate within the context of the EES. That is to say, while gender equality certainly did not lose its legitimacy as governance objective, it became an issue of minor concern rather than being presented as absolutely necessary.

However, since the most important conceptual debate on the activation agenda is taking place in the transnational arena of the EES, most citizens do not have the chance to contribute their favoured notions of subjectivity, their experiences, or their priorities with regard to rights or societal resources. The conceptual debate within the EES is generally carried out – despite rhetorical commitments to participation and partnership – in a highly exclusive way and kept at a considerable distance from citizens and even parliaments. Hence, its interventions are extremely one-sided and citizens do not get a chance to participate in renegotiating the political knowledge behind welfare and citizenship. The focus on contestations as constitutive elements driving the historical development of both the conceptual activation debate and citizenship has also uncovered that access to and influence within respective debates are distributed very differently. Most significant, voices contesting the development of its gender dimension had either been lacking access to or influence in the activation debates within the EES or the member states. However, what would be necessary in the context of the transnational activation debate within the EU is a strengthened element of political citizenship.

With regard to promoting this goal in the future, two key challenges are crucial. The first and more general problem consists in promoting the very idea of direct participation, which still seems to be counterintuitive to many and is often met with scepticism and prejudice.[4] Closely connected with this general problem, the second challenge is to find concrete procedures and examples of how such participation could work. For this purpose, again, it has to be emphasised that there are certainly many options of participatory practices and, equally important, that it will be impossible to theoretically design and apply a perfect practice in advance and/or without regard to a particular context.

However, the EU discourse on governance in general and the EES in particular contain an explicit, though in many cases rhetorical, promise of participation which might be used for contesting current practices of political knowledge formation and creating opportunities for increasing the substantive involvement of citizens in EU policy-making in the future.[5] In fact, the EU has already made some attempts in this direction – although the legitimacy generating potential of those processes remains contested (see, for example, Boussaguet & Dehousse 2008; Héritier 1999; Magnette 2003). Moreover, there are actual examples of how policy-making has been made more open and inclusive in other fields. For instance, attempts of including citizens, stakeholders or clients have been made in fields as diverse as healthcare and social policy (see, for example, Barnes, Newman, & Sullivan 2007; Beresford 2000, 2002; Lister 2004, 2007), planning and public policy (see, for example, Gomart & Hajer 2003; Hajer 2005), or even science and technology (see, for example, Joss & Durant 1995; Misa, Schot, & Rip 1995; Rowe, Marsh, & Frewer 2004).

Most research on such participatory processes agrees that they always contain certain ambivalences and should be carefully examined. For example, policy-makers are mostly able to set the rules and the limits of a participatory practice (see all the examples mentioned above). Examining such processes in detail and reflecting on how they could improve our understanding about conceptual debates and enhance their governance in practice would clearly exceed the scope of this book. However, it is an immensely interesting and extremely relevant challenge for future research in this context. From a more general point of view and taking seriously Kostakopoulou's claim that citizenship studies is always about what is as well as what should be (Kostakopoulou 2008), the goal should be moving from 'activated citizenship' in the narrow context of the labour market to 'active citizenship' with regard to all aspects of politics.

Notes

1   While this crucial aspect of subjectivity is neglected in many theoretical accounts of citizenship, it is especially pointed out by studies on Foucault's concepts of governmentality in general and neo-liberalism in particular (Foucault 1991, 2004a, 2004b).

2   For accounts on how substantive citizenship practices are blurring the boundaries between national and EU citizenship, see Bader (1999), Delanty (2000), Meehan (1993), Shaw (1998), or Wiener (1998).

3   For a perspective on (EU gender equality) law as 'opportunity structure' see Shaw (2002).
4   For example, Carole Pateman (1970) argued that strong resistance against direct participa-
    tion of citizens was mostly based on concerns about the stability of democratic institutions
    or about the intellectual capacities that would be required to participate.
5   Most significant, the White Paper on European Governance identified 'better involvement'
    as one of four priorities calling, for instance, for a 'reinforced culture of consultation and
    dialogue' (European Commission 2001b: 16).

Interview no.	Institution or position
1	European Commission, DG REGIO
2	European Commission, DG EMPL
3	European Commission, DG EMPL
4	European Commission, DG EMPL
5	European Commission, DG EMPL
6	European Commission, DG EMPL
7	European Commission, DG EMPL
8	Office of the Northern Ireland Executive in Brussels
9	Policy Consultant
10	European Women's Lobby
11	DGB (GER)
12	European Trade Union Institute for Research, Education and Health and Safety (ETUI-REHS)
13	German Women's Council (GER)
14	DGB (GER)
15	Academic (GER)
16	Federal Ministry for Labour and Social Affairs (GER)
17	DGB (GER)
18	DGB, German Women's Council (GER)
19	Federal Ministry for Labour and Social Affairs (GER)
20	TUC (UK)
21	Equal Opportunities Commission (UK)
22	European Women's Lobby; formerly national activist (UK)
23	Joint International Unit DfES & DWP (UK)
24	Employment Office (HU)
25	Women's NGO (HU)
26	Academic (HU)
27	Ministry of Employment Policy and Labour (HU)
28	Academic (HU)
29	Academic (HU)
30	Academic (HU)
31	Women's NGO (HU)
32	Women's NGO/Business Association (HU)
33	Women's NGO/Business Association (HU)
34	Women's/employment NGO (HU)
35	Equal Treatment Authority (HU)
36	Equal Treatment Authority (HU)
37	Member of the European Parliament (HU)
38	Journalist, feminist activist (HU)

References

Ainley, P. (1998). 'Towards a Learning Society or Towards Learningfare?' *Social Policy Review*, 9, 51–67.

Armstrong, K. (2005). 'Inclusive Governance? Civil Society and the Open Method of Coordination', in S. Smismans (ed.), *Civil Society and Legitimate European Governance*. Cheltenham: Edward Elgar.

Ashiagbor, D. (2005). *The European Employment Strategy. Labour Market Regulation and New Governance*. Oxford: Oxford University Press.

Aust, A. (2003). Policy Map Germany: Labour Market Policy, Social Assistance and Women's Employment, Long-term Care. *WRAMSOC Working Paper*, www.kent.ac.uk/wramsoc/workingpapers/secondyearsreports/policymaps/germanpolicymap.pdf, accessed 20 January 2006.

Bäcker, G. (2006). 'Was heißt hier "geringfügig"? – Minijobs als wachsendes Segment prekärer Beschäftigung.' *WSI-Mitteilungen*, 56(05), 255–261.

Bader, V. (1999). 'Citizenship of the European Union. Human Rights, Rights of the Citizens of the Union and of the Member States.' *Ratio Juris*, 12(2), 153–181.

Bader, V. (2002). 'Institutions, Culture, and Identity of Transnational Citizenship: How Much Integration and "Communal Spirit" is Needed?', in K. Eder, C. Crouch & D. Tambini (eds), *Citizenship, Markets and the State*. Oxford: Oxford University Press.

BAG (2002). Zu den 15 Eckpunkten der Regierungskoalition zur Umsetzung des Reformkonzepts der Hartz-Kommission. BAG Stellungnahme, 10 September 2002, www.frauenbeauftragte.de/bag/sn0209hartz.htm, accessed 14 August 2005.

Barnes, M., Newman, J., & Sullivan, H. (2007). *Power, Participation and Political Renewal. Case Studies in Public Participation*. Bristol: Policy Press.

Bauböck, R. (ed.) (2006). *Migration and Citizenship: Legal Status, Rights and Political Participation*. Amsterdam: Amsterdam University Press.

Beckmann, P., & Kempf, B. (1996). 'Arbeitszeit und Arbeitszeitwünsche von Frauen in West- und Ostdeutschland.' *Mitteilungen aus der Arbeitsmarkt- und Berufsforschung*, 29(3).

Behning, U., Foden, D., & Serrano Pascual, A. (2001). 'Introduction', in U. Behning & A. Serrano Pascual (eds), *Gender Mainstreaming in the European Employment Strategy*. Brussels: ETUI.

Behning, U., & Serrano Pascual, A. (2001). 'Comparison of the Adaptation of Gender Mainstreaming in National Employment Policies', in U. Behning & A. Serrano Pascual (eds), *Gender Mainstreaming in the European Employment Strategy*. Brussels: ETUI.

Bellamy, K., & Rake, K. (2005). *Money Money Money – Is it Still a Rich Man's World? An Audit of Women's Economic Welfare in Britain Today*. London: Fawcett Society.

Bellamy, R., Castiglione, D., & Santoro, E. (eds) (2004). *Lineages of European Citizenship: Rights, Belonging and Participation in Eleven Nation-States*. Basingstoke: Palgrave.

Bellamy, R., & Warleigh, A. (eds) (2001). *Citizenship and Governance in the European Union*. London/ New York: Pinter/Continuum.

Bendix, R. (1964). *Nation-Building and Citizenship. Studies of our Changing Social Order*. New York: John Wiley.

Benhabib, S. (ed.) (1996). *Democracy and Difference: Contesting the Boundaries of the Political*. Princeton: Princeton University Press.

Beresford, P. (2000). 'Service Users' Knowledge and Social Work Theory: Conflict or Collaboration.' *British Journal of Social Work*, 30(4), 489–503.

Beresford, P. (2002). 'Participation and Social Policy: Transformation, Liberation or Regulation.' *Social Policy Review, 14*, 265 – 290.

Betzelt, S. (2007). 'Hartz IV aus Gender-Sicht. Einige Befunde und viele offene Fragen.' *WSI-Mitteilungen*, 60(6), 298–304.

Betzelt, S. (2008). 'Hartz IV – Folgen für Ungleichheit und das Gender Regime. Universelle Erwerbsbürgerschaft und Geschlechter(un)gleichheit.' *ZeS Report, 13*(1), 1–8.

Beveridge, F. (2006). 'Building against the Past: The Impact of Mainstreaming on EU Gender Law and Policy.' Paper presented at *Exchanging Ideas on Europe 2006. Visions of Europe: Key Problems, New Trajectories*. UACES 36th Annual Conference and 11th Research Conference, 31 August–2 September, Limerick.

Beveridge, F. (2007). 'Building against the Past: The Impact of Mainstreaming on EU Gender Law and Policy.' *European Law Review*, 32(2), 193–212.

Beveridge, F., & Nott, S. (2002). 'Mainstreaming: A Case for Optimism and Cynicism.' *Feminist Legal Studies*, 10(3), 299–311.

Biró, I., & Szabó, E. M. (1999). Institutional Mechanisms for the Advancement of Women in Hungary, www.karat.org/documents/hungary_mechanisms.shtml, accessed 12 May 2005.

Blair, T. (1997). Prime Minister's Speech to the CBI Conference. 11 November 1997, www.number10.gov.uk/output/Page1072.asp, accessed 3 December 2006.

Blair, T. (1998). *The Third Way. New Politics for the New Century*. London: The Fabian Society.

BMFSFJ (2001). Vereinbarung zwischen der Bundesregierung und den Spitzenverbänden der deutschen Wirtschaft zur Förderung der Chancengleichheit von Frauen und Männern in der Privatwirtschaft vom 2.07.2001, www.bmfsfj.de/Politikbereiche/ gleichstellung,did=6408.html, accessed 20 November 2006.

BMFSFJ (2003). Das neue Gesetz zur Gleichstellung in der Bundesverwaltung und in den Gerichten des Bundes (Bundesgleichstellungsgesetz – BGleiG) 2nd, www. bmfsfj.de/RedaktionBMFSFJ/Broschuerenstelle/Pdf-Anlagen/PRM–24204- Broschure-BGleiG,property=pdf.pdf, accessed 20 November 2006.

BMFSFJ (2005). Implementierung von Gender Mainstreaming in die Arbeit der Bundesregierung, www.gender-mainstreaming.net/RedaktionBMFSFJ/ RedaktionGM/Pdf-Anlagen/gm-implementierung,property=pdf,bereich=gm, rwb=true.pdf, accessed 20 November 2006.

BMFSFJ (2006a). *Erziehungsgeld, Elternzeit. Das Bundeserziehungsgeldgesetz*. Berlin: Bundesministerium für Familie, Senioren, Frauen und Jugend.

BMFSFJ (2006b). *Kindertagesbetreuung für Kinder unter drei Jahren. Bericht der Bundesregierung über den Stand des Ausbaus für ein bedarfsgerechtes Angebot an*

Kindertagesbetreuung für Kinder unter drei Jahren. Berlin, July.

Borchorst, A. (1998). 'Feminist Thinking about the Welfare State', in B. B. Hess, J. Lorber & M. M. Ferree (eds), *Revisioning Gender: New Directions in the Social Sciences*. London: Sage.

Boss, A., Christensen, B., & Schrader, K. (2005). Anreizprobleme bei Hartz IV: Lieber ALG II statt Arbeit? *Kieler Diskussionsbeiträge, 421*, www.uni-kiel.de/ifw/pub/kd/2005/kd421.pdf, accessed 9 January 2006.

Bothfeld, S., Klammer, U., Klenner, C., Leiber, S., Thiel, A., & Ziegler, A. (2005). *WSI-FrauenDatenReport 2005 – Handbuch zur wirtschaftlichen und sozialen Situation von Frauen*. Berlin: Edition Sigma.

Bothfeld, S., Schmidt, T., & Tobsch, V. (2005). Erosion des männlichen Ernährermodells? Die Erwerbstätigkeit von Frauen mit Kindern unter drei Jahren. Forschungsbericht an das BMFSFJ, www.bmfsfj.de/Kategorien/Forschungsnetz/forschungsberichte,d id=59416.html, accessed 2 April 2007.

Boussaguet, L., & Dehousse, R. (2008). Lay people's Europe: A Critical Assessment of the First EU Citizens' Conferences. *European Governance Papers (EUROGOV), No. C–08–02*, www.connex-network.org/eurogov/pdf/egp-connex-C–08–02.pdf, accessed 14 September 2008.

Brandt, T. (2006). 'Bilanz der Minijobs und Reformperspektiven.' *WSI-Mitteilungen*, 59(8), 446–452.

Brubaker, W. R. (1992). *Citizenship and Nationhood in France and Germany*. Cambridge, MA: Harvard University Press.

Brush, L. D. (1998). 'Gender, Work, Who Cares? Production, Reproduction, Deindustrialization, and Business as Usual', in B. B. Hess, J. Lorber & M. M. Ferree (eds), *Revisioning Gender: New Directions in the Social Sciences*. London: Sage.

Büchs, M., & Friedrich, D. (2005). 'Surface Integration: Dealing with the EES and the OMC/incl. in Germany', in J. Zeitlin & P. Pochet (eds), *The Open Method of Co-ordination in Action: The European Employment and Social Inclusion Strategies*. Brussels: PIE Peter Lang.

Bundesregierung (2002). Bericht der Bundesregierung zur Berufs- und Einkommenssituation von Frauen und Männern, 24 April 2002, www.bmfsfj.de/RedaktionBMFSFJ/Abteilung4/Pdf-Anlagen/PRM-19920-Bericht-der-Bundesregierung-zu,property=pdf.pdf, accessed 22 November 2006.

Carmel, E. (2005). 'Governance and the Constitution of a European Social', in J. Newman (ed.), *Remaking Governance: Peoples, Politics and the Public Sphere*. Bristol: Policy Press.

Castle-Kanerova, M., & Jordan, B. (2001). 'The Social Citizen?', in R. Bellamy & A. Warleigh (eds), *Citizenship and Governance in the European Union*. London, New York: Continuum.

Castles, S., & Davidson, A. (2000). *Citizenship and Migration: Globalization and the Politics of Belonging*. Basingstoke: Palgrave.

CBI (1989). *Towards a Skills Revolution, Report of the Vocational Education and Training Taskforce*. London: Confederation of British Industry.

CDU/CSU, & SPD (2005). *Gemeinsam für Deutschland. Mit Mut und Menschlichkeit.*, *Koalitionsvertrag von CDU, CSU und SPD*, 11 November.

CEDAW (2006). *Consideration of Reports Submitted by States Parties Under Article 18 of the Convention on the Elimination of All Forms of Discrimination against Women. Sixth Periodic Report of States Parties – Hungary*. CEDAW/C/HUN/6. New York, 15 June.

Chamberlayne, P. (1990). 'Neighbourhood and Tenant Participation in the GDR', in B. Deacon & J. Szalai (eds), *Social Policy in the New Eastern Europe: What Future for Socialist Welfare?* Aldershot: Avebury.

Charmaz, K. (2000). 'Grounded Theory: Objectivist and Constructivist Methods', in N. K. Denzin & Y. S. Lincoln (eds), *Handbook of Qualitative Research* (2nd edn). London: SAGE.

Charmaz, K. (2005). *Constructing Grounded Theory: A Practical Guide through Qualitative Analysis.* London: SAGE.

Clarke, J. (2004). *Changing Welfare, Changing States: New Directions in Social Policy.* London: SAGE.

Clarke, J., & Newman, J. (1997). *The Managerial State.* London: SAGE.

Council of Europe (1998). *Gender Mainstreaming. Conceptual Framework, Methodology and Presentation of Good Practices. Final Report of Activities of the Group of Specialists on Mainstreaming (EG-S-MS).* EG-S-MS (98) 2. Strasbourg.

Council of the EU (1997). *Council Resolution of 15 December 1997 on the 1998 Employment Guidelines.* 98/C 30/01. Brussels, 15 December.

Council of the EU (1999). *Council Resolution of 22 February 1999 on the 1999 Employment Guidelines.* 1999/C 69/02. Brussels.

Council of the EU (2000a). *Council Decision of 27 November 2000 Establishing a Community Action Programme to Combat Discrimination (2001 to 2006).* 2000/750/EC. Brussels.

Council of the EU (2000b). *Council Directive of 27 November 2000 Establishing a General Framework for Equal Treatment in Employment and Occupation.* 2000/78/EC. Brussels.

Council of the EU (2000c). *Council Directive of 29 June 2000 Implementing the Principle of Equal Treatment between Persons Irrespective of Racial or Ethnic Origin.* 2000/43/EC. Brussels.

Council of the EU (2000d). *Council Recommendation of 14 February 2000 on the Implementation of Member States' Employment Policies.* 2000/164/EC. Brussels.

Council of the EU (2001). *Council Decision of 20 December 2000 Establishing a Programme Relating to the Community Framework Strategy on Gender Equality (2001–2005).* 2001/51/EC. Brussels.

Council of the EU (2002). *Directive 2002/73/EC of the European Parliament and of the Council of 23 September 2002 Amending Council Directive 76/207/EEC on the Implementation of the Principle of Equal Treatment for Men and Women as Regards Access to Employment, Vocational Training and Promotion, and Working Conditions.* 2002/73/EC. Brussels.

Council of the EU (2003a). *Council Decision of 22 July 2003 on Guidelines for Member States' Employment Policies.* 2003/578/EC. Brussels.

Council of the EU (2003b). *Council Recommendation of 22 July 2003 on the Implementation of Member States' Employment Policies.* 2003/579/EC. Brussels.

Council of the EU (2004a). *Council Recommendation on the Implementation of Member States' Employment Policies.* 2004/741/EC. Brussels, 14 October.

Council of the EU (2004b). *Joint Employment Report 2003/2004.* 7069/04. 5 March. Brussels.

Council of the EU (2007). *Recommendation for a Council Recommendation on the 2007 Up-Date of the Broad Guidelines for the Economic Policies of the Member States and the Community and on the Implementation of Member States' Employment Policies.* 7456/07. 15 March. Brussels.

Council of the EU (2008). *Council Recommendation on the 2008 Update of the Broad Guidelines for the Economic Policies of the Member States and the Community and on the Implementation of Member States' Employment Policies.* 8276/08. 6 May. Brussels.

Council of the EU (2009). *Country-Specific Integrated Recommendations – Report from the Council to the European Council.* 7444/09 10 March. Brussels.

Crespo, E., & Serrano Pascual, A. (2004). 'The EU's Concept of Activation for Young People: Towards a New Social Contract?', in E. Crespo & A. Serrano Pascual (eds), *Are Activation Policies Converging in Europe? The European Employment Strategy for Young People.* Brussels: ETUI.

Crompton, R. (ed.). (1999). *Restructuring Gender Relations and Employment: The Decline of the Male Breadwinner.* Oxford: Oxford University Press.

Deacon, B., & Hulse, M. (1997). 'The Making of Post-communist Social Policy: The Role of International Agencies.' *Journal of Social Policy*, 26(1), 43–62.

Delanty, G. (1995). *Inventing Europe: Idea, Identity, Reality.* London: Macmillan.

Delanty, G. (2000). *Citizenship in a Global Age: Society, Culture, Politics.* Buckingham: Open University Press.

Deutscher Bundestag (2003). *Regierungserklärung durch den Bundeskanzler. Mut zum Frieden und zur Veränderung.* Berlin.

Deutscher Frauenrat (2001a). *Gleichstellungsgesetz für die Privatwirtschaft bleibt auf der Tagesordnung. Beschluss vom 11.11.2001.* Berlin: Deutscher Frauenrat.

Deutscher Frauenrat (2001b). Sommerschlussverkauf. Gleichstellung in der Wirtschaft. *Press Release*, 4 July, www.frauenrat.de/module/press/press.details.aspx?S_ID=4 9566020620061127165656143117641045567308663331&NWS_ID=504&NWS_ SYS_ID=144242121&NWS_MDT_ID=0001&SN=0&VIEW=SUCHE, accessed 27 November 2006.

Deutscher Frauenrat (2009a). *Ernüchternde Bilanz.* Press Release, 24 November.

Deutscher Frauenrat (2009b). *Gleichstellungsgesetz für die Privatwirtschaft tut not.* Press Release, 1 December.

DfEE (1998). *Meeting the Childcare Challenge Green Paper.* Cm 3959. London.

DGB-Bundesvorstand (2003). *Stellungnahme des Deutschen Gewerkschaftsbundes (DGB) zum Entwurf der Bundesregierung sowie der Koalitionsfraktionen eines 'Vierten Gesetzes für moderne Dienstleistungen am Arbeitsmarkt'.* Berlin: Deutscher Gewerkschaftsbund.

DGB (2001a). DGB-Bundesfrauenkonferenz hält an Gleichstellungsgesetz fest. Press Release 363: 26 November, www.dgb.de/presse/pressemeldungen/pmdb/ pressemeldung_single?pmid=1563, accessed 24 November 2006.

DGB (2001b). DGB: Frauenförderung ist Investition in die Zukunft. Press Release 279: 11 September, www.dgb.de/presse/pressemeldungen/pmdb/pressemeldung_ single?pmid=1480, accessed 24 November 2006.

DGB (2001c). Engelen-Kefer: Gleichstellungsgesetz für die Privatwirtschaft ist un-verzichtbar. Press Release 094: 23 March, www.dgb.de/presse/pressemeldungen/ pmdb/pressemeldung_single?pmid=1268, accessed 24 November 2006.

DGB (2001d). Schulte: Gleichstellung braucht Verbindlichkeit. Press Release 362: 22 November , www.dgb.de/presse/pressemeldungen/pmdb/pressemeldung_ single?pmid=1562, accessed 24 November 2006.

Dietz, M. (1992). 'Context is All: Feminism and Theories of Citizenship', in C. Mouffe (ed.), *Dimensions of Radical Democracy: Pluralism, Citizenship, Community.* London: Verso Books.

DJB (2001). Zur Vereinbarung zwischen der Bundesregierung und den Spitzenverbänden der deutschen Wirtschaft zur Förderung der Chancengleichheit von Frauen und Männern in der Privatwirtschaft. Press Release 3 July, www.djb.de/Kommissionen/kommission-arbeits-gleichstellungs-und-wirtschaftsrecht/pm–29/

DJB (2002a). DJB kritisiert das Verfahren der Hartz-Kommission und fordert frauenpolitische Korrekturen. Press Release 16 August, www.djb.de/Kommissionen/kommission-recht-der-sozialen-sicherung-familienlastenausgleich/pm–96/, accessed 27 November 2006.

DJB (2002b). Juristinnenbund fordert die Umgestaltung des Ehegattensplittings zu einer Individualbesteuerung. Press Release 11 October, www.djb.de/Kommissionen/kommission-recht-der-sozialen-sicherung-familienlastenausgleich/pm–100/, accessed 27 November 2006.

DJB (2002c). Zum Bericht zur Berufs- und Einkommenssituation von Frauen und Männern des BMFSFJ vom 24. April 2002. Press Release 4/2002, www.djb.de/Kommissionen/kommission-oeffentliches-recht-europa-und-voelkerrecht/pm–89/, accessed 27 November 2006.

DJB (2003). Kommission Recht der Sozialen Sicherung, Familienlastenausgleich. Tätigkeitsbericht 2001–2003, www.djb.de/Kommissionen/kommission-recht-der-sozialen-sicherung-familienlastenausgleich/SozialeSicherung_bericht2003/, accessed 28 November 2006.

DJB (2006a). *Hintergrundpapier zur aktuellen Diskussion über eine Reform der Besteuerung von Ehe und Familie*. Berlin, 26.06.2006.

DJB (2006b, 26.06.2006). Kann Familiensplitting fortschrittlich sein? Press Release 27 June, www.djb.de/Kommissionen/kommission-recht-der-sozialen-sicherung-familienlastenausgleich/pm06–19-Splitting/, accessed 27 November 2006.

DJB (2006c). Reform der Familienbesteuerung – ein Thema des Deutschen Juristentags vom 19.–22.9.2006 in Stuttgart. Press Release 18 June, www.djb.de/Kommissionen/kommission-recht-der-sozialen-sicherung-familienlastenausgleich/pm06–17-Familienbesteuerung/, accesed 27 November 2006.

Dombos, T., Horváth, A., & Krizsán, A. (2007). 'Where did Gender Disappear? Anti-Discrimination Policy in the EU Accession Process in Hungary' In M. Verloo (ed.), *Multiple Meanings of Gender Equality. A Critical Frame Analysis of Gender Policies in Europe*. Budapest & New York: Central European University Press.

Dörre, K. (2005). 'Prekarität – Eine arbeitspolitische Herausforderung.' *WSI-Mitteilungen*, 58(5), 250–258.

DSS (1998). *New Ambitions for Our Country: A New Contract for Welfare* (no. Cm 3805). London: HMSO.

DTI (2004). *Creating Wealth from Knowledge. The DTI Five Year Programme*. London: HMSO.

DWP (2001). *Opportunity for All – Making Progress, Third Annual Report*. Cm 5260. London.

DWP (2002). *Opportunity for All, Fourth Annual Report*. Cm 5598. London.

DWP (2004). *Building on New Deal: Local Solutions Meeting Individual Needs*. London.

DWP (2005a). *Five Year Strategy. Opportunity and Security throughout Life*. Cm 6447. London.

DWP (2005b). *Opportunity for All, Seventh Annual Report*. Cm 6673. London.

DWP (2006a). *A New Deal for Welfare: Empowering People to Work, Green Paper*. Cm 6730. London.

DWP (2006b). *Opportunity for All, Eighth Annual Report 2006. Strategy Document.* Cm 6915-i. London.

DWP (2007a). *In Work Better Off: Next Steps to Full Employment.* Cm 7130. London.

DWP (2007b). *Ready for Work: Full Employment in our Generation.* Cm 7290. London.

DWP (2008). *Raising Expectations and Increasing Support: Reforming Welfare for the Future.* CM 7506. London.

Eberhardt, E. (2005). 'Equal Opportunities, Mainstreaming and Reconstruction of Gender in Hungary.' Paper presented at *ECPR General Conference*, 8–11 September, Budapest.

EHRC (2008). Legal Strategy 2008–9, www.equalityhumanrights.com/uploaded_files/legal_strategy_0809.doc, accessed 1 February 2010.

EHRC (2009). Enforcement and Compliance Policy, www.equalityhumanrights.com/uploaded_files/legal_strategy_0809.doc, accessed 1 February 2010.

Einhorn, B. (1993). *Cindarella Goes to Market: Citizenship, Gender, and Women's Movements in East Central Europe.* London: Verso.

Einhorn, B. (1996). 'Gender and Citizenship in East Central Europe After the End of State Socialist Policies for Women's Emancipation', in B. Einhorn, M. Kaldor & Z. Kavan (eds), *Citizenship and Democratic Control in Contemporary Europe.* Cheltenham: Edward Elgar.

Einhorn, B., Kaldor, M., & Kavan, Z. (eds). (1996). *Citizenship and Democratic Control in Contemporary Europe.* Cheltenham: Edward Elgar.

EIRO online (2003). Increasing Emphasis on Equal Opportunity and Gender Issues. *European Industrial Relations Observatory Online*, 22 May, www.eiro.eurofound. eu.int/2003/05/feature/hu0305101f.html, accessed 19 March 2006.

Employment Taskforce (2003). *Jobs, Jobs, Jobs – Creating more Employment in Europe. Report of the Employment Taskforce chaired by Wim Kok.* Brussels.

Engelbrech, G., & Reinberg, A. (1997). 'Beschäftigungskrise trifft im Westen vor allem die Männer, im Osten die Frauen.' *IAB Kurzbericht*, 9, 15 September.

Engelen-Kefer, U. (2005). 'Die Hartz-Gesetze – eine Zwischenbilanz des DGB.' Paper presented at *Fachtagung der Arbeitnehmerkammer Bremen*, 8 February. Bremen.

EOC (2003). Towards Equality and Diversity – Making it Happen. A Response from the Equal Opportunities Commission, www.eoc.org.uk/PDF/making_it_happen. pdf, accessed 5 July 2006.

EOC (2006a). *Gender Equality Duty Code of Practice. England and Wales.* London: Equal Opportunities Commission.

EOC (2006b). Statement: EOC Responds to Cadman Equal Pay Ruling, www.eoc.org. uk/Default.aspx?page=19515, accessed 18 December 2006.

Esping-Andersen, G. (1990). *Three Worlds of Welfare Capitalism.* Cambridge: Polity Press.

Esping-Andersen, G. (ed.). (2002). *Why We Need A New Welfare State.* Oxford: Oxford University Press.

European Commission (1993). *White Paper on Growth, Competitiveness and Employment: The Challenges and Ways forward into the 21st Century.* COM (1993) 700 final. 5 December 1993. Brussels.

European Commission (1996). *Incorporating Equal Opportunities for Women and Men into All Community Policies and Activities.* COM (1996) 67 final. 21 February. Brussels.

European Commission (1999). *1999 Regular Report from the Commission on Hungary's Progress Towards Accession.* COM (1999) 505 final. 30 October. Brussels.

European Commission (2000). *Towards a Community Framework Strategy on Gender Equality (2001–2005).* COM(2000) 335 final. 7 June. Brussels.

European Commission (2001a). *2001 Regular Report on Hungary's Progress towards Accession.* SEC (2001) 1748. 13 November. Brussels.

European Commission (2001b). *European Governance. A White Paper.* COM (2001) 428 final. 25 July. Brussels.

European Commission (2001c). *European Social Fund Support for the European Employment Strategy.* COM (2001) 16 final. 23 July. Brussels.

European Commission (2002a). *Impact Evaluation of the EES. Background Paper – Equal Opportunities for Women and Men.* EMCO/29/060602/EN_REV 1. Brussels.

European Commission (2002b). *The Lisbon Strategy – Making Change Happen, Communication from the Commission to the Spring European Council in Barcelona.* COM (2002)14 final. 15 January. Brussels.

European Commission (2002c). *Streamlining the Annual Economic and Employment Policy Coordination Cycles.* COM (2002) 487 final. 3 September. Brussels.

European Commission (2002d). *Taking Stock of Five Years of the European Employment Strategy.* COM (2002) 416 final. 17 July. Brussels.

European Commission (2003a). *European Commission Adopts an Instrument for European Economic Governance, Press Release.* IP/03/508. 8 April. Brussels.

European Commission (2003b). *The Future of the European Employment Strategy (EES): 'A Strategy for Full Employment and Better Jobs for All'.* COM (2003) 6 final. 14 January. Brussels.

European Commission (2003c). *Progress in Implementing the Joint Assessment Papers on Employment Policies in Acceding Countries.* COM (2003) 37 final. 30 January. Brussels.

European Commission (2003d). *Progress in Implementing the Joint Assessment Papers on Employment Policies in Acceding Countries – Updated Version.* COM (2003) 663 final. 6 November. Brussels.

European Commission (2005a). *Common Actions for Growth and Employment: The Community Lisbon Programme.* COM (2005) 330 final. 20 July. Brussels.

European Commission (2005b). *Delivering on Growth and Jobs: A New and Integrated Economic and Employment Co-ordination Cycle in the EU. Companion document to the Communication to the Spring European Council 2005 {COM (2005) 24}"Working Together for Growth and Jobs".* SEC(2005) 193. 3 February. Brussels.

European Commission (2005c). *Integrated Guidelines for Growth and Jobs (2005–2008).* COM (2005) 141 final. 12 April. Brussels.

European Commission (2005d). *Working Together for Growth and Jobs. A New Start for the Lisbon Strategy, Communication to the Spring European Council from President Barroso in Agreement with Vice-President Verheugen.* COM (2005) 24 final. 2 February. Brussels.

European Commission (2005e). *Working together for Growth and Jobs. Next Steps in Implementing the Revised Lisbon Strategy, Commission Staff Working Paper.* SEC (2005) 622/2. 29 April. Brussels.

European Commission (2006a). *Indicators for Monitoring the Employment Guidelines. 2006 Compendium.* 30 November. Brussels.

European Commission (2006b). *A Roadmap for Equality between Women and Men 2006–2010*. COM (2006) 92 final. 1 March. Brussels.

European Commission (2006c). *Time to Move up a Gear. Country Chapters (Part II), Communication from the Commission to the Spring European Council*. COM (2006) 30 final. 25 January. Brussels.

European Commission (2006d). *'A Year of Delivery': Implementing the Renewed Lisbon Strategy for Growth and Jobs. Country Assessments*. COM (2006) 816 final PART II. 12 December. Brussels.

European Commission (2007a). *Keeping up the Pace of Change. Country Assessments*. COM (2007) 803 final PART II. 11 December. Brussels.

European Commission (2007b). *Tackling the Pay Gap between Women and Men*. COM(2007) 424 final. 18 July. Brussels.

European Commission (2009a). *Companion Document: Implementation of the Lisbon Strategy Structural Reforms in the Context of the European Economic Recovery Plan – a more detailed Overview of Progress across the EU in the specific macro- and micro-economic as well as the employment Areas*. COM(2009) 34 Volume II final. 28 January. Brussels.

European Commission (2009b). *Implementation of the Lisbon Strategy Structural Reforms in the Context of the European Economic Recovery Plan: Annual Country Assessments – a detailed Overview of Progress made with the Implementation of the Lisbon Strategy Reforms in Member States in 2008*. Brussels.

European Council (1993). *European Council in Copenhagen, 21–22 June 1993. Conclusions of the Presidency*. Brussels.

European Council (1995). *Madrid European Council 16 December 1995. Presidency Conclusions*. Brussels.

European Council (2000). *Lisbon European Council 23 and 24 March. Presidency Conclusions*. Brussels.

European Council (2002). *Barcelona European Council 15 and 16 March 2002. Presidency Conclusions*. Brussels.

European Council (2003). *Brussels European Council. 20 and 21 March 2003. Presidency Conclusions*. Brussels.

European Council (2004). *Brussels European Council. 25 and 26 March 2004. Presidency Conclusions*. Brussels.

European Council (2005). *Brussels European Council 22 and 23 March. Presidency Conclusions*. 7619/1/05 REV 1. Brussels.

European Council (2006). *Brussels European Council 23 and 24 March. Presidency Conclusions*. 7775/1/06 REV 1. Brussels.

European Council (2009). *Country-Specific Integrated Recommendations. Report from the Council to the European Council 7444/09*. 10 March. Brussels.

Evans, M., Eyre, J., Millar, J., & Sarre, S. (2003). *New Deal for Lone Parents: Second Synthesis Report of the National Evaluation. Prepared for the Department for Work and Pensions*. Bath: Centre for Analysis of Social Policy, University of Bath.

Fagan, C. (2002). Assessment of the National Action Plan for Employment 2002 from a Gender Perspective, www.mbs.ac.uk/research/european-employment/projects/gender-social-inclusion/documents/NAP2002_UK.pdf, accessed 21 November 2006.

Fagan, C., Grimshaw, D., & Rubery, J. (2006). 'The Subordination of the Gender Equality Objective: the National Reform Programmes and 'Making Work Pay' Policies', *industrial Relations Journal*, 37(6), 571–592.

Fagan, C., & Hebson, G. (2004). *'Making Work Pay' Debates from a Gender Perspective: a Comparative Review of Some Recent Policy Reforms in Thirty European Countries*. Manchester: EGGSIE.

Fairclough, N., & Wodak, R. (1997). 'Critical Discourse Analysis', in T. A. van Dijk (ed.), *Discourse as Social Interaction (= Discourse Studies: A Multidisciplinary Introduction, Vol. II)*. London: SAGE.

Faist, T. (2001). 'Social Citizenship in the European Union: Nested Membership.' *Journal of Common Market Studies*, 39(1), 37–58.

FCO (2005). *Prospects for the EU in 2005. The UK Presidency of the European Union*. London.

Ferge, Z., & Juhász, G. (2004). 'Accession and Social Policy: The Case of Hungary.' *Journal of European Social Policy*, 14(3), 233–251.

Ferrera, M. (2003). 'European Integration and National Social Citizenship. Changing Boundaries, New Structuring?'. *Comparative Political Studies*, 36(6), 611–652.

Ferrera, M. (2005). *The Boundaries of Welfare*. Oxford: Oxford University Press.

Fodor, E. (2005). *Women at Work. The Status of Women in the Labour Markets of the Czech Republic, Hungary and Poland* (No. 3). Geneva: United Nations Research Institute for Social Development (UNRISD).

Fodor, E., Glass, C., Kawachi, J., & Popescu, L. (2002). 'Family Policies and Gender in Hungary, Poland, and Romania.' *Communist and Post-Communist Studies*, 35, 475–490.

Foucault, M. (1991). 'On Governmentality', in G. Burchell, C. Gordon & P. N. Miller (eds), *The Foucault Effect: Studies in Governmentality*. Chicago: University of Chicago Press.

Foucault, M. (2004a). *Die Geburt der Biopolitik. Geschichte der Gouvernementalität II. Vorlesung am Collège de France 1978–1979*. Frankfurt: Suhrkamp.

Foucault, M. (2004b). *Sicherheit, Territorium, Bevölkerung. Geschichte der Gouvernementalität I. Vorlesung am Collège de France 1977–1978*. Frankfurt: Suhrkamp.

Fraser, N. (1994). 'After the Family Wage: Gender Equity and the Welfare State.' *Political Theory*, 22(4), 591–618.

Freedland, M., & King, D. (2003). 'Contractual Governance and Illiberal Contracts: Some Problems of Contractualism as an Instrument of Behaviour Management by Agencies of Government.' *Cambridge Journal of Economics*, 27(3), 465–477.

Freud, D. (2007). *Reducing Dependency, increasing Opportunity: Options for the Future of Welfare to Work*. London: DWP.

Fultz, E., Ruck, M., & Steinhilber, S. (2003). Gender Dimensions of Social Security Reform in Central and Eastern Europe. Case Studies of the Czech Republic, Hungary and Poland, www.ilo.org/public/english/region/eurpro/budapest/download/gender.pdf, accessed 30 May 2006.

Gal, S., & Kligman, G. (2000). *The Politics of Gender after Socialism: A Comparative-Historical Essay*. Princeton, NJ: Princeton University Press.

Gallie, W. B. (1956). 'Essentially Contested Concepts.' *Proceedings of the Aristotelian Society*, 56 (ns), 167–198.

Gerhard, U., Knijn, T., & Lewis, J. (2002). 'Contractualization', in B. Hobson, J. Lewis & B. Siim (eds), *Contested Concepts in Gender and Social Politics*. Cheltenham: Edward Elgar.

Germany (1999). *Employment Action Plan 1999*.

Germany (2000). 'National Employment Action Plan 2000.'

Germany (2001). *National Action Plan for Employment Policy 2001*.

Germany (2002). *National Action Plan for Employment Policy 2002*.

Germany (2003). *National Action Plan for Employment Policy 2003*.

Germany (2004). *National Action Plan for Employment Policy 2004*.

Germany (2005). *Nationales Reformprogramm Deutschland: Innovation forcieren – Sicherheit im Wandel – Deutsche Einheit vollenden*.

Germany (2006). *National Reform Program Germany 2005–2008. Implementation and Progress Report*, 15 August.

Germany (2007). *National Reform Programme Germany 2005–2008. Implementation and Progress Report 2007*.

Germany (2008). *Germany's National Reform Programme 2008–2010. Building on Success – Continuing with the Reforms for More Growth and Jobs*. Berlin.

Germany (2009). *National Reform Programme. Germany 2008–2010. Implementation and Progress Report 2009*. Berlin.

Gerntke, A., Klute, J., Troost, A., & Trube, A. (eds). (2002). *Hart(z) am Rande der Seriösität? Die Hartz-Kommission als neues Modell der Politikberatung und -gestaltung? Kommentare und Kritiken*. Münster, Hamburg, London: Lit Verlag.

Giddens, A. (1976). *New Rules of Sociological Method: A Positive Critique of Interpretive Sociologies*. London: Hutchinson.

Giddens, A. (1995). *A Contemporary Critique of Historical Materialism* (2nd edn). Basingstoke: Macmillan.

Giddens, A. (1998). *The Third Way: The Renewal of Social Democracy*. Cambridge, Oxford: Polity Press.

Goetschy, J. (1999). 'The European Employment Strategy: Genesis and Development.' *European Journal of Industrial Relations*, 5(2), 117–1137.

Gomart, E., & Hajer, M. (2003). 'Is that Politics? For an Inquiry into Forms in Contemporary Politics', in B. Joerges & H. Nowotny (eds), *Social Studies of Science and Technology: Looking Back Ahead*. Amsterdam: Kluwer Academic Publishers.

Goven, J. (2001). 'New Parliament, Old Discourse? The Parental Leave Debate in Hungary', in S. Gal & G. Kligman (eds), *Reproducing Gender: Politics, Publics, and Everyday Life After Socialism*. Princeton, NJ: Princeton University Press.

Gransee, U. (2005). 'Mehr "Fordern" als "Fördern". Die Folgen von Hartz I–IV für ArbeitnehmerInnen in Niedersachsen', in H. Baumeister, U. Gransee & K.-D. Zimmermann (eds), *Die Hartz-'Reformen'. Die Folgen von Hartz I–IV für ArbeitnehmerInnen. Ein Projekt der Arbeitnehmerkammer Bremen und des DGB-Bezirks Niedersachsen – Bremen – Sachsen-Anhalt*. Hamburg: VSA-Verlag.

Gregg, P. (2008). *Realising Potential: a Vision for Personalised Conditionality and Support*. London: DWP.

Grint, K. (1998). *The Sociology of Work. An Introduction* (2nd edn). Cambridge: Polity Press.

Habermas, J. (1992). 'Citizenship and National Identity: Some Reflections on the Future of Europe.' *Praxis International*, 12(1), 1–19.

Hajer, M. A. (2005). 'Setting the Stage: A Dramaturgy of Policy Deliberation.' *Administration & Society*, 36(6), 624–647.

Hammar, T. (1994). *Democracy and the Nation State: Aliens, Denizens and Citizens in a World of International Migration*. Aldershot: Avebury.

Hanagan, M., & Tilly, C. (eds). (1999). *Extending Citizenship, Reconfiguring States*. Lanham, MD: Rowman & Littlefield.

Handler, J. F. (2004). *Social Citizenship and Workfare in the United States and Western Europe: the Paradox of Inclusion*. Cambridge: Cambridge University Press.

Haney, L. (2002). *Inventing the Needy. Gender and the Politics of Welfare in Hungary*. Berkeley, CA: University of California Press.

Hantrais, L., & Letablier, M.-T. (1996). *Families and Family Policies in Europe*. Harlow: Ardison Wesley Longman.

Harkness, S. (2002). *Low Pay, Times of Work and Gender*. Manchester: Equal Opportunities Commission.

Héritier, A. (1999). 'Elements of Democratic Legitimation in Europe: an Alternative Perspective.' *Journal of European Public Policy*, 6(2), 269–282.

Hickel, R. (2003). 'Hartz-Konzept: Arbeitslose effektiver in billige Jobs – Deregulierungsschub auf den Arbeitsmärkten.' *Aus Politik und Zeitgeschichte* 06–07, 7–9.

Hielscher, V. (2006). 'Reorganisation der Bundesagentur für Arbeit: "Moderner Dienstleister" für wen?'. *WSI-Mitteilungen*, 59(3), 119–124.

High Level Group (2004). *Facing the Challenge – The Lisbon Strategy for Growth and Employment. Report from the High Level Group Chaired by Wim Kok*. Brussels.

Hindess, B. (1998). 'Divide and Rule: the International Character of Modern Citizenship.' *European Journal of Social Theory*, 1(1), 57–70.

HM Treasury (2000). Chancellor Gordon Brown Calls for Enterprise for All. New Figures Show Differences in Small Business Creation around the Country. HM Treasury Press Release 80/00, www.hm-treasury.gov.uk/newsroom_and_speeches/press/2000/press_80_00.cfm, accessed 16 January 2007.

HM Treasury (2001). Speech by the Chancellor of the Exchequer to the Institute of Directors. HM Treasury Press Release 125/01, http://archive.treasury.gov.uk/press/2001/p125_01.html, accessed 16 January 2007.

HM Treasury (2002a). *Budget 2002 – The Strength to Make Long-term Decisions: Investing in an Enterprising, Fairer Britain*. HC 592. 17 April 2002. London.

HM Treasury (2002b). *Towards Full Employment in the European Union*. July 2002. London.

HM Treasury (2003a). *Budget 2003 – Building a Britain of Economic Strength and Social Justice*. London.

HM Treasury (2003b). *Every Child Matters, Green Paper*. Cm 5860. London.

HM Treasury (2004a). *Budget 2004 – Prudence for a Purpose: A Britain of Stability and Strength*. HC 301. 17 March. London.

HM Treasury (2004b). *Choice for Parents, the Best Start for Children: A Ten Year Strategy for Childcare*. London.

HM Treasury (2005a). *Budget 2005. Investing for Our Future: Fairness and Opportunity for Britain's Hard-Working Families*. HC 372. London.

HM Treasury (2005b). Speech by the Rt Hon Gordon Brown MP, Chancellor of the Exchequer at the CBI Annual Dinner. HM Treasury Press Release 48/05, www.hm-treasury.gov.uk/newsroom_and_speeches/press/2005/press_48_05.cfm, accessed 16 January 2007.

Hungary (2001). *Joint Assessment of the Employment Policy Priorities of Hungary*. Budapest.

Hungary (2004). *National Action Plan for Employment 2004*.

Hungary (2005a). Beijing +10 Evaluation of the Implementation of the UN World Congress on Women (Beijing, 1995) Platform for Action in Hungary, www.

un.org/womenwatch/daw/Review/responses/HUNGARY-English.pdf, accessed 19 December 2006.

Hungary (2005b). *National Reform Programme for Growth and Employment 2005–2008.* Budapest.

Hungary (2006). *Revised National Lisbon Action Programme for Growth and Employment.* Budapest.

IHF (2000a). '*Women's Status in Hungary*: A Perspective on Women's Human Rights. Vienna: International Helsinki Federation for Human Rights.

IHF (2000b). *Women 2000 – An Investigation into the Status of Women's Rights in Central and South-Eastern Europe and the Newly Independent States.* Vienna: International Helsinki Federation for Human Rights.

Ingham, H., & Ingham, M. (2003). 'Enlargement and the European Employment Strategy', in*dustrial Relations Journal*, 34(5).

Ingham, M., Ingham, H., Býçak, H., & Altinay, M. (2005). 'The Impact of (More) Enlargement on the European Employment Strategy', *Industrial Relations Journal*, 36(6), 456–477.

Isin, E. F., & Wood, P. (1999). *Citizenship and Identity.* London: Sage.

Jacobson, D. (1996). *Rights Across Borders: Immigration and the Decline of Citizenship.* Baltimore, MD: Johns Hopkins University Press.

Jacobsson, K. (2004). 'Soft Regulation and the Subtle Transformation of States: The Case of EU Employment Policy.' *Journal of European Social Policy*, 14(4), 355–370.

Jayasuriya, K. (2001). 'Autonomy, Liberalism and the New Contractualism.' *Law in Context*, 18(2), 57–78.

Jayasuriya, K. (2002). 'The New Contractualism: Neo-Liberal or Democratic?'. *Political Quarterly*, 73(3), 309–320.

Jenson, J. (2007). 'The European Union's Citizenship Regime. Creating Norms and Building Practices.' *Comparative European Politics*, 5(1), 53–69.

Jenson, J. (2008). 'Writing Women Out, Folding Gender In: The European Union "Modernises" Social Policy.' *Social Politics: International Studies in Gender, State & Society*, 15(2), 131–153.

Jenson, J., & Pochet, P. (2006). 'Employment and Social Policy Since Maastricht: Standing up to European Monetary Union', in R. M. Fishman & A. M. Messina (eds), *The Year of the Euro: The Cultural, Social, and Political Import of Europe's Common Currency.* Notre Dame, IN: University of Notre Dame Press.

Jenson, J., & Saint-Martin, D. (2006). 'Building Blocks for a New Social Architecture: The LEGO(TM) Paradigm of an Active Society', *Policy & Politics*, 34(3), 429–451.

Joss, S., & Durant, J. (1995). *Public Participation in Science: The Role of Consensus Conferences in Europe* London: Science Museum.

Kakucs, N. (2009). 'Lost in Translations? Implementing Gender Mainstreaming in Hungary.' Paper presented at *5th ECPR General Conference*, 10–12 September, Potsdam.

Kalina, T., & Voss-Dahm, D. (2005). 'Mehr Minijobs = mehr Bewegung auf dem Arbeitsmarkt? Fluktuation der Arbeitskräfte und Beschäftigungsstruktur in vier Dienstleistungsbranchen.' *IAT-Report*, 2005(7).

Kalina, T., & Weinkopf, C. (2006). 'Mindestens sechs Millionen Niedriglohnbeschäftigte in Deutschland: Welche Rolle spielen Teilzeitbeschäftigung und Minijobs?'. *IAT-Report*, 2006(03).

Karagiannaki, E. (2007). 'Exploring the Effects of Integrated Benefit Systems and Active Labour Market Policies: Evidence from Jobcentre Plus in the UK.' *Journal of Social Policy*, 36(2), 177–195.

King, D., & Wickham-Jones, M. (1999). 'From Clinton to Blair: The (Democratic) Party Origins of Welfare to Work.' *Political Quarterly*, 70(1), 62–74.

Kingsmill, D. (2001). *Report into Women's Employment and Pay*. London.

Klement, C., & Rudolph, B. (2006). *Arbeitsmarktpartizipation von Frauen im Transformationsprozess. Sozio-ökonomische Realität in den EU-Beitrittsländern Polen, Tschechien und Ungarn* (No. Nr. 13/2006). Nürnberg: Institut für Arbeitsmark- und Berufsforschung (IAB).

Kohaut, S., & Möller, I. (2009). 'Vereinbarungen zur Chancengleichheit: Kaum Fortschritte bei der betrieblichen Förderung.' *IAB Kurzbericht*, 26/2009.

Kollonay Lehoczky, C. (2002). 'Female Employment in the Candidate Countries (ambivalent responses to controversial "emancipation").' Paper presented at *Quality in Employment and Enlargement of the European Union*, 18–19 October, Brussels.

Kollonay Lehoczky, C. (2005a). 'The Significance of Existing EU Sex Equality Law for Women in the New Member States. The Case of Hungary.' *Maastricht Journal of European and Comparative Law*, 12(4), 467–493.

Kollonay Lehoczky, C. (2005b). 'Work and Family Issues in the Transitional Countries of Central and Eastern Europe. The Case of Hungary', in J. Conaghan & K. Rittich (eds), *Labour Law, Work, and Family*. Oxford: Oxford University Press.

Korintus, M., & Vajda, G. (2002). WP 4: Surveying Demand, Supply and Use of Care – Hungary. *Care Work. Current Understandings and Future Directions in Europe*, http://144.82.31.4/reports/WP4HungaryNationalReport.pdf, accesed 18 December 2006.

Kostakopoulou, D. (2005). 'Ideas, Norms and European Citizenship: Explaining Institutional Change.' *Modern Law Review*, 68(2), 233–267.

Kostakopoulou, D. (2007). 'European Union Citizenship: Writing the Future.' *European Law Journal*, 13(5), 623–646.

Kostakopoulou, D. (2008). *The Future Governance of Citizenship*. Cambridge: Cambridge University Press.

Krizsán, A., & Zentai, V. (2003). Policy Frames and Implementation Problems: The Case of Gender Mainstreaming. State of the Art and Mapping of Competences in Hungary, www.mageeq.net/docs/hungary.pdf, accessed 12 April 2004.

Krizsán, A., & Zentai, V. (2006). 'Gender Equality Policy or Gender Mainstreaming? The Case of Hungary on the Road to an Enlarged Europe.' *Policy Studies*, 27(2), 135–151.

Kymlicka, W., & Norman, W. (1994). 'Return of the Citizen: A Survey of Recent Work on Citizenship Theory.' *Ethics*, 102(2), 352–381.

LAG AzuP (2005). '"Kann ich mir dieses Buch noch leisten oder kaufe ich bei Aldi lieber Winterschuhe?" Einblicke in die Grundstimmung von Betroffenen', in H. Baumeister, U. Gransee & K.-D. Zimmermann (eds), *Die Hartz-'Reformen'. Die Folgen von Hartz I–IV für ArbeitnehmerInnen. Ein Projekt der Arbeitnehmerkammer Bremen und des DGB-Bezirks Niedersachsen – Bremen – Sachsen-Anhalt*. Hamburg: VSA-Verlag.

Larsen, T. P., & Daguerre, A. (2003). UK Policy Maps. *WRAMSOC Working Paper*, www.kent.ac.uk/wramsoc/workingpapers/secondyearsreports/policymaps/ukpolicymap.pdf, accessed 20 January 2006.

Lascoume, P., & Le Galès, P. (2007). 'Introduction: Understanding Public Policy through its Instruments from the Nature of Instruments to the Sociology of Public Policy Instrumentation.' *Governance*, 20, 1–21.

Leibfried, S. (2005). 'Social Policy. Left to the Judges and the Markets?' In H. Wallace, W. Wallace & M. A. Pollack (eds), *Policy-Making in the European Union* (5th edn).

Oxford: Oxford University Press.

Leibfried, S., & Pierson, P. (eds). (1995). *European Social Policy: Between Fragmentation and Integration*. Washington DC: The Brookings Institution.

Leitch, S. (2006). *Prosperity for all in the Global Economy – World Class Skills*. London.

Leschke, J., Schmid, G., & Griga, D. (2006). On the Marriage of Flexibility and Security: Lessons from the Hartz-Reforms in Germany. *WZB Discussion Paper, SP I 2006-108*, http://skylla.wz-berlin.de/pdf/2006/i06-108.pdf, accessed 26 October 2006.

Lewis, J. (2001). 'The Decline of the Male Breadwinner Model: Implications for Work and Care'. *Social Politics: International Studies in Gender, State & Society*, 8(2), 152–169.

Lewis, J. (2004). 'Auf dem Weg zur "Zwei-Erwerbstätigen"-Familie', in S. Leitner, I. Ostner & M. Schratzenstaller (eds), *Wohlfahrtsstaat und Geschlechterverhältnis im Umbruch*. Wiesbaden: VS Verlag für Sozialwissenschaft.

Lewis, J., & Giullari, S. (2005). 'The Adult Worker Model Family, Gender Equality and Care: the Search for new Policy Principles and the Possibilities and Problems of a Capabilities Approach'. *Economy and Society*, 34(1), 76–104.

Lewis, J., & Ostner, I. (1995). 'Gender and the Evolution of European Social Policy', in S. Leibfried & P. Pierson (eds), *European Social Policy. Between Fragmentation and Integration*. Washington DC: The Brookings Institution.

Lister, R. (2003a). *Citizenship: Feminist Perspectives* (2nd edn). Basingstoke: Palgrave Macmillan.

Lister, R. (2003b). 'Investing in the Citizen-Workers of the Future: Transformations in Citizenship and the State under New Labour'. *Social Policy and Administration*, 37(5), 427–443.

Lister, R. (2004). 'A Politics of Recognition and Respect: Involving People with Experience of Poverty in Decision-Making that Affects their Lives', in J. Andersen & B. Siim (eds), *The Politics of Inclusion and Empowerment. Gender, Class and Citizenship*. Basingstoke & New York: Palgrave Macmillan.

Lister, R. (2006). 'Children (but not Women) First: New Labour, Child Welfare and Gender'. *Critical Social Policy*, 26(2), 315–335.

Lister, R. (2007). 'From Object to Subject: Including Marginalised Citizens in Policy Making'. *Policy and Politics*, 35(3), 437–455.

Maas, W. (2007). *Creating European Citizens*. Lanham, MD: Rowman & Littlefield.

Magnette, P. (2003). 'European Governance and Civic Participation: Beyond Elitist Citizenship?'. *Political Studies*, 51(1), 144–160.

Magnusson, L., Mosesdottir, L., & Serrano Pascual, A. (2003a). 'Gender Mainstreaming and Equal Pay in the European Employment Strategy', in L. Magnusson, L. Mosesdottir & A. Serrano Pascual (eds), *Equal Pay and Gender Mainstreaming in the European Employment Strategy*. Brussels: ETUI.

Magnusson, L., Mosesdottir, L., & Serrano Pascual, A. (eds). (2003b). *Equal Pay and Gender Mainstreaming in the European Employment Strategy*. Brussels: ETUI.

Magnusson, L., & Strath, B. (eds). (2004). *A European Social Citizenship? Preconditions for Future Policies from a Historical Perspective*. Brussels: P.I.E. Peter Lang.

Maier, F. (2000a). Gender Impact Assessment & the Employment Strategy in Germany, www.mbs.ac.uk/research/european-employment/projects/gender-social-inclusion/documents/GIA_Germany.pdf, accessed 24 November 2006.

Maier, F. (2000b). German National Employment Action Plan: Expert Evaluation, www.mbs.ac.uk/research/european-employment/projects/gender-social-inclusion/documents/G_NAPev.pdf, accessed 24 November 2006.

Maier, F. (2001). Gender Equality and the European Employment Strategy. Evaluation of the 2001 German National Action Plan for Employment, 31 May, www.mbs.ac.uk/research/european-employment/projects/gender-social-inclusion/documents/DE2001.pdf, accessed 15 November 2006.

Maier, F. (2003, 31.05.2001). Assessment of the National Action Plans for Employment from a Gender Perspective. Germany 2003, 31 May, www.mbs.ac.uk/research/european-employment/projects/gender-social-inclusion/documents/NAP2003_DE.pdf, accessed 15 November 2006.

Mann, M. (1987). 'Ruling Class Strategies and Citizenship.' *Sociology*, 21(3), 339–354.

Marinetto, M. (2003). 'Who Wants to be an Active Citizen? The Politics and Practice of Community Involvement.' *Sociology*, 37(1), 103–120.

Marshall, T. H. (1992). 'Citizenship and Social Class', in T. H. Marshall & T. Bottomore (eds), *Citizenship and Social Class*. London: Pluto Press.

Mather, J. D. (2005). 'The Court of Justice and the Union Citizen.' *European Law Journal*, 11(6), 722–743.

Meehan, E. R. (1993). *Citizenship and the European Union*. London: Sage.

Mehta, L. (2005). 'Citizenship and the Right to Water: Lessons from South-Africa's Free Basic Water Policy', in N. Kabeer (ed.), *Inclusive Citizenship: Meanings and Expressions*. London and New York: Zed Books.

Miller, D. (2000). *Citizenship and National Identity*. Oxford: Polity Press.

Mills, J., Bonner, A., & Francis, K. (2006). The Development of Constructivist Grounded Theory. *International Journal of Qualitative Methods*, 5(1), www.ualberta.ca/~iiqm/backissues/5_1/PDF/MILLS.PDF, accessed 28 October 2006.

Misa, T., Schot, J., & Rip, A. (eds) (1995). *Managing Technology in Society: the Approach of Constructive Technology Assessment*. London: Pinter.

Montgomery, K. A. (2003). 'Introduction', in R. E. Matland & K. A. Montgomery (eds), *Women's Access to Political Power in Post-Communist Europe*. New York: Oxford University Press.

Mosesdottir, L. (2001). 'The Case of Sweden', in U. Behning & A. Serrano Pascual (eds), *Gender Mainstreaming in the European Employment Strategy*. Brussels: ETUI.

Münch, R. (2001). *Nation and Citizenship in the Global Age*. Basingstoke: Palgrave.

Nagy, B. (2004). Assessment of the 2004 National Action Plan for Employment from a Gender Perspective. Hungary, http://ec.europa.eu/employment_social/gender_equality/docs/2005/hungary-napemp_en.pdf, accessed 21 November 2006.

NANE, & HCWG (2002). Shadow Report, The Joint Report of the Women Against Violence (NANE) Association and the Habeas CorpusWorking Group (HCWG) on the Realization of the Convention on the Elimination of All Forms of Discrimination AgainstWomen in Hungary incorporated with the Critical Examination of the Report of the Hungarian Government Presented at the 2002 August Session of the CEDAW Committee of the UN 4 August 2002, http://hc.netstudio.hu/allaspont/report/cedaw.shadow.report.pdf, accessed 30 May 2006.

Naumann, I. K. (2005). 'Child Care and Feminism in West Germany and Sweden in the 1960s and 1970s.' *Journal of European Social Policy*, 15(1), 47–63.

Newman, J. (2005a). 'Introduction', in J. Newman (ed.), *Remaking Governance. Peoples, Politics and the Public Sphere*. Bristol: Policy Press.

Newman, J. (2005b). 'Participative Governance and the Remaking of the Public Sphere', in J. Newman (ed.), *Remaking Governance. Peoples, Politics and the Public Sphere*. Bristol: Policy Press.

Noaksson, N., & Jacobsson, K. (2003). The Production of Ideas and Expert Knowledge in OECD. The OECD Jobs Strategy in Contrast with the EU Employment Strategy. *Score Rapportserie*, 2003(7), www.score.su.se/pdfs/2003–7.pdf#search=%22score %20noaksson%20jacobsson%22, accessed 3 October 2006.

Nowotny, H., Gibbons, M., & Scott, P. (2001). *Re-Thinking Science. Knowledge and the Public in an Age of Uncertainty.* Cambridge: Polity Press.

Offe, C. (2008). 'Governance – "Empty Signifier" oder sozialwissenschaftliches Forschungsprogramm?'. *Politische Vierteljahresschrift – Sonderheft*, 41, 61–76.

Ohmae, K. (1995). *The End of the Nation State: The Rise of Regional Economies.* London: Harper Collins.

Okin, S. M. (1998). 'Gender, the Public and the Private', in A. Phillips (ed.), *Feminism and Politics.* Oxford: Oxford University Press.

Olsen, E. D. H. (2008). 'The Origins of European Citizenship in the First Two Decades of European Integration.' *Journal of European Public Policy*, 15(1), 40 – 57.

Open Society Institute (2005). *Equal Opportunities for Women and Men: Monitoring Law and Practice in New Member States and Accession Countries of the European Union.* Budapest: Open Society Institute – Network Women's Program.

OPTEM (2002). Study on Integrating Gender Mainstreaming into Employment Policies Covering Public-Authority Officials Responsible for Employment Policies and Social Partners in the 15 Member States of the European Union. Final Report, http://ec.europa.eu/employment_social/employment_strategy/eval/survey/ survey_gender_en.pdf, accessed 7 November 2006.

Oschmiansky, F. (2003). 'Faule Arbeitslose? Zur Debatte über Arbeitsunwilligkeit und Leistungsmissbrauch.' *Aus Politik und Zeitgeschichte*, B 06–07, 10–16.

Oschmiansky, F. (2004). 'Reform der Arbeitsvermittlung (Erhoehung der Geschwindigkeit einschliesslich neue Zumutbarkeit und PSA)', in W. Jann & G. Schmid (eds), *Eins zu Eins? Eine Zwischenbilanz der Hartz Reformen am Artbeitsmarkt.* Berlin: Edition Sigma.

Pateman, C. (1970). *Participation and Democratic Theory.* Cambridge: Cambridge University Press.

Pateman, C. (1989). *The Disorder of Women.* Stanford, CA: Stanford University Press.

Peters, M., Dorenbos, R., van der Ende, M., Versantvoort, M., & Arents, M. (2004). *Benefit Systems and their Interaction with Active Labour Market Policies. Final Report.* Brussels: DG Employment, Social Affairs and Equal Opportunities.

Pfister, T. (2005). 'Citizenship and Globalization.' *Ethnopolitics*, 4(1), 105–113.

Pfister, T. (2008). 'Mainstreamed away? Assessing the Gender Equality Dimension of the European Employment Strategy.' *Policy & Politics*, 36(4), 521–538.

Pfister, T. (2009). 'Governing the Knowledge Society. Studying Lisbon as Epistemic Setting', in: Kröger, Sandra (ed.), What Have we Learnt: Advances, Pitfalls and Remaining Questions of OMC Research. *European Integration Online Papers, special issue 1* (13), http://eiop.or.at/eiop/index.php/eiop/article/view/2009_006a/114, accessed 14 January 2009.

Phillips, A. (1991). *Engendering Democracy.* Cambridge, Oxford: Polity Press.

Phillips, A. (1993). *Democracy and Difference.* Cambridge, Oxford: Polity Press.

Pollert, A. (2003). 'Women, Work and Equal Opportunities in Post-Communist Transition.' *Work, Employment and Society*, 17(2), 331–357.

Pollert, A. (2005). 'Gender, Transformation and Employment in Central Eastern Europe.' *European Journal of Industrial Relations*, 11(2), 213–230.

Pollert, A., & Fodor, E. (2005). *Working Conditions and Gender in an Enlarged Europe.*

Dublin: European Foundation for the Improvement of Living and Working Conditions.

Preuss, U. K. (1995a). 'Citizenship and Identity: Aspects of a Political Theory of Citizenship', in R. Bellamy, V. Bufacchi & D. Castiglione (eds), *Democracy and Constitutional Culture in the Union of Europe*. London: Lothian Foundation Press.

Preuss, U. K. (1995b). 'Problems of a Concept of European Citizenship.' *European Law Journal*, 3(1), 267–281.

Prime Minister's Delivery Unit (2006). Capability Review of the Department for Work and Pensions. *Civil Service Capability Reviews*, www.civilservice.gov.uk/reform/capability_reviews/publications/pdf/Capability_Review_DWP.pdf, accessed 4 December 2006.

Prospect (2006a). Cadman Union Lines up New Tribunal Cases, www.prospect.org.uk/news/newsstory.php?news=380, accessed 13 December 2006.

Prospect (2006b). Prospect Victory in European Landmark Pay Claim *News*, www.prospect.org.uk/news/newsstory.php?news=379, accessed 13 December 2006.

Reihs, S. (2005). 'Hartz-Reformen am Arbeitsmarkt und Gender-Mainstreaming – eine schwierige Beziehung?!' Paper presented at *'Damit Sie auch morgen noch kraftvoll zubeißen können!' Gesundheit, Arbeit, Rente – Sozialpolitik aus Frauensicht*, 24 February. Bad Boll.

Rhodes, M. (1995). 'A Regulatory Conundrum: Industrial Relations and the Social Dimension', in S. Leibfried & P. Pierson (eds), *European Social Policy. Between Fragmentation and Integration*. Washington DC: The Brookings Institution.

Rhodes, M. (2005). 'Employment Policies', in H. Wallace, W. Wallace & M. A. Pollack (eds), *Policy-Making in the European Union* (5th edn). Oxford: Oxford University Press.

Rosenberg, D. (1991). 'Shock Therapy: GDR Women in Transition from a Socialist Welfare State to a Social Market Economy.' *Signs*, 17(1), 129–151.

Rosenfeld, R. A., Trappe, H., & Gornick, J. C. (2004). 'Gender and Work in Germany: Before and After Reunification.' *Annual Review of Sociology*, 30, 103–124.

Rowe, G., Marsh, R., & Frewer, L. J. (2004). 'Evaluation of a Deliberative Conference.' *Science Technology Human Values*, 29(1), 88–121.

Rubery, J. (2000). Evaluation of UK National Action Plan: A Gender Equality Perspective, www.mbs.ac.uk/research/european-employment/projects/gender-social-inclusion/documents/UK_NAPev.pdf, accessed 6 December 2006.

Rubery, J. (2001). Evaluation of the UK National Action Plan 2001: A Gender Equality Perspective, www.mbs.ac.uk/research/european-employment/projects/gender-social-inclusion/documents/UK2001.pdf, accessed 21 November 2006.

Rubery, J. (2002). 'Gender Mainstreaming and Gender Equality in the EU: the Impact of the EU Employment Strategy', in*dustrial Relations Journal*, 33(5), 500–522.

Rubery, J. (2003). Gender Mainstreaming and Gender Equality in the UK National Action Plan on Employment. *Assessment of the National Action Plans for Employment from a Gender Perspective*, www.mbs.ac.uk/research/european-employment/projects/gender-social-inclusion/documents/NAP2003_UK.pdf, accessed 21 November 2006.

Rubery, J. (2004). Gender Mainstreaming and Gender Equality in the UK National Action Plan on Employment. *Assessment of the 2004 National Action Plan for Employment from a Gender Perspective*, http://ec.europa.eu/employment_social/gender_equality/docs/2005/uk-napemp_en.pdf, accessed 21 November 2006.

Rubery, J., & Grimshaw, D. (2001). *The Gender Pay Gap: a Research Review*. Manchester: Equal Opportunities Commission.

Rubery, J., Grimshaw, D., Fagan, C., Figueiredo, H., & Smith, M. (2003). 'Gender Equality still on the European Agenda – but for how Long?'. *Industrial Relations Journal*, 34(5), 477–497.

Rubery, J., Grimshaw, D., Figueiredo, H., Smith, M., & Donnelly, R. (2005). The National Reform Programme 2005 and the Gender Aspects of the European Employment Strategy. The Co-ordinators' Synthesis Report Prepared for the Equality Unit, European Commission, http://ec.europa.eu/employment_social/gender_equality/docs/2006/final_nrp_synthesis_2005_en.pdf, accessed 21 November 2006.

Sabel, C. F., & Zeitlin, J. (2007). Learning from Difference: The New Architecture of Experimentalist Governance in the European Union. *European Governance Papers (EUROGOV)*, No. C-07-02, www.connex-network.org/eurogov/pdf/egp-connex-C-07-02.pdf, accessed 3 March 2008.

Schmid, G. (2003). 'Moderne Dienstleistungen am Arbeitsmarkt: Strategie und Vorschläge der Hartz-Kommission.' *Aus Politik und Zeitgeschichte*, 06–07, 3–6.

Sedelmeier, U. (2009). 'Post-accession Compliance with EU Gender Equality Legislation in post-communist new member States.' *European Integration Online Papers*, 13(2).

Serrano Pascual, A. (2007). 'Reshaping Welfare States: Activation Regimes in Europe', in A. Serrano Pascual & L. Magnusson (eds), *Reshaping Welfare States and Activation Regimes in Europe*. Brussels: PIE Peter Lang.

Serrano Pascual, A., & Crespo Suarez, E. (2007a). 'The Government of Activation Policies by EU Institutions', *international Journal of Sociology and Social Policy*, 27(9–10), 376–386.

Serrano Pascual, A., & Crespo Suarez, E. (2007b). 'Political Production of Individualised Subjects in the Paradoxical Discourse of the EU Institutions', in R. van Berkel & B. Valkenburg (eds), *Making it Personal. Individualising Activation Services in the EU*. Bristol: Policy Press.

Shaw, J. (1997). 'The Many Pasts and Futures of Citizenship in the European Union.' *European Law Review*, 22(6), 554–572.

Shaw, J. (1998). 'The Interpretation of European Union Citizenship.' *Modern Law Review*, 61(3), 293–317.

Shaw, J. (2002). 'The European Union and Gender Mainstreaming: Constitutionally Embedded or Comprehensively Marginalised?'. *Feminist Legal Studies*, 10(3), 213–226.

Shaw, J. (2007). *The Transformation of Citizenship in the European Union: Electoral Rights and the Restructuring of Political Space*. Cambridge: Cambridge University Press.

Shaw, J., & Wiener, A. (1999). The Paradox of the 'European' Polity. *Jean Monnet Working Paper,* 10/99, www.jeanmonnetprogram.org/papers/99/991001.html, 20 September 2004.

Siim, B. (2000). *Gender and Citizenship. Politics and Agency in France, Britain and Denmark*. Cambridge: Cambridge University Press.

Sloat, A. (2004). Legislating for Equality: The Implementation of the EU Equality Acquis in Central and Eastern Europe. *Jean Monnet Working Paper*, 08/04, www.jeanmonnetprogram.org/papers/04/040801.pdf, accessed 12 November 2005.

Soysal, Y. N. (1994). *Limits of Citizenship: Migrants and Postnational Membership in Europe*. Chicago: University of Chicago Press.

SPD, & Bündnis 90/Die Grünen (1998). *Aufbruch und Erneuerung – Deutschlands Weg ins 21. Jahrhundert, Koalitionsvereinbarung zwischen der Sozialdemokratischen Partei Deutschlands und Bündnis 90/Die GRÜNEN.* 20 October. Bonn.

SPD, & Bündnis 90/Die Grünen (2002). *Erneuerung – Gerechtigkeit – Nachhaltigkeit. Für ein wirtschaftlich starkes, soziales und ökologisches Deutschland. Für eine lebendige Demokratie.* 16 October. Berlin.

Squires, J. (2005). 'Is Mainstreaming Transformative? Theorising Mainstreaming in the Context of Diversity and Deliberation.' *Social Politics: International Studies in Gender, State & Society,* 12(3), 366–388.

Strauss, A., & Corbin, J. (1998). *Basics of Qualitative Research. Techniques and Procedures for Developing Grounded Theory* (2nd edn). Thousand Oaks, CA: SAGE.

Streeck, W. (1995). 'From Market Making to State Building? Reflections on the Political Economy of European Social Policy', in S. Leibfried & P. Pierson (eds), *European Social Policy. Between Fragmentation and Integration.* Washington DC: The Brookings Institution.

Streeck, W. (2003). No Longer the Century of Corporatism. Das Ende des "Bündnisses für Arbeit". *MPIfG Working Paper,* 03(4), www.mpi-fg-koeln.mpg.de/pu/workpap/wp03-4/wp03-4.html, accessed 18 November 2006.

Szabo, S. (2003). *Gender Assessment of the Impact of EU Accession on the Status of Women in the Labour Market in CEE. National Study: Hungary.* Budapest: Social Innovation Foundation.

Taux, E. (2005). '"Arbeit wird billig wie Dreck" Gegen Ausgrenzung, Vereinzelung und Verschlechterung der Lebensverhältnisse', in H. Baumeister, U. Gransee & K.-D. Zimmermann (eds), *Die Hartz-'Reformen'. Die Folgen von Hartz I–IV für ArbeitnehmerInnen. Ein Projekt der Arbeitnehmerkammer Bremen und des DGB-Bezirks Niedersachsen – Bremen – Sachsen-Anhalt.* Hamburg: VSA-Verlag.

Taylor-Gooby, P., & Daguerre, A. (2002). Welfare Reform in the UK. 1985–2002. *WRAMSOC Working Paper,* www.kent.ac.uk/wramsoc/workingpapers/firstyearreports/nationalreports/ukcountryreport.pdf, accessed 20 January 2006.

Taylor-Gooby, P., Larsen, T., & Kananen, J. (2004). 'Market Means and Welfare Ends: The UK Welfare State Experiment.' *Journal of Social Policy,* 33, 573–592.

Therborn, G. (1977). 'The Rule of Capital and the Rise of Democracy.' *New Left Review,* 103, 3–41.

Thompson, M., Vinter, L., & Young, V. (2005). *Dads and their Babies: Leave Arrangements in the First Year* (no. 37). London, Manchester: Equal Opportunities Commission/NOP World.

Tilly, C. (1999). 'Conclusion: Why Worry about Citizenship?' In M. Hanagan & C. Tilly (eds), *Extending Citizenship, Reconfiguring States.* Lanham, MD: Rowman & Littlefield.

Tilly, C. (ed.). (1975). *The Formation of Nation States in Western Europe.* Princeton, NJ: Princeton University Press.

Titscher, S., Meyer, M., Wodak, R., & Vetter, E. (2000). *Methods of Text and Discourse Analysis. In Search of Meaning.* London: Sage.

Trube, A. (2005). '"Besser irgendeine Arbeit als keine Arbeit" – Kritik einer qualitätsblinden Arbeitsmarkt- und Sozialpolitik.' *WSI-Mitteilungen,* 58(4), 1–8.

Trubek, D. M., & Zeitlin, J. (eds). (2003). *Governing Work and Welfare in the New Economy: European and American Experiments.* Oxford: Oxford University Press.

TUC (2006). *Low Pay Commission Review 2006. The TUC Evidence.* London: TUC.

Tully, J. (1995). *Strange Multiplicity: Constitutionalism in an Age of Diversity*. Cambridge: Cambridge University Press.

Turner, B. S. (1990). 'Outline of a Theory of Citizenship.' *Sociology*, 24(2), 189–217.

Turner, B. S. (1994). 'Postmodern Culture/Modern Citizen', in B. van Steenbergen (ed.), *The Condition of Citizenship*. London: Sage.

United Kingdom (1998). *Employment Action Plan*.

United Kingdom (1999). *Employment Action Plan*.

United Kingdom (2000). *UK Employment Action Plan for 2000*.

United Kingdom (2002). *UK Employment Action Plan 2002*.

United Kingdom (2003). *United Kingdom Employment Action Plan 2003*.

United Kingdom (2004). *UK National Action Plan for Employment 2004*.

United Kingdom (2005). *Lisbon Strategy for Growth and Jobs. UK National Reform Programme 2005*. London.

United Kingdom (2006). *Lisbon Strategy for Growth and Jobs. UK National Reform Programme – Update on Progress*. London: HM Treasury.

United Kingdom (2007). *Lisbon Strategy for Growth and Jobs. UK National Reform Programme – Update on Progress*. London: HM Treasury.

United Kingdom (2008). *Lisbon Strategy for Growth and Jobs. UK National Reform Programme*. London: HM Treasury.

United Kingdom (2009). *Lisbon Strategy for Growth and Jobs. UK National Reform Programme 2009*. London: HM Treasury.

United Nations (1995). *Report of the Fourth World Conference on Women. Beijing, 4–15 September 1995*. A/CONF.177/20. 17 October. Beijing.

United Nations (2002). *Report of the Committee on the Elimination of Discrimination against Women, Twenty-sixth session (14 January–1 February 2002); Twenty-seventh session (3–21 June 2002); Exceptional session (5–23 August 2002);*. A/57/38. New York.

Valkenburg, B. (2007). 'Individualising Activation Services: Thrashing out an Ambigious Concept', in R. van Berkel & B. Valkenburg (eds), *Making it Personal: Individualising Activation Services in the EU*. Bristol: Policy Press.

van Berkel, R., & Møller, I. H. (2002a). 'The Concept of Activation', in R. Van Berkel & I. H. Møller (eds), *Active Social Policies in the EU. Inclusion through Participation?* Bristol: Policy Press.

van Berkel, R., & Møller, I. H. (2002b). 'Introduction', in R. Van Berkel & I. H. Møller (eds), *Active Social Policies in the EU. Inclusion through Participation?* Bristol: Policy Press.

van Berkel, R., & Roche, M. (2002). 'Activation Policies as Reflexive Social Policies', in R. Van Berkel & I. H. Møller (eds), *Active Social Policies in the EU. Inclusion through Participation?* Bristol: Policy Press.

van Berkel, R., & Valkenburg, B. (2007). 'Introduction: The Individualisation of Activation Services in Context', in R. van Berkel & B. Valkenburg (eds), *Making it Personal: Individualising Activation Services in the EU*. Bristol: Policy Press.

Vandenberg, A. (2000). 'Contesting Citizenship and Democracy in a Global Era', in A. Vandenberg (ed.), *Citizenship and Democracy in a Global Era*. Basingstoke: Macmillan.

van Dijk, T. A. (1993). 'Principles of Critical Discourse Analysis.' *Discourse & Society*, 4(2), 249–283.

van Dijk, T. A. (1997). 'Discourse as Interaction in Society', in T. A. van Dijk (ed.), *Discourse as Social Interaction (= Discourse Studies: A Multidisciplinary Introduction,*

Vol. II). London: SAGE.

van Dijk, T. A. (2001). 'Critical Discourse Analysis', in D. Schiffrin, D. Tannen & H. E. Hamilton (eds), *The Handbook of Discourse Analysis.* Oxford: Blackwell.

Verloo, M., Maratou-Alipranti, L., Tertinegg, K., & van Beveren, J. (2005). 'Framing the Organisation of Intimacy as a Policy Problem across Europe.' *The Greek Review of Social Research*, 117(B), 119–147.

Vincent-Jones, P. (2000). 'Contractual Governance: Institutional and Organizational Analysis.' *Oxford Journal of Legal Studies*, 20(3), 317–351.

Voet, R. (1998). *Feminism and Citizenship.* London: Sage.

Vogel, B. (1999). 'Arbeitslosigkeit in Ostdeutschland. Konsequenzen für das Sozialgefüge und für die Wahrnehmung des gesellschaftlichen Wandels.' *SOFI Mitteilungen*, 27(1999).

Walters, W. (2004). 'Some Critical Notes on "Governance".' *Studies in Political Economy*, 73 (spring/summer), 27–46.

White, S. (2004). 'Welfare Philosophy and the Third Way', in J. Lewis & R. Surender (eds), *Welfare State Change. Towards a Third Way?* Oxford: Oxford University Press.

Wiener, A. (1997). Accessing the Constructive Potential of Union Citizenship. *European Integration Online Papers*, 1/17, 23 September, http://eiop.or.at/eiop/texte/1997-017a.htm, accessed 11 December 2006.

Wiener, A. (1998). *European Citizenship Practice. Building Institutions of a Nonstate.* Boulder, CO and Oxford: Westview.

Wiener, A. (2003). 'Citizenship', in M. Cini (ed.), *European Union Politics.* Oxford: Oxford University Press.

Wiener, A. (2005). 'Bürgerschaft in neuen Grenzen: Zur sozialen Konstitution politischer Ordnung in Europa', in H. Huget, C. Kambas & W. Klein (eds), *Grenzüberschreitungen. Differenz und Identität im Europa der Gegenwart.* Wiesbaden: VS Verlag für Sozialwissenschaften.

Wodak, R. (2003). 'Critical Discourse Analysis', in C. Seale, *et al.* (eds), *Qualitative Research Practice.* London: SAGE.

Wodak, R., & Meyer, M. (eds). (2001). *Methods of Critical Discourse Analysis.* London: Sage.

Women and Equality Unit (1998). Policy Appraisal for Equal Treatment, www.womenandequalityunit.gov.uk/archive/gender_mainstreaming/equal.htm, accessed 6 December 2006.

Women and Work Commission (2005). *A Fair Deal for Women in the Workplace. An Interim Statement.* London: Women and Equality Unit.

Women and Work Commission (2006). *Shaping a Fairer Future, Report Presented to the Prime Minister by Baroness Prosser of Battersea*, February 2006. London.

Work and Pensions Committee (2006a). *The Efficiency Savings Programme in Jobcentre Plus. Volume I. Report, together with Formal Minutes, Second Report of Session 2005–06.* HC 834-I. 18 March. London.

Work and Pensions Committee (2006b). *The Efficiency Savings Programme in Jobcentre Plus: Government Response to the Committee's Second Report of Session 2005–06, Second Special Report of Session 2005–06.* HC 1187. 15 June. London.

Yaxley, D., Vinter, L., & Young, V. (2005). *Dads and their Babies: The Mothers' Perspective* (no. 41). London, Manchester: Equal Opportunities Commission/NOP World.

Yeatman, A. (1995). 'Interpreting Contemporary Contractualism', in J. Boston (ed.), *The State under Contract.* Wellington, New Zealand: Bridget Williams Books.

Yeatman, A. (1997). 'Contract, Status and Personhood', in G. Davis (ed.), *The New Contractualism*. Basingstoke: Palgrave Macmillan.

Young, I. M. (1989). 'Polity and Group Differences: A Critique of the Ideal of Universal Citizenship.' *Ethics*, 99(2), 250–274.

Young, I. M. (1990). *Justice and the Politics of Difference*. Princeton, NJ: Princeton University Press.

Zeitlin, J. (2003). 'Introduction. Governing Work and Welfare in a New Economy: European and American Experiments', in J. Zeitlin & D. M. Trubek (eds), *Governing Work and Welfare in the New Economy: European and American Experiments*. Oxford: Oxford University Press.

Zeitlin, J. (2005a). 'Introduction: The Open Method of Coordination in Action', in J. Zeitlin & P. Pochet (eds), *The Open Method of Co-ordination in Action: The European Employment and Social Inclusion Strategies*. Brussels: P.I.E. Peter Lang.

Zeitlin, J. (2005b). Social Europe and Experimentalist Governance: Towards a New Constitutional Compromise? *European Governance Papers (EUROGOV), No. C-05-04*. www.connex-network.org/eurogov/pdf/egp-connex-C-05-04.pdf, accessed 8 January 2005.

Note: page numbers in *italics* refer to illustrations

access to societal resources 4, 13, *22*, 23, 26,
    47–8, 64, 96–7, 101
   promise 14, 24, 91, 98
activating welfare state 1–2, 8, 78, 95–7, 100
active labour market policies 38, 82, 97–8,
    104
Act on Equal Treatment and Promotion of
    Equal Opportunities 81–2, 84, 86–9, 94
adult worker model 2, 20, 57, 71, 93–4, 97
   socialist adult worker model 41, 75, 100
   see also gender contract; gender norms;
    male breadwinner/female caregiver
    model
affirmative action *see* positive action
Agenda 2010 45, 52
Alliance for Jobs 42, 44–5, 53
ambivalence 5, 24, 49, 66, 86, 97, 107, 110
Amsterdam Treaty 10–11, 28, 30, *34*, 79, 82
anti-discrimination 25, 55, 77, 79–81, 86–9

BA *see* Federal Employment Service
belonging 21–3
   see also identity
benefit 8, 12, 23, 46–9, 51, 53–4, 58–60, 62,
    64–5, 75, 83–5, 92, 96, 98–100
BEPGs *see* Broad Economic Policy
    Guidelines
Blair, Tony 57–8, 60, 70–1
Bokros, Lajos 75
Broad Economic Policy Guidelines 10, 33, 38
Brown, Gordon 57–8, 60, 71

Cameron, David 71
categories 91, 95, 101, 103–5
CEDAW *see* Convention/Committee on the
    Elimination of Discrimination against
    Women
Childcare strategy (UK) 61–2, 64, 71
Citizenship of the European Union 2, 21,
    24–6, 107, 110n2
citizenship perspective 2, 4–6, 8, 10, 13, 16,
    24, 29, 47, 89, 109
citizenship practices 3, 13–14, 21, 23–6, 46,
    64–5, 74, 85, 89, 95, 101, 103, 107, 109,
    110n2
citizen-worker 68, 101
competitiveness 7, 11, 27, 53, 61, 70, 97, 102
conceptual debate
   concepts 5, 11–14, 18, 23, 25, 36, 48, 54,
    58, 86, 91–2, 95, 103–6
   discursive mechanisms 104
   ontological issues 23, 100, 102, 104
   transformation 8, 14, 33, *34*, 35, 55, 95
   transnational 1, 5, 8, 14, 91, 101, 107, 109
conflicts 44, 56, 92–4, 103–4
Conservatives (UK) 57, 59, 64, 71
contractualisation 98–101
control 8, 12, 23–4, 47, 65, 68, 108
   see also discipline
Convention/Committee on the Elimination
    of Discrimination against Women
    77–8, 80, 88, 108
Copenhagen criteria 78

DGB *see* German Trade Union Federation
difference 18, 20
Directorate for Equal Opportunities 79
discipline 7–8, 14, 24, 47, 51, 64–5, 96–7,
    101, 108
diversity 4, 16, 20, 23, 68, 73, 92, 108
   see also difference
duties
   differentiated 64–5, 71, 98
   individualised 14, 91, 99–101
   new 24, 64, 96, 101
   to work 26n5, 48, 64, 95–6

East Germany 41, 100
ECJ *see* European Court of Justice
economic citizenship 29, 45, 67, 76, 85–6,
    101
education 6, 14, 20, 23, 29, 42–3, 45, 47,
    58–9, 61, 64, 67, 77, 93, 95, 98, 106
   early childhood 59, 61, 97
   see also skills
EES *see* European Employment Strategy

EHRC *see* Equality and Human Rights
    Commission
employability 38, 40, 54–5, 58, 104
employment growth 29–30, 32, *34*, 65, 92,
    94–5
employment rate 3–4, 8, 19, 47, 67, 74, 84–5,
    90, 103, 105
    female 30–1, *34*, 39, 40n2, 51, 86
Employment Taskforce *34*, 36–8, 70
empowerment 8, 12, 23–4, 51, 68
Equality and Human Rights Commission 69
Equal Opportunities Commission 68–9,
    72n3
Equal Pay Act 63, 66–7
Equal Treatment Act *see* Act on Equal
    Treatment and Promotion of Equal
    Opportunities
Equal Treatment Authority 81, 84, 86, 88,
essential contestedness 3, 17–18, 20, 48
EU *see* European Union
EU citizenship *see* Citizenship of the
    European Union
European Council 10, 28, 31–2, *34*, 36–9,
    78–80
European Court of Justice 25, 27–8, 56, 69,
    79
European Employment Strategy
    EMCO *see* Employment Committee
    Employment Committee 54–5, 56n5, 82
    gender equality dimension 2, 5, 27–9, 32,
        35–6, 40, 45, 86, 91, 94, 97, 102, 104–7,
        109
    guidelines 11, 28–31, 33, *34*, 36, 38–9, 49,
        51, 63, 82
    recommendations 11, 25, 29, 31, *35*, 38–9,
        49–51, 66–7, 69, 82, 86–7, 101
European Pact for Gender Equality 39
European Union
    accession 78–9, 81–2, 84, 86–7, 94
    citizenship *see* Citizenship of the
        European Union
    enlargement 4, 30, 73–4, 78
    membership 77, 79, 89
exclusion 1–2, 4–5, 10, 13–14, 16, 22–3, 29,
    52–3, 56, 65, 84, 90, 97, 101, 103, 105–8
    from full citizenship 2, 19–20, 24
    social exclusion 53, 99,
    see also inequality

family policy 14, 23, 30, 41, 48, 53, 55, 61–2,
    76, 87, 92, 94, 98
fathers 46, 62
Fawcett Society 67

Federal Employment Service 43–4, 46, 52, 54
feminism 16, 18–19, 29, 88–9
feminist movement *see* feminism
Fiatal Demokraták Szövetsége 76–8, 81–2,
    87
FIDESZ *see* Fiatal Demokraták Szövetsége
flexibility 7, 9, 11, 29, 37–8, 48, 51, 53–4, 57,
    68, 70, 75, 83–4, 92–4, 106
    see also competitiveness; responsibility
future 6–7, 31, 37, 59, 61–3, 68, 70, 95, 97,
    108

gender contract 2, 4, 19, 22, 24, 71
gender equality
    fragility 36, 105
    functional requirement 5, 14, *34*, 65
    human right 5, 14, 35, 39, 55, 80, 87–8, 93,
        97, 102, 106
    quantitative *34*, 84, 87, 92, 97, 105
Gender Equality Duty 63, 65, 93
gender gaps 3, 30, 33, 37, 40n3
    gender pay gap 19, 30–1, 39, 40n3, 49–50,
        63–4, 66–7, 98, 104, 106
gender mainstreaming 25, 26n8, 30–5,
    37, 39, 40n2, 43–5, 52, 55, 63, 68, 71,
    78–82, 84, 86–9, 94, 104–6
gender norms 20, 53, 57, 73, 92–6
    see also adult worker model; gender
        contract; male breadwinner/female
        caregiver model
German Trade Union Federation 51–2
German Women's Council 52
governance 1, 4, 8–10, 12, 23, 33, 82, 84, 89,
    94, 109–10
    new modes of governance 25, 103
Government Office for Equal Opportunities
    80, 88
grounded theory methodology 5
Gyurcsany, Ferenc 82

Hartz Commission 44
health and safety 27, 30
health care 45, 65, 92
homo oeconomicus 107
    see also subjectivity
human capital *see* social capital

identity 21–3, 26n6
    see also belonging
inequality 1–2, 19, 28, 31, 39–40, 49, 64–5,
    76, 92, 94, 98, 105–6
    see also exclusion

JobCentre Plus 60, 70

knowledge 6–7, 11–12, 55, 70, 83, 110
  knowledge-based economy 10, 31, 36
  political knowledge production 14, 91,
    103, 107, 109
  socially robust 103
Kok, Wim *34*, 36–8, 70
Kostakopoulou, Dora 8, 26n3, 110

labour market participation 2, 7, 12, 20, 29,
    37, 40n3, 56, 58, 75–6, 83, 85, 92
  see also employment rate
labour market segregation 30, 66–7, 76, 84,
    93, 104
Labour (UK) 61, 67, 68, 71
  New Labour 57–60, 62, 64, 99
Levai, Katalin 79–80
Linke, the 45, 52–4
Lisbon agenda *see* Lisbon Strategy
Lisbon Strategy 10, 32–3, 37, 52, 54–5, 102
    re-launch *34–5*, 38–9, 70, 82, 86
  see also Strategy for Growth and Jobs
lone parents 59–61, 65–7, 104
  see also New Deal for Lone Parents

Maastricht Treaty 24, 28
Magyar Szocialista Párt 79–83
Major, John 57
male breadwinner/female caregiver model
    2–3, 20, 41, 53, 57, 62, 71, 94
Marshall, T. H. 17–18, *22*, 26n5, 98
maternal leave 62, 84, 97
  see also parental leave
meaning 2–3, 9–13, 25, 29, 32, 35–6, 38, 40,
    48, 64, 68, 92, 95, 99–100, 104, 108
  meaning making 14, 91, 103, 109
Merkel, Angela 41, 45, 53, 99
modernisation 1, 3–5, 10, 14, 18, 27, 31–2,
    40–2, 45, 52–3, 56, 63, 69, 97
MSZP *see* Magyar Szocialista Párt

New Deal 60, 62, 64, 70
  New Deal for Lone Parents 59, 65, 97

OECD *see* Organisation for Economic Co-
    operation and Development
OMC *see* open method of coordination
open method of coordination 10, 31, 33, *34*,
    103
Orban, Victor 76, 78–9
Organisation for Economic Co-operation
    and Development 11, 15n2, 71

parental leave 23, 46, 48, 55, 62, 65, 71, 76,
    95, 98
pay gap *see* gender pay gap
personal autonomy 5, 20, 23, 49, 92, 98
political citizenship 1, 5, 14, 107, 109
    participation 4, 13–14, 18, 21–4, 26, 85,
    107–10, 111n4
political community 18, 26n6
  see also political membership
political membership 5–6, 13, 16–18, 24,
    107, 109
  see also political community
positive action 30, 43–5, 105
productivity growth 29, 95, 97

quantitative targets 14, 31, 84, 108

responsibility 6–7, 43, 47–8, 50, 52–4, 69, 83,
    92, 96, 99–100, 106
rights
  human rights 16, 46, 55, 69, 79–80, 87–8,
    93, 101, 106
  new rights 48, 65, 89, 94, 98, 108–9
  see also gender equality; social citizenship
Rubery, Jill 31

sanction 11, 23, 47–8, 51–3, 56, 58–9, 81
  see also control; discipline
Schröder, Gerhard 41, 44–6, 51, 56, 99
Secretariat for the Representation of Women
    79
Sex Discrimination Act 63, 66
single parents *see* lone parents
skills 37–8, 54, 58–9, 61, 64–6, 83, 95, 97
social capital 6–7, 24, 37, 52, 68, 92, 97, 100,
    104, 107–8
  see also human capital; social investment
social citizenship 5, 7, 17–18, 25, 92, 98,
    100–1
  social rights 5, 19, 25, 47, 53, 56, 58, 85
social inclusion 7, 31, 58, 108
social investment 37–8, 48, 61–2, 70, 84,
    93–5, 97, 100
  see also human capital; social capital
Sozialdemokratische Partei Deutschlands
    41–2, 44–5, 52–3, 55, 57, 94
SPD *see* Sozialdemokratische Partei
    Deutschlands
Strategy for Growth and Jobs *34*, 38, 40,
    49–50, 84
  see also Lisbon Strategy
subjectivity 9, 100, 105, 107, 109, 110n1
  see also homo oeconomicus

supply-side 6–7, 12, 24, 52, 54, 83
surveillance *see* control

Thatcher, Margaret 57
Trade Union Congress 68
TUC *see* Trade Union Congress

UN *see* United Nations
unequal pay *see* gender pay gap
United Nations 78, 86
   World Conference on Women
     (Beijing 1995) 30, 77

urgency *34*, 36–7, 45

van Berkel, Rik 6, 8
von der Leyen, Ursula 46, 48, 50, 53

welfare paradigm 1, 6
welfare to work 60, 65–6, 68
Wiener, Antje 21–3, 110n2
Woman and Work (Frau und Beruf) 42–4
Women and Equality Unit 63
women's policy 42–4